D1070675

PSYCHOLOGICAL THOUGHT FROM PYTHAGORAS TO FREUD

An Informal Introduction

Psychological Thought from Pythagoras to Freud

AN INFORMAL INTRODUCTION

Gardner Murphy

An Original Harbinger Book

Harcourt, Brace & World, Inc., New York

 First edition. Library of Congress Catalog Card Number: 68-25371. Printed in the United States of America.

Chapter 1 first appeared as "Pythagorean Number-Theory and Its Implications for Psychology" in the *American Psychologist,* XXII:1 (June 1967), pp. 423–431. Copyright © 1967 by the American Psychological Association and reprinted by permission. Chapter 7 first appeared in the *Bulletin of the Menninger Clinic,* XXXII, pp. 86–101. Copyright © 1968 by the Menninger Foundation and reprinted by permission.

The quoted material on pages 124–127, 135 is from *The Autobiography of Charles Darwin and Selected Letters,* edited by Francis Darwin, Dover Publications, Inc., New York 10014. The lines on pages 35–36, and 37, from the William Ellery Leonard translation of Lucretius's *Of the Nature of Things* are reprinted, from the Everyman's Library edition, with the permission of E. P. Dutton & Co., Inc., and J. M. Dent & Sons Ltd. The quoted material on pages 144–145, and 163 is from *The Thought and Character of William James* by Ralph Barton Perry, used by permission of Atlantic–Little, Brown and Co. Copyright 1935, by Henry James.

To my favorite Greek philosophers:

Peter, Pitsa, Anemona, Lina, Thomas

Preface

During the winter, 1966–1967, I gave a series of lectures to The Menninger School of Psychiatry. The emphasis was upon a few great personalities and a few great ideas, landmarks in the history of Western psychology from the Greeks to the beginning of the present century. Though they have been edited with a view to a larger audience, they are still essentially lectures, selecting a few main issues that remain important today. It is impossible to deal with *contemporary* psychology in any such brief compass, and explanations are due to the thoughtful reader for an attempt to compress whole mountain ranges of ideas into a page or two here. A little later, if I have occasion—with good fortune—to revise my *Historical Introduction to Modern Psychology,* the difference will be great indeed between a systematic effort of that sort and an introductory sketch that alone is possible in the present lecture series.

I wish to express my gratitude to Dr. Donald A. Neher, who suggested the publication of these lectures; to Mrs. Kay Stoner, who so expertly made tape-recordings into typescripts; and to Mrs. Susan Irza, whose secretarial and editorial skills did much to make them readable.

GARDNER MURPHY

The Menninger Foundation, Topeka, Kansas
February, 1968

Contents

PSYCHOLOGICAL THOUGHT FROM PYTHAGORAS TO FREUD

An Informal Introduction

I

The Mathematical View of Life and Mind: Pythagoras

❦

When Lois Murphy and I had the delightful course by Ruth Benedict at Columbia University entitled "The Religions of Preliterate Peoples," we learned the following from the philosophy of the Dakotah Indians: As the units of time are four—the day, the night, the month, and the year—and as the seasons of man's life are four—infancy, childhood, adulthood, and old age—and as the fingers are four . . . and as the toes are four . . . and as the sum of the thumbs and the big toes is four . . . we decided we were encountering a number-obsessed people. Perhaps we ourselves are another number-obsessed people. I thought I would explore this question. Numbers are vital to our life. It may be worth while to understand their role in our thinking.

It is not my intention to regale you, like Major General Stanley in *Pirates of Penzance,* with many cheerful facts about the square on the hypotenuse. Rather, I hope to direct attention to the "golden numbers," of arithmetic and geometry, inclining to the view that "God made the whole numbers, man everything else." I shall offer a few little signposts planted by Egyptians to mark distances, a few little numbers that make for Mendeleev the all-or-none difference between one traditional atom and another; a few little odd facts about black-body radiations that give us Planck's world of the quantum and discontinuity; a few little reminders that we must, in two profound meanings of the term, find "safety in numbers"; and a few unanswerable questions, I believe, as to where number cathexis carries us, from the soundest reality testing to the wildest extravaganza of irrationality.

Not much is known about Pythagoras or about any of his immediate followers. They shared the fascination and excitement of those who made discoveries that transcend the world of ordinary communication, and maintained the secret fraternity of their silence through the whole great period of their discoveries. They taught a wide range of things that puzzle us. The basic thing about them, for the history of science, is that they discovered the role of number in that vast enterprise which we call science. Together with the atomists on the one hand and the Platonists on the other, they defined the basis for an ordered cosmic structure, an ordered structure of human individuality, and a social order. We may make many mistakes as to what they taught, but this is of secondary importance. The main thrust of what they taught is very plain. The danger is not that we falsely attribute this or that to them, but that we go wrong in our contemporary thinking about what numbers are, how they can be used, where they hold the priceless key to reality, and where they lead off into a solipsistic world, in which the manipulation of numbers bends back upon itself in a self-contained fantasy, remote from that numbered world which it is our scientific task to perceive and to use. Absolutely nothing I offer will be new to the mathematician. But there is enough, I believe, of direct importance to psychologists in the rich Pythagorean tradition to be worth our listening closely to it.

There are three great personalities from pre-Socratic philosophy to whom I especially invite attention. There is Heraclitus, the man who said that we never step twice into the same river; the man who in the expanding trade between Greeks and Mesopotamians reminded us that all things can be changed into gold or into fire and back again. He taught that strife is the father of all things, and that all things flow. There was the atomist, Democritus, who conceived the world to be made of minute moving particles, some larger, some smaller, some constituting what we call our bodies; some, what we call our minds. He laid the foundation for all modern material atomism. There was Pythagoras, of the island of Samos, who fled a local despot and set up his school in Croton in the south of Italy about 530 B.C. His school was a fraternity or a secret society lost in the immensity of number and of measurement, and, like many Greek schools, concerned both with cosmic and with human problems, with epistemology and with aesthetics and ethics. He taught that quantity, specifically number, was the key to all reality, and it is for this that we revere him.

Two great discoveries heralded the arrival of Pythagorean number theory. First, in tuning the lyre it was discovered that there is a certain unity or blending of tone when one string is just twice as long as another, the octave, that there is a good acceptable sweet chord when the ratio of length is 3 to 2, again that good chords are produced by a relation such as 4 to 3. Using four strings it was found that the combinations 1 to 2, 3 to 2, and 4 to 3 were especially delicious to the lover of tone. There was something about simple numbers that gave beauty. More complex numerical relationships appeared when the lyre was not quite properly tuned, and the relation was something like 15 to 8. These strings, when simultaneously struck, gave a discord. There was thus a direct relation between arithmetical simplicity on the one hand and beauty on the other. It was not far from this to a doctrine of harmony in nature—for example, in the courses of the stars or the rhythms and ordered time relations of pageantry and the dance, and the basic physiological relation to life. In this conception of order there is a preoccupation and fascination with whole numbers. Of course, the mystic three, the mystic four, the mystic seven, are virtually universal human concerns. There is luck in odd numbers, specifically three and seven, and bad luck in thirteen, according to the culture. There is also a feeling that numbers are almost persons, almost benign and malignant entities in nature, with an emotional investment or cathexis in the number system as a whole. The child is early aware that he has two hands, two eyes. He must count out, he must re-establish rhythms after falling or sobbing or getting lost in his own little dyadic pat-a-cake of life. This idea of the sacredness of numbers was of course enormously accentuated with the discovery of the amazing fact that the right triangle, familiar from Egyptian measurements of the land, was so invested with nature's universal harmony that the square on the hypotenuse was exactly equal to the sum of the squares on the other two sides—not somewhere near, not by an approximation of a one percent error, not probabilistically or in terms of averages, but literally, absolutely, eternally, and indisputably, as a necessary numerical relationship.

Many a Greek temple showed likewise a subtle and marvelous concern with manipulation of arithmetical relations between columns, capitals, interspaces between columns, and the relations of lengths and widths appreciated by the beauty-loving eye, long before they were discovered by the individual to be based upon numerical realities. In other words, the world of geometry speaks to us in the same language as the world of the musician's lyre, and both speak in terms of the basic numerical relations of the body. Music and the time arts, geometry and the space arts, gave the Pythagoreans boldness to speculate that order, rhythm, balance, numerical simplicity, are likewise a clue to the ordering of human affairs through systems of morals, politics, and law.

Another celebrated discovery of the Pythagoreans related to the interdependence of the integers that add up to ten. Imagine the front elevation of a traditional pile of cannonballs, with one at the top, two below that, three underneath, and four at the base. The total is ten. Ten contains, in rational order, the first four cardinal numbers. But the form of the two-dimensional figure, if properly ordered, is an equilateral triangle; thus the three enters into the company of the ten in an especially intimate way. I learned once from a numerologist in New Haven why the prevailing color on the face of the earth is green. Count out from the sun. The sun is one, Mercury two, Venus three, the Earth four. Now count the colors of the rainbow. Red is one, orange two, yellow three, and green four. Does it not follow that in the kingdom of the number system the earth must be green? Or does it? This is the fine flavor of number mysticism which stretches all the way from the greatest mathematical genius to the schizoid confusion of symbols with the things symbolized.

But this is not the only kind of passion with which the lovers of number are tortured. Deep in our culture is the belief that numbers, like people, have distinctive qualities. The clean square four, the ragged, cruel, unfortunate thirteen—they have family resemblances and tribal affinities. Indeed, who can quite say they have not? In anthropology we encounter the moieties, and the people who live on one side of the river and on the other. And in the number world we have the odds and the evens, the prime numbers and those that can be factored, and countless other categories. These qualities often lead to their being loved and hated, sought and avoided.

There are in our tradition easily recognizable and very intense feelings about quality and the importance of each of the individual integers. Take them then from one to ten, or beyond. One is of course the center and root of all numerical thinking. There is no number at all if the one is itself uncertain. "One is one and all alone and ever more shall be so." Two represents the fundamental duality, the male and the female, the Yang and the Yin, the odd and the even, as bases of the eternal polarities based on opposition or directionality. Three is the great tripod, the universal system in which simple opposition is transcended—the father, the mother, and the child; the trinity of body, mind, and spirit; Osiris, Isis, and Horus. And of course three is lucky—the third time never fails.

The four is a pair of pairs, the consummation of the polarities, north, south, east, and west. Five is a hand, a fistful of fingers, the combination of the polarity and the mystic triad, so structured in its fearful symmetry that it appears in evolution as the five-toed form from which endless diversification has appeared in feet or paws or hands. There are countless creatures to whom this supple and majestic symmetry is essential for balance, locomotion, and grasping. How much is biology, how much culture, how much the inscrutable fiveness of elementary symmetry? Six is another kind of two and three—not a simple summation, but a multiplication that appears in the hexagonal cell of the insect's constructiveness. It appears in the perfect cube because there are really three dimensions, and there are really six basic theses of the simplest reality. Mathematicians with their theories of the group have done many wonderful things with boxes of sixes.

As we go on, we realize another enormously mysterious and mystifying number, the seven, which is a six plus a one, a four plus a three, and we know intuitively why there had to be seven heavenly bodies to constitute the harmony of the spheres, seven wonders of the ancient world, seven candles in the mystic candelabra. Seven is lucky. More than that, it is a number fundamental in human constructiveness. Another challenging relation of two and three appears in the eight, which is a two to the third power. And the sublime rhythm that represents the number of the muses, the three times three—the nine.

We have only now to put our two hands together to find suddenly the root of all western numerical construction, the decimal or digital possibilities. As Frank Lorimer says, the decade is a two hands of years, and a century is a two hands of two hands of years. Alone in its oddity stands eleven, claiming its arch intimacy with the ten on the one side and the tremendous twelve on the other—twelve, with its facets of two and three, its divisibility into all the fundamental forces we have tried to describe. When this magnificence has been exhausted, is there anything strange about the threatening quality of the lonely, residual thirteen? It negates the number twelve and in utter Satanism rejects the sublime unity of the whole number ritual that all the foregoing have laid down.

Each may play this game in his own way, remembering the sacredness of the score, the diabolism of forty stripes save one, the seventy years that define the span of man's life, the one-hundred and forty-four thousand of the majestic vision of the Revelation, and so on. My wife showed me during the summer the family section of *Grit* for July 3, 1966:

> The number 40 has played a role of great importance in world history.
>
> Jesus fasted 40 days. Moses spent 40 days and 40 nights on Mount Sinai at the time he got the Ten Commandments. . . .
>
> A quarantine extends to 40 days. In old English law, the privilege of sanctuary was for 40 days. . . .

From the sublime now to the ridiculous. I myself discovered at the age of five a basic numerical clue to human personality. I discovered that there were odd-numbered people—generous, friendly, free-roving, simple, direct, earthy, lovable people—and that there were even-numbered people—restrained, orderly, correct, demanding, and ultimately inscrutable people. The odd-ball, minority-group kinds of people with Irish names like myself were comfortable in their oddness. Most of the Anglo-Saxons who lived in the little Massachusetts town that was my home were even-numbered in every respect, in their politics, their religion, their philosophy of life, the way they said good morning, the way they called in the dogs. Think back—did you not also make a great discovery about numbers and people? When you took statistics, did you really find that all numbers were equal or that some were "more equal than others"?

Aristotle of course had the theory of the golden mean. He was speaking a language already somewhat familiar to his fourth-century compatriots, who flourished long after the time of the Pythagoreans. But Aristotle had virtually no interest in mathematics, virtually no understanding of the Pythagorean vision. Despite his brilliant derivation of an ethical system from the theory of the golden mean, he left the main course of Greek thought to develop number theory in other directions. The Platonists, however, through the extraordinary mathematical cosmogony of the *Timaeus*, saw the implications for man's moral and ideal fulfillment. Plato indeed made a journey to the Pythagorean establishment in southern Italy, and came back a man broadened in terms of his mathematics. Over the gate of the Academy the inscription appeared: "Only mathematicians enter here," and in one of his wisest intellectual bouts with an especially alert questioner, Socrates himself is reported to have said: "They err not only with respect to lack of knowledge in general, but in particular with respect to that kind of knowledge which is called measuring."

If we think of Socrates and Plato as drawing away from crass mathematical atomism and the early forms of a hard-boiled physicalist scientific naturalism, we wholly miss the boat, and we flounder hopelessly in a sea of confusion. For the whole point, from the Greek outlook, was to find the value of numbers as guides to order, and not only to physical but to esthetic and ideal order. Naturally, this led to mystical applications that neither the Pythagoreans nor the Platonists shunned. It is not, however, with these mystical applications that we are here concerned, except insofar as we may note that preoccupations with numbers and the attribution of vast importance to them in the basic cosmic and human meanings was inevitably associated with the conception of cognitive drives as superior to the simpler physical or physiological drives; and to the idea, especially associated with Plato, that man is most completely man when he thinks in terms of generalizations and abstractions representing a pure, cognitive attachment to the known or knowable world, man being driven on by an orderly nature of the knowing process syntonic with—we might almost say isomorphic with—the ordered nature of the world he hopes to know.

Pythagorean number theory was kept alive in the West largely through Plato's *Timaeus*. The historian and the philosopher are concerned to know how it fared in the great Catholic system of St. Thomas Aquinas and his intellectual descendants in northern Italy at the time of the Renaissance. One of the questions that the scholars, acting as subjects in the celebrated Würzburg experiments, were asked to reflect about and answer, was couched in these words: "Was the Pythagorean theorem known to the Middle Ages?" The most important question for us is whether it was known when modern science took shape. Part of the answer lies in the fact that at the University of Padua in northern Italy mathematics was flourishing in Renaissance times, and the great Galileo Galilei was Professor of Mathematics at Padua. So sure was he of the soundness of a mathematical approach to reality that he apparently belittled his own *experiments* as being necessary only for beginners who did not see the inner necessity of nature's laws. Kurt Lewin opposed an Aristotelian to a Galilean principle, in the sense that the latter looks for laws having, as he said, exceptionless validity—that is, the necessity of mathematical logic. This does not cover all the historical facts; for Galileo, hearing of a telescope in the Netherlands, pushed telescopic observation about Jupiter's moons and other objects to a point where it intrigued and shocked the classicists of his day. He and his pupil, Torricelli, exchanged messages with lanterns to see whether the speed of light was really infinite, and, as Conant has reminded us, he speculated on the failure of hand pumps that had to draw water more than about twenty-five feet, looking for empirical considerations (mistakenly, as it happened) in the tendency of the column of water to break of its own weight.

Some say that he had earlier begun his mathematical investigation by watching the swinging of a lamp in the cathedral at Pisa, and that his approach to the laws of the falling body is a clean-cut instance of an empirical determination of something that followed of necessity from the mathematics of the relations of velocity to acceleration, a straight question of arithmetic and geometry. Galileo, in short, married empiricism to mathematical deduction. But so had Pythagoras; so had the great astronomers of Egypt. Mathematics was the tool that operated when continually fed with good raw material. It is possible, but likewise idle, to say that the development of science could have been carried through without benefit of Pythagoras. The empirical fact stands clear: Pythagorean thinking was of the very essence of the applied mathematics that we find in the history of science. It was because number theory and its application to arithmetic and geometry was clear and exciting that empirical observations took the shape that we call science.

Historians of psychology have not forgotten that as Galileo's thought was causing an electrical storm in Western Europe, Descartes was inventing analytical geometry, that amazing science which showed that an orderly equation derived from the study of conic sections will lay out upon a plane the exquisite three-petal and four-petal roses inherent in the bare abstractions of an equation. Certainly nothing could more dramatically satisfy the triumphant Pythagorean prediction that the worlds of beauty, of music, of architecture, and indeed of structure and symmetry of human thought, lie in the ordered relations of the numbers themselves. Newton carried the torch further, and with the impact of his thinking the eighteenth century became the intellectualist century, or, as it has been called, the century of the Enlightenment. Voltaire, armed with mathematics in one hand and skepticism in the other, gave us the ordered but essentially nonhuman universe in which Laplace could conceive of "celestial mechanics" and a "system of the world." The physician David Hartley, having reference to Newton's Laws of the Pendulum, which in turn went back to Galileo's Laws of the Pendulum, created an "association psychology" based squarely upon the elementary mathematics of the sine wave incorporated in the functions of the "white medullary substance of the brain."

But it was Herbart who saw the radical implications. It was Herbart who conceived of elementary concepts, or psychic atoms, pushing upon one another like the molecules in a gas; he saw them colliding and interfering with each other's movements, and under other conditions coalescing or structuring themselves into larger wholes. He saw the mind as a dynamic system of energies running an ordered course. He saw the difference between the ideas at a conscious level upon which we can make direct observations, and those below threshold which act, in the darkness of unconsciousness, exactly as if they were in the light of consciousness. He saw the phenomena of assimilation, integration, and the apperception mass, and realized the structural potentialities from which dynamic potentialities must emerge. All this he did, of course, with the aid of a well-defined conception of energies, and with the benefit of the new differential and integral calculus that came from Newton and Leibnitz. A giant indeed he was, with but few equals in either ancient or modern times—who saw the necessity of formal assumptions about elements, their relations, their energies, their dynamic interdependence,their capacities for synthesis. He went on, in a life of intense usefulness, to build educational institutions and to make more rational the ordered acquisition of facts and ideas in the mind of the child. It was to a large degree from Herbart that Fechner derived his conception of the threshold, and the rich system of psychophysical methods and psychological measurements that dominated experimental psychology in its first decade. It was from this kind of a systematic experimental quantitative psychology that a psychology of individual differences was built.

Indeed, in his presidential address to the American Psychological Association in 1956, Cronbach showed the massive place of quantitative method in the whole structure of modern psychology. Cronbach's analysis showed that systematic quantitative thinking was even more of the basic substance or essence of psychology than was experimental or other inductive methodology. As the slogan of the Psychometric Society expresses it, the trend and aim of scientific psychology is to create a "quantitative rational science," and of course the realization of this whole trend in our own day lies in the preoccupation with the construction of mathematical models.

No form of psychology can escape this mathematical thrust. We may think of it as the very essence of the modern quest for truth, almost as Plato did; or we may think of it as a force that, hand in hand with materialist atomism and mechanism, debases our ideal and distorts our vision. But normative judgments of these types do not seem to impede too greatly the spread of mathematics, which is so deeply ingrained in our whole modern way of thinking. Indeed Freud, whose thinking is as radically qualitative as any you could devise, made more and more of the economic principle with its quantitative approach to the resolution of conflict, and his invention of the polarities and of systems of threes may well represent the same cathexis upon numbers, the same love of abstract quantitative relationships, that is the very essence of Pythagoreanism.

Gestalt psychology began protesting against atomism and mechanism, yet found very early, in Köhler's doctrine of the physical gestalt, the tendency of organismic operations to take the simplest mathematical form, leading on to the generalization of the principles of prägnanz and the law of closure. These tell us why, in a complex heterogeneous field, the relatively simple, ordered, symmetrical, rhythmic, or structured will tend to press its way in, and to press out the components of randomness, confusion, or noise, which have the same stimulus intensity but are doomed to vastly less effective roles in biological and psychological life. The mathematical obsession or aspiration —however you view it—has seeped and percolated, pressed forward and invaded everything in psychology. Laws, however stated, soon become quantitative laws, as in Thorndike's dictum: "Whatever exists must exist in some quantity, and therefore can be measured."

In Heinz Werner's magnificent developmental system, at first the global or undifferentiated world is not ready for numbers; at the second level it is the world of identifiable and measurable components; at the third level these components find articulate structured interrelations, one with another, and we have the quantitative, the quasi-geometrical system that universal science would expect. We look everywhere now for isomorphism, identity of form, between physical, physiological, and psychological realities, assuring ourselves—possibly correctly, though we don't know for sure—that number and number systems apply equally to the object, to the subject, to the cosmos, to the person, to the infinitely large, and to the infinitely small.

I have moved ahead rapidly in praise of the Pythagoreans because I believe that we seldom realize the enormous dependence upon them that is characteristic of our work in dealing with human beings, and the enormous strength of the preoccupation with numbers that feeds in, together with a reality principle, to make psychology one special kind of number system. I would simply ask, as objectively as I know how, and without knowing the answer: "Are we overinvested in number?" There is not the slightest doubt that number theory and number preoccupation help us toward the discovery of many kinds of reality. There is likewise no doubt that numbers lead into various types of mysticism, which becomes so fascinating, so enriching, and so sustaining that one finds it difficult indeed to come back to the world of plain things and the immediate world to be dealt with. Number mysticism makes us believe that symmetry, order, and rhythm have direct predictive power as to what will actually be observed. This has often led us astray. The colossal achievement of Fechner, for example, produced a colossal scientific and mystical output. He was going to measure sensations in the full meaning of the term. But several decades of cautious inductive work have shown the great limitations in time and place upon Fechner's type of generalizations.

I have another grave question to put regarding the adequacy of the whole formulation I have been using. I have not distinguished between number theory as such and quantitative theory in general. Of course, all of us recognize and use the principles of continuity and discontinuity all the time. We know that people, for example, come in whole numbers, and we laugh when the statistician tells us that there are 2.3 children in the average family, or that you have a certain fractional chance of dying of cancer. The very nature of the mathematical operations, however, which have followed from the practical art of measurement and likewise from the beautiful methods of Newton and his followers, have represented the real as continuous and continuity as the only modality of a true science. We teach our pupils about continuities, linear relationships, normal curves. Nature may hate a vacuum, but not more intensely than we hate the gaps that would appear in discontinuous distributions, or in particular from true quantum principles. The profound revolution in physics, coming from Max Planck's discovery of a constant h in black-body radiation, which has served as a prototype for unit thinking, whole number thinking, in so much of modern physics, has almost completely passed psychology by. We have, in our devotion to the mathematics of the continuum, forgotten—or almost forgotten—the Pythagoreans' adoring attitude toward whole numbers. We have forgotten that nature—that is, the sidereal universe and our own Mother Earth; life, including amoeba and man; and psychology, including perception, memory, emotion, and thought—often comes in whole chunks. Very often, when properly observed, these identifiable chunks are discontinuous with other chunks. Some of these chunks happen to be called whole individuals, and we have idiographic as well as nomothetic methods to employ. But there are many discontinuities also within the individual, many potential "split brain monkeys" lurking within our own inner selves and sometimes becoming painfully manifest.

The quantum principle, dating from the year 1900, may manifest itself in large units, or in small. Planck's discovery appears to indicate that action comes in unit packages, as we might expect from the new electron theory that just preceded it. I do not believe we have yet fully grasped the importance of this principle in behavior study or in the analysis of our immediate awareness. The all-or-nothing law in neurophysiology and the related all-or-nothing law that applies to rods, cones, and receptors generally, gives discrete psychophysiological units that are concealed behind the misleading appearance of continuity. S. S. Stevens won the Warren Prize for demonstrating the quantal basis of musical pitch. As Mary Shirley showed, growth is a matter of "saltatory" chunks, unit spurts, behind the apparently smooth maturational process. Affectivity, fears, rages, and other dynamic processes come in quantum terms when first excited, and it may well be that the affective life really comes in psychophysiological integer units too. There are, in personality structure and in the social order, stupid, stubborn lines that say: "Thou shalt not cross." In fact, everywhere in society there are discontinuities so enormous that you can wonder, when you look at them, why we have the stupidity to assume the universality of continuities.

The heart of the difficulty appears to lie in misunderstanding the process of abstracting. For whole numbers are an abstraction. The "threeness" that is present in three apples and three pears is not apprehended at the lowest sensory level but at the level of cognition. If, by using the word *real* we mean that we operate rationally, construct systems, and make predictions on the basis of whole numbers thus abstracted, the numbers are certainly real. They are, of course, one step away from sensory reality and one step toward some other kind of reality. If we speak of the square root of three, we are carrying out a further abstraction: we are asking what can happen if two equal quantities multiplied by one another give three. Then we can perfectly well go on to emphasize that the square roots of negative numbers—which involve a still further abstracting process—can be multiplied by one another and come back giving the less puzzling reality of a whole negative number. There may be abstractions upon abstractions, and the abstracting process itself can be psychologically very real. Sometimes, after many such abstractions, we come back and stub our toes upon simple sensory qualities that have been predicted through these abstractions. I am not inveighing against the abstractions as unreal, or the process of manipulating them as scientifically unsound. On the contrary, I am endeavoring to justify higher-order abstractions by the same process of legitimization which applies to simpler, lower-order abstractions.

But there is always, in science, a further empirical test. Take a simple factoring job with two answers, one of which is the square root of a positive number, and the other of which is the square root of a negative number; there is good reason to say that the intellect must choose one as a real answer to the problem and reject the other. If the examination of evidence shows discontinuity as one possibility and continuity as another, it is an empirical question as to which one will fit the facts. I am raising the question of whether we are aware of this at all in contemporary psychology. We have a strong tendency to believe that continuities are in some deep sense real, that linear relations and normal distributions, multiple factor analysis, and most of the machinery of calculation, and inherently the normalization, the linearization, and the adjustment of data through the use of inverse squares and of logarithmic restatement of bizarre distribution forms, are all carried out in the name of intelligibility and ultimately in the name of truth.

The result is, of course, that we force data, sometimes slightly but sometimes profoundly, into channels that are conceived to make them more real, but can only in fact make them less real in the sense of confronting nature as she is. My statistical friends frequently remind me that the fundamental methods of dealing with discontinuous data in the biological sciences are relatively primitive and grossly incomplete. The result is that we forget the quantum principles that Schrödinger emphasizes in his definition of life and of evolution; we turn away from the discontinuities and the pure numbers, the step functions, or the jump processes with which nature is so well equipped, so full indeed that the theory of the electron, the theory of the cell, the theory of the individual, would all be utterly confused if we insisted upon continuities. What we have done, in the light of mathematics since the seventeenth century, is to defy the fundamental sense in Pythagorean number theory and to rely almost wholly upon the higher-order abstractions that make use of continuities, linearities, normalities, which nature so often contradicts. It is not the mathematics that is intellectually crippling, nor can mathematics ever take the side of one metaphysical proposition against another, but the uses of mathematics can become blind, as can any tool revealed by the sociology of knowledge.

My task has been to suggest our enormous emotional investment or cathexis in numbers—not just the danger of looking for discontinuities and quantum principles when they do not exist, but the very much greater danger that we look for higher-order abstractions relating to numbers rather than respecting empirical stepwise quantum numerical realities with which nature is shot through. It is only the empirical use of Pythagorean number theory, only the investigation of the tough problem of whether nature is working in terms of units or continua, that can save us from the pitfalls inherent in the assumptions of modern psychology. Fifty years ago psychology unwittingly turned at the crossroads in the direction of naïve continuity theory, but the issue is not really closed, and if wrong decisions have been made they can be reconsidered.

Over and above the general cathexis upon numbers and ways of manipulating them, psychology is, of course, shot through with preference for specific numbers. A p value (probability value), for example, at a level of .05 is significant, but at .06 is not significant, I suppose because few of us have six fingers. Here we have misplaced the discontinuity, that is, where there is a real continuity we have made a gulf between .05 and .06, or indeed for certain problems, .01 rather than .02. When I was a graduate student at Columbia, a critical ratio had to be three, and a doctor's dissertation had to report a nonsignificant difference between two means if the critical ratio was 2.7. There had to be thirty subjects to make possible the use of a Pearson correlation coefficient. Despite the nonlinearities with which nature is so replete, we may not use the assumptions about eta or nonlinear relations unless we have massive evidence against linearity.

It would of course take us further into metaphysics to ask whether there is more than our own human ways of thinking that produces this universality of mathematical laws to be found in science—whether, in short, the world is, in reality, ordered mathematically. If the reader is as much of a Pythagorean as I am, he will have to believe that it is; but if he is as critical as he ought to be, he has to doubt it. Neither science nor metaphysics is ready to say anything final on this issue.

There is, however, one profound question from the time of the Pythagoreans, and much alive today, that we do have to attempt briefly to answer in conclusion. This is the question of the isomorphism, the ultimate unity of form, found in comparing the rhythms and symmetries and quantitative laws of our life, and the rhythms and symmetries of stars and oceans, of cells and electrical particles, that emerge from scientific study. Research in the biology and psychology of the last few decades has shown a rich abundance of quantitatively known behavior principles, principles of perception, memory, and thought; they make up, as I said, a fair part of modern psychology. As in the case of Fechner's "outer psychophysics" and "inner psychophysics," and as in the case of Köhler's physical *Gestalten,* the laws that describe the within also describe the world without.

It is not simply a question of one system of realities fitting another. It is a question of their being one and the same, in two different guises. Isomorphism, or identity of form, forces us to the recognition that the same reality of adaptation or learning or forgetting or generalization appears in different levels of observation because it is the same reality refracted through different media. That the curve of forgetting looks like the curve of a declining gas pressure as more and more elements are lost is not an odd coincidence, but a statement that parabolic declines of this sort are a mathematical necessity for particles free from outside influences. James Miller and his collaborators have undertaken, with some success, to show that some basic laws apply at different levels in nature, and as in Herbert Spencer's and Heinz Werner's broad evolutionary schemes, we may say that the mathematical order is the same in all these different concepts for the simple reason that there are cosmic universals relating to observable realities in general, and to the mathematics of their change in time. Psychology will thus become isomorphic with physiology, with psychoanalysis, with linguistic and with moral change and development insofar as there are observables subject to the same possibilities of measurement.

If this is mystical, make the most of it. If it be materialistic, follow the consequences in terms of the research that seems most pressing. This is not the first time in history that the mystical and the materialistic have been suspected under the cover of a very broad groping generalization. Such ideas are fascinating, likewise dangerous. Pythagoreans fled despots because their secret society was dangerous. But my point is that they really *were* dangerous. There is no deity that we worship more abjectly today than number theory in its two-theory form, the quantum and the continuity form. It would be wise to know at which shrine we are worshiping in each of our scientific endeavors, and to know in the last analysis what we think of that strange prophetic figure who defined both these deities, and apparently worshiped them both. I will conclude with a quotation from one of the great biologists of this century, D'Arcy Thompson:

> A "principle of discontinuity," then, is inherent in all our classifications, whether mathematical, physical or biological; and the infinitude of possible forms, always limited, may be further reduced and discontinuity further revealed by imposing conditions—as, for example, that our parameters must be whole numbers, or proceed by *quanta,* as the physicists say. The lines of the spectrum, the six families of crystals, Dalton's atomic law, the chemical elements themselves, all illustrate this principle of discontinuity. In short, nature proceeds *from one type to another* among organic as well as inorganic forms; and these

types vary according to their own parameters, and are defined by physico-mathematical conditions of possibility. In natural history Cuvier's "types" may not be perfectly chosen nor numerous enough, but *types* they are; and to seek for stepping-stones across the gaps between is to seek in vain, for ever.[1]

[1] D'Arcy W. Thompson, *On Growth and Form* (2nd ed., Cambridge: Harvard Univ. Press, 1952), II, 1094.

2

The Materialist View of Life and Mind: Democritus, Epicurus, and Lucretius

It would puzzle a fifth-century Greek if he could know that an "atomic age" was coming later. We think of ourselves in terms of the Atomic Age, but we do not *begin* to be atomic in the sense in which the early Greek philosophers were, who had a passion for dissecting, cleaving, chopping, and getting down to residual elements that no mortar and pestle could ever achieve, and then asking: "What's the still finer unit?" You hear a batch of eight- and ten-year-olds talking together and saying: "But it's as small as it can be." "No, I could chop it smaller." And you get to the conceptual level: "Is there something so small that it hasn't *any* size?" And until our society has made clear to the youngsters that they should not deal with these impractical questions, you find them asking all over the map about the infinitely small and the infinitely big: "But what happens when you get to the end of the universe?" "There *isn't* anything more!" "There is a wall!" "But there's got to be something *on the other side!*" That is to say, the Greeks were like eight- and ten-year-olds who were confronting what they could not understand. But they had the capacity to make marks on paper, a few fragments of which still come down to us and tell us about the atomism of the early Greeks.

Of course, there has always been this theme of the extremes: the infinitely little and the infinitely big. In a way they are symmetrical. Eddington tells us the number of particles in the human body, and in the universe; he argues that man is geometrically at the mid-point between the infinitely little and the infinitely big. As Jonathan Swift said: "Big fleas have little fleas on their backs to bite 'em, little fleas have littler still, and so on ad infinitum."

Now, of course, we have to start with somebody that left marks on paper, and we usually begin with Leucippus, and then concentrate upon Democritus, a Thracian who came to Athens, as did many philosophers, for an extended stay. He was concerned with three problems that have ordinarily been regarded as the problems of materialism. Actually, they are the problems of atomism of all sorts, of which materialism is only one special case. The first problem is: "What is the stuff of which the world is made?"—assuming that it must be homogeneous, that is, assuming that there could not conceivably be two or more ultimately distinctive kinds of stuff. And the second question is: "What are its elemental, invisible, and indivisible forms?" For example, are they of different shapes? Are they of different consistencies? Are they of different qualities? Or shall we be so strict in our atomism and in the purity of our conceptualization that we should say that all of the ultimate parts of which the world is made are alike? For example, they could all be spherical. That, because of its mathematical beauty, was a major assumption often made, and was apparently an assumption of the earliest atomism.

Then there is, of course, the third question: "What do the particles move in?" And this is what the Greeks called the problem of the *void*. The same children who struggled to define what is the infinitely little had to have something for the infinitely little to move in; and we can talk of it as space. Or if we are very sophisticated in terms of space-time, we can create for ourselves a thing that does not exist—the vacuum, the hole in the doughnut. It is the problem of "nonbeing." It has to have a kind of existence if things that are real can move in it. And this is the insoluble, but perennial, problem known to the Greek atomists as the void.

Now if we formulate the three problems—what is the stuff, what are its forms, and what does it move in—then we have the basis for an atomist theory.

Democritus was a psychologist. That is to say, he saw how atomism applied to the problems of the soul, the problems of memory and perception, as well as the pleasure-pain dimension. His atomism involves the notion of heterogeneous types of particles. There can be particles in motion, each one behaving in terms of its size and its quality, bumping fortuitously against others exactly as we have in the kinetic theory of gases in modern physics. And we simply have specially smooth, spherical particles to make up the soul. These particles are scattered through the body, and therefore there is no reason to presume that they would be able to hang together after death. There are, then, religious implications that become clear as one goes further.

The process of perception is handled with great charm. We are dealing with symbols. *Eidolon* in the Greek means that which stands for, represents, or serves as an image for a physical object; an eidolon is a *representation* of a thing. Now all objects give off such representations—*eidola.* That is to say, they project into the space around them tiny copies of themselves. The ideas which we receive are all, directly or indirectly, ultimately based upon these representations from the senses. The senses are the recipients of these eidola, which are formed as the original objects are because they are copies, and which impinge upon our sense organs. If we are doubtful about all this, we can just look at the pupil of the eye and see the evidence that they saw in it. The eye receives these little copies in great quantity and organizes them into perceptual patterns. Typically thought will be excited by these eidola, propelled and impinging upon the sense organs and ultimately causing an internal commotion, which is itself ultimately a copy of the thing outside.

As one of the later commentators says: "They attributed sight to certain images of the same shape as the objects, which were continually streaming off from the objects of sight and impinging on the eye." We have to assume that the oral tradition, together with fragments of writing, were transmitted without much distortion and that this was the classical theory of perception so widely held by the atomists.

This is primitive "realism." It is an assertion that what we see is really there. It has the properties we attribute to it, as contrasted with the theory of self-deception—also very widely entertained among the Greeks and among the moderns—to the effect that the percept is subjective response to objective stimulus; this view holds that we recast, we do not copy, what is given to us from outside.

The second point is that there is a difference between truth-conveying perceptual responses—those which cling to the reality of the situation—and truth-distorting or negating types of perception. Democritus and his peers recognized that there are certain cases where the theory of the eidolon will not work. There are hallucinations. There are illusions. "Is this a dagger which I see before me?" asks Macbeth. Or is it something, he asks, "from the heat-oppressed brain?" "Here, let me clutch thee"; he grasps for the dagger and cannot touch it. He is now convinced that his senses have been deceiving him, in other words, that the eidolon is not just a copy of a real externally placed object. How should we handle this problem philosophically? It was solved by Democritus exactly as it was solved two thousand years later by John Locke. If we look at the moon we are perceptually correct and in contact with the moon insofar as we see a disc; or, if with more refined photographs or telescopic observations, we say that it is a sphere in which the shadows and so on are *interpreted* in a certain way. But that it is lemon-colored, we say, is not *in* the moon; that is a creation of our minds. In the same way, as we listen to music or as we feel with the fingers, there are raw sensory impressions that may be integrated in various ways to give a deceptive result. Perhaps we do not really hear what we think we hear. There are tonal qualities that are just not given in the composition. But we hear them. There are, of course, in everyday conversations thousands of cases where we not only make misinterpretations, but actually fill in gaps, as in the proofreader's illusion, in which we see letters that simply are not there. We are now no longer dealing with "primary qualities," as John Locke later called them, but with "secondary qualities," that is, qualities that arise subjectively from the nature of the observer. They are due, if I understand Democritus correctly, to the fact that there is internal commotion of parts of the body, and that the pure, original activity of the eidolon has been confused by bumping, let us say, into another eidolon or another internal confusing or distorting factor in the body. There is the distinction, then, between sensation, which always "tells the truth," and perception, which tells the truth if we integrate the sensations properly, as contrasted with the illusion or hallucination that supervenes when we put the parts together in the wrong way.

This is particularly dramatic when we compare the senses that give refined structure, like sight and hearing and touch, with those weak in structure, like taste and smell, where the contribution of subjectivity is so very great. Here is another direct quotation from Democritus: "By convention are sweet and bitter, hot and cold, by convention is colour; in truth are atoms and the void. . . . In reality we apprehend nothing exactly, but only as it changes according to the condition of our body and of the things that impinge on or offer resistance to it."

Relatively little gets into us to make up our own internal copy of the external world. But this all depends on what we call physical properties—size, shape, motion, number. Here is one of the few points of contact with the Pythagorean mathematical way of thinking. Aside from these physical properties, with their physical and mathematical structures, we are dealing mostly with raw quality.

After much beating of this theme we come, of course, to the skeptical note: "Can you really believe anything at all from your senses, if the secondary qualities play such a large part?" To which I think Democritus has a beautiful reply: ". . . Wretched mind, do you, who get your evidence from us, yet try to overthrow us? Our overthrow will be your downfall." If we go so far as to deny the reality orientation of the senses, then all that you build up from the senses by way of perception, or even cognition, contains within it the inherent flaws and defects and the misleading indications that are there. The senses, in other words, have to do their job to provide the raw material with which the hifalutin philosopher can construct his theory of reality.

Now we can go to the other extreme and deny the senses any raw, primitive, truth-giving value. But it is quite plain that, long before Plato, the issue of the necessary reliance of man upon his senses, despite their tricky quality, was clearly understood by Democritus.

There are also some ethical notes here and there in the Democritean thinking which were developed among the later materialists. In connection with the question of whether life is good or can be made good, what the qualities of the good life really are, Democritus had this to say: "The cheerful man, who is eager for just and lawful deeds, rejoices whether waking or sleeping and is strong and free from care; but he that cares nought for justice and does not the things that are right finds all such things joyless, when he remembers them, and is afraid and reproaches himself." This is to be encountered in the Proverbs, too, and also in Chinese Buddhism and in the middle period of Indian philosophy. This idea is that it is only in the just, the humane, the decent, the right, that the pleasant can be found, and that a steady quality of cheerfulness is only obtainable when certain basic postulates of appropriate behavior have been defined. Then comes a note that is even more like the Book of Proverbs: "Happiness does not reside in cattle or gold; the soul is the dwelling-place of one's good or evil genius." If anyone still believes that materialism has to mean baseness of character, this is a good answer from Democritus.

By all odds the great materialist of the ancient period is Epicurus, the most misunderstood and most maligned of Greek philosophers, largely because of the issue that I have just tried to bring out. Epicurus believed in pleasure; he believed in cheerfulness; he believed in rightness. He talked, however, to an era that had been climbing the sky. Remember how Socrates was accused of treading on air, stepping over the clouds in his search for the good. The Athenians (and other Greeks, too) were inclined to be skeptical about such hifalutin ideas. Socrates' words, as given us by Plato, portrayed the ideal, which many people held to be out of touch with the physical, the immediate, the concrete. Greek philosophy appeared to many to be moving to a point in which humble, everyday, touchable things were of little value. On top of this, the Greek city-states had been shattered by the Peloponnesian War, a thirty-years' war of destruction between brothers. The Greeks were always having *little* wars, which they could patch up between the city-states, but the Peloponnesian War was a strangling process that destroyed a great deal of the wealth, and, more important than that, most of the morale, most of the confidence in life on the part of the people of the Greek city-states. It led to what Gilbert Murray called "a failure of nerve." There was a tendency to fall back on things that were simple and direct and inherently good, whether ideally justified or not. Epicurus belonged to this post-Peloponnesian War period, in which a serious person had to defend philosophy, yet could at the same time look for something that was safe despite all wars and further carnage among brothers.

Epicurus defined the problem almost as it was defined by Democritus, in terms of simplicity, freedom from suffering, and a life of order. Materialism was supported partly in these terms, and partly for a reason that we might not suspect: Materialism could free men from the fear of what happens after death (just as Hamlet has it in the soliloquy), and from fear of the gods. For Epicurus the gods exist, but they do not bother about mankind, and they do not have to be placated. A here-and-now philosophy, then, will suffice, provided that the use of material objects can be understood, and provided that a world of personal and social order can be built upon a physical order that man understands. In order to do this the philosophies of the period must be structured both in physical terms and in terms of the moral sciences. Philosophy had to create a kind of a world in which human beings could live without fear and without mutual predatory designs on one another.

Epicurus was so sure of the soundness of the materialistic approach that he built into his ethical scheme notions that had been well expressed by Leucippus and Democritus. He accepted, for example, the notion of perception as the reception of sense impressions (*eidola,* page 25). But he adds that the higher order processes can deceive us; we can come to wrong conclusions because, as he puts it, there is an error not in the senses, but in the "opinions" based upon them. The material particles that constantly bump into one another are capable of producing failures of orientation. It is possible that bad consequences come from an essentially correct perception of an issue if there is an inadvertent mixing of different kinds of evidence. It is therefore important for the philosopher to conclude only that which is supported from *many* sources. In this sense he inveighs against the idealists of the period who have complicated life and made it unlivable in this period of degradation and despair. The hedonism—Greek word *hedone,* which means simply pleasure—is supported, simply because it is the only way to define the goodness of life once freed of the fear of the gods and the fear of death. But a great deal of attention is given to health and to disease—even what we would call mental disease—in the sense that the particles interfering with one another's normal activity can cause a material failure of function. His discussion of the process of disease and the way the disease influences the operation of the mind sounds very modern. We get this very clearly in Lucretius, the Latin poet who systematizes the doctrines of Epicurus.

Why is it so difficult to make clear a hedonism of this sort, so that it can be understood in the modern period? Pleasure is not taken at face value, but has been identified with specific or particular pleasures. Pleasure has become utterly disreputable. It is very curious that what seems to be self-evidently good to most people, as they look at the tragedies of human life—first, getting rid of pain, and, second, creating some sense of well-being—is usually defined in terms of something debasing, lowering the worth of life. This was the severe position of the Stoic school, rivals of the Epicureans. There have been many strictures on Epicurus. I offer a few illustrations, in a little dialogue between the critic and the Epicurean. (1) What is inherently pleasant must inevitably be temporary. Reply: But what is not temporary? (2) Pleasure must be seen in terms of relativism. Reply: But what is there that is not to be seen in terms of relativism? (3) Pleasure must be seen in terms of something that is short of the ideal. Reply: But what that we encounter is not short of the ideal? The three ways in which one may shoot one's darts into the living form of Epicurus are all defined in terms of the supposed depravity of the concern with pleasure.

Socrates himself had the extraordinary integrity to see that the ideal would itself have to comprise a state of happiness, and that there is no dissociation between the ideal and the pleasant. It is very curious that in the doctrines relating to Epicurus it is systematically assumed that he was "a gluttonous man and a wine-bibber." It is curious, because if we read what Epicurus has to say, we note that he recommends frugality, simplicity, self-control—constantly and over and over again in all sorts of ways—on the ground that most of the short pleasures and most of the uncalculated pleasures leave damage and therefore ultimately pain. He is constantly arguing, in the name of pleasure, for what are commonly called the "higher" pleasures, the kinds of pleasures that do not lead to these three typical non-pleasures.

If we look further for reasons for the lack of respect generally held for Epicurus's very simple and orderly doctrine of pleasure, we find them in the nature of a changing society—notably the parallel development, after the Peloponnesian War, of the conservatism of the Greek city-states and the Stoic doctrine. The gentlemen who stood on the porch, or *stoa,* defined for themselves a world in which that is good which is in conformity with nature. Nature is simple, orderly, businesslike, involves self-control, involves a limitation of passion, except for a passionate concern with rectitude and with continuity and consistency, the kind of image that we have with regard to Cato the censor, or later, the slave, Epictetus, who taught the doctrine of nobility in the face of torment and accusation, and, of course, Emperor Marcus Aurelius, of the third century of the Christian era. Stoicism involved a limitation of the claims of pleasure.

Actually, many of the doctrines of the Stoic and of the Epicurean are quite similar. If we go back to the source materials that we find in Diogenes Laertius, who wrote systematic comparisons of these philosophic figures, we find a close parallel between the two systems. Yet we find that the Stoic had a logical and a popular advantage, in the sense that he who lampoons the lowly, the simple, and the obvious—and implies that life is more complex, noble, and austere—is always able to put his antagonist in a difficult position. The same was true later of Puritanism. It is well remarked that the reason that the Puritans objected to bear-baiting was not that it hurt the bears, but that it gave pleasure to the spectators. The same way of looking at life is involved, I think, in Charles Lamb's beautiful remark, when he had been accused of trying to be funny, that it is "full as good as trying to be dull." We ordinarily believe that the funny, the pleasant, the jocular, the amusing, are inevitably cheap, even though some of the world's greatest literary productions are quite properly called comedies, in the sense that they give life a perspective in which joy can still reign despite the temporary and adventitious rule of misery or brutality.

From such a point of view Epicurus was willing to admit the reality of all sorts of practical limitations upon psychological hedonism. Yet he held that though it is extraordinarily difficult to live a life that is really happy, it is still worth the effort. This was socially, as well as personally, possible.

Epicurus maintained a liberal school. For example, women were, as a matter of course, present in the Epicurean school. Why did this kind of modern idea become involved? The answer appears to be that the old Greek standards of the city-states were, as we say, Spartan. Of course, Sparta was just one of the city-states, and the most military, and the one with least regard for women. But most Greeks, through most of the classical period, entertained both the conception that women belonged at home and the conception that we find appearing in Plato's *Republic,* that some women may be able some of the time to function as well as men, but that after all you have to be realistic and not demand too much.

This is quite contrary to the Epicurean spirit, which as a matter of fact became a sort of prophetic or evangelistic spirit, in the sense that Epicurus actually founded a school whose devotees came and stayed with him a long time and then carried the word elsewhere. Epicurus wrote epistles, very much as Paul the Apostle wrote epistles to the early churches. Epicurean philosophy became, as we see it in the Roman period, a world school. Marius the Epicurean (a brain-child of Walter Pater) speaks to men of good will who have started life without the gods.

Now, of course, this sounds to an idealist, who has created a belief in powers beyond any human understanding, as if it were claiming too much, and it sounds as if it would certainly have to crash as a result, failing to establish an anchorage point on some reality outside of human experience. It is actually a nature philosophy, exactly as Stoicism became a nature philosophy.

But the Stoics won the "battle for the mind." Today, if we

say, "I'll take it philosophically," we are quoting the approach of the Stoics. To take it philosophically! Does that mean to take it in the way Epicurus did? We would never do that, because Epicurus lost the battle and was put down in the records of mankind as a lover of immediate and ill-considered joys. That is why I do not think anybody in the whole history of philosophy has been more handily dismissed and excluded in terms of the discrepancies between what he actually offered and what he has been understood to offer.

We have, in the case of Lucretius, a very different story to tell. We have a great Epicurean who was in the first place capable of magnificent expression. His *On the Nature of Things* is one of the great poems of antiquity, of the first century B.C., the classical period of golden Latin, the same period as Caesar and Cicero, the period of the New Empire and the Pax Romana. Here is one of the really extraordinary expressions of human thought about the origins of life, the origins of human society, and the conditions under which man can come to terms as a humanist with his own potentialities, without needing more. This is essentially the story of Lucretius, an evolutionary biologist, teaching much of Darwinism, much of Weismann and the "continuity of the germ plasm," with some of our modern ideas about mutations. One has to compare two or three different translations of Lucretius before one convinces oneself that this is not just a translator's fantasy; that there really *is* there in the Latin a most extraordinary conception.

First, the materiality of the universe, taking over from Democritus and from Epicurus the idea of tiny particles that first make up lower plants and simpler animals, and then, with individual growth and with the development of species, become more complex. We can be reasonably sure that the coherence of this presentation is that of Epicurus because we know that Epicurus wrote a great deal, systematically, and we have the devoted acolyte's constant genuflections to the great master. I do not mean to say that Lucretius created something never glimpsed in the Greek period—that would not be true—but he did have the capacity to take the philosophical tradition of materialism as it existed then and to give it this vital form.

We can organize his essential thought around the expression that life arose from the "fortuitous concourse of atoms." It turns out that the term *fortuitous* means *unforeseeable,* but not *random.* It might be easy for us to say that everything is left to chance, but in fact nothing is left to chance. That is, in the evolutionary system, every movement of every particle is determined by its previous position and the course of its present angular momentum and so forth. In other words, there is no chance element in it at all; it is fortuitous only in the sense that no human being would be able to extrapolate from one position to another. We have a systematic determinism in which man is caught, and in which, if his thought is itself fully determined in a wise direction, he may be able to carry through a theory of perception and a theory of judgment essentially as given by Epicurus, but seen in a fuller context with many more illustrations. Then follow pages upon pages of natural history—the differences, for example, in the way in which bees, fishes and birds, and small mammals think and behave. These are delightful observations that many other Latin poets like Vergil, lovers of nature, were accustomed to describe, but here with an exceptionally complete and clear picture of the process of change—the fact that life is constantly evolving from one form to another. Then towards the end of this book comes his beautiful picture of social evolution from the simple brutal self-contained to the community, the psychology of interdependent persons.

Here is one little passage from Lucretius about the nature of the soul, trying to take the position we are familiar with from Democritus and Epicurus, that mind and soul have their own existence, that they are knowable, that they consist of material particles, that they are important in the problems of health and disease, and that at the same time they are so utterly *dependent upon the body that they cannot exist without it:* "Thus, since within the body itself of man/ The mind and soul are by such great diseases/ Shaken, so miserably in labour distraught,/ Why, then, believe that in the open air,/ Without a body, they can pass their life,/ Immortal, battling with the master winds?"[1] He is talking to Romans, who, like the earlier Greeks, are afraid of existence beyond death, and afraid of the risks that might be involved. This is offered not as a prayer, but as a comfort regarding fears of posthumous existence. Then this beautiful phrase, all of this physiological psychology in one phrase: "The nature of the mind and soul is bodily."

He goes on from these more general statements to many comments on the way the senses operate, which, if we seek a comparison with early medicine and Hippocrates, stands up very favorably as a medical view of how the senses mediate reality. Here is a passage about the sense of touch. I think first I will describe the experience, because the poetry might be a little bit too delicate to get at one reading. We know that a blind man with a stick feels, not just the stick, but the *ground*. That is, the tapping operation gives him a kind of touch even though it is mediated through the white stick that he is using. Lucretius notes that when we tap on a rock, we know that we are not just tapping a surface; we feel, as it were, the whole rock beyond the tactual impression that we get from the tips of the fingers. In his words: ". . . whene'er we thump/ With finger-tip upon a stone, we touch/ Not the rock's surface . . . [we] rather feel/ The very hardness deep within the rock."[2] There is sensitive observation like this all through Lucretius; little sensitive, delicate phenomenological interpretations.

It would be unjustified to spend so much time on the sheer physics of these philosophers were it not for the fact that the delicacy of the psychology is so frequently found in the midst of a physical analysis. Then, if we are inclined to think of Lucretius' message as being, as most Roman philosophy is,

[1] William Ellery Leonard (trans.), Lucretius's *Of the Nature of Things* (New York: E. P. Dutton & Co., Inc., 1950), p. 110.
[2] *Ibid.*, p. 145.

mostly a carbon copy of the Greek, and to think of Lucretius as not very subtle or very complicated, we must consider the exquisite ethical outcome of his teaching. The ethical emphasis we found in Epicurus is hope for mankind in discovering a life capable of joy, and of sharing this vision and setting up schools to carry this optimistic message to the world. We find the same in Lucretius. This is rather remarkable in the Roman society of the first century B.C., a pretty hard society, a pretty cruel society, a society not only of the Pax Romana, but of crucifixion as a routine method of disposing of robbers and so forth, a society in which one would not think very much gentleness would be available. But it is found all through Lucretius.

When John Benjamin, the well-known analyst in Denver, came to talk to us a few years ago in Topeka, he wanted to show us that the understanding of physiological man, the physiological roots of human motivation and thought, might actually exalt human self-respect; he read us the following passage from Lucretius:

> . . . Nor may we suppose
> Evil can e'er be rooted up so far
> That one man's not more given to fits of wrath,
> Another's not more quickly touched by fear,
> A third not more long-suffering than he should.
> And needs must differ in many things besides
> The varied natures and resulting habits
> Of humankind—of which not now can I
> Expound the hidden causes, nor find names
> Enough for all the divers shapes of those
> Primordials whence this variation springs.
> But this meseems I'm able to declare:
> Those vestiges of natures left behind
> Which reason cannot quite expel from us
> Are still so slight that naught prevents a man
> From living a life even worthy of the gods.[3]

In today's language, there is a lot of evil in us, yes, but not too much but that we can control it. Humanism may be inadequate

[3] *Ibid.*, pp. 103–104.

and far from ideal, humanity may have a lot of flaws and a lot of things that frighten us or shame us, but still all of that put together is so slight in the total picture that "naught prevents a man from living a life even worthy of the gods."

I want to refer forward for a moment to the modern materialisms that come essentially from these same sources. The conception of material particles could not make very much headway without research involving instrumentation. In the Alexandrian laboratories, and dissection rooms, and in the Alexandrian library, these ideas were known, but not essentially advanced beyond Lucretius because microscopes consisted only of the Archimedes hand-lens. They were not good enough to advance the work. Subsequent materialisms in the Western world were still philosophical materialisms and were not pushed in the direction of asking how far the very small could be observed and classified. It was not until the seventeenth century that the Dutch Leeuwenhoek with his lenses was able to describe red blood cells and bacteria; it was not until the beginning of the nineteenth century, thanks to the techniques of the chemists, that it was possible for Dalton to talk about atoms and atom theory, beginning to use this traditional lore from the Greeks as the world of the observables became more and more controlled.

The development of materialism as a philosophy waited upon further ways of observing the material. And of course, when we begin quantifying, when we begin thinking as Pythagoras did, some of these materials that we work with do not look so simple. Materialism reached a certain philosophical limit as far as utility to explain the universe is concerned. What it could do was to take another direction, and not necessarily for the good of philosophy. What materialism did was to get into a pitched battle with the various forms of mind-body dualism, which teach that mind is one thing, body something else. The same thing happened in India that happened with the Greeks and Romans, and, of course, with Christianity; materialism took on battle proportions until the Church suppressed it. Materialism was held to be opposed to all the spiritual values that had sprung from a dualistic system, a soul-versus-body system. This is the reason why modern materalism, beginning in the sixteenth or seventeenth century, has to fight a very difficult action against dualistic and particularly Christian doctrines of mind and body. It had to begin with two strikes against it, with the assumption that there is something inherently crude, dirty, base, subhuman, about a material structure; that the only good can lie in an opposition between the material and the ideal. When Thomas Hobbes, in the seventeenth century, talked about the material basis of life, "Hobbism" became a whipping boy for all serious, decent, idealistic English thinkers. And when La Mettrie, in France a century later, wrote an extraordinary essay called *Man a Machine,* he was not considered worthy of serious philosophical attention. One thing that was lost by this series of events was the ethical contribution that the materialists had made.

I think that this has happened over and over again. The very fact, however, that the materialism of the Greeks was so much more sophisticated than the materialism of ancient India or of ancient China led inevitably to a certain defensive reaction against it, a feeling that here was something pretty formidable—it had to be fought. We are likely, in the modern era, therefore, to lose the moral, particularly the humanistic, virtues inherent in Greek materialism. Remember that while most of the atomists were materialists, the central idea of atoms is really not the same as the idea of the material origin of all reality. Fortunately the atomist, with his notion of elementary particles, did not have to fight quite the same battle. When materialism says roughly and crudely that the body, the whole society, and whatever we claim to be of importance to human values, has to be reduced to some nonspiritual, some corporeal basis, this starts the battle. But to say the universe begins with tiny particles does not involve quite the same spiritual battle. When, therefore, atomism got started in the modern era (say in the sixteenth or seventeenth century), atomism, as contrasted with materialism, had a relatively good chance immediately to influence science, while science could remain agnostic as to what the atoms were, and whether they would turn out to be anything like the material particles that Leucippus and Democritus described. We have gotten into the habit of equating atomism and materialism. But I suggest that these are really different issues, that on the whole philosophy has damaged itself by lining up a series of imaginary ethical issues in such a way as to disparage the approach of Greek materialism. On the other hand, Greek atomism has come through relatively unscathed. If we want to see the whole perspective of Greek philosophy we have to see how natural, how inevitable, it was for the Greeks to look for an atomic basis for reality, and how natural it was for an atomic basis for reality to be sought again in modern times.

We have, then, a good deal that we can still use—particularly the idea that there are ultimate units into which complex totals can be divided; that their mode of behavior is important; that human life is to some degree dependent upon these particles; that the ethical values arise in a natural way from the very fact that life has this simple orderly basis; and that even the social aspects, even the *future* social aspects, of humanity's hopes may not be damaged through understanding those rudimentary aspects of nature to which the early atomists gave their attention. It remains to ask whether this conception of the Greeks, this particular conception of atoms, will really fit within the structure of contemporary thinking. But those issues belong to a later time.

3

The Functionalist View of Life and Mind: Plato and Aristotle

I would not have the arrogance to try to deal with a topic as vast as the present one except from one frame of reference—that of trying to put into a single concept something shared by some of the greatest of minds in human history. And I am going to define rather arbitrarily the common theme for the great high classical philosophical development in Greece in terms of the concept of *process* or *function*. We have seen in earlier discussions how the concept of number can be a key to all of the systematic thinking of the last twenty-five hundred years, and we encountered the concept of atoms or particles, from which larger aggregates are formed, in discussing Democritus, Epicurus, and Lucretius. But there is another way of thinking that has captured the imagination of mankind, the conception of process or function. There can be no doubt at all that, in spite of the deep antithesis between the teacher, Plato, and the pupil, Aristotle, the concept of function comes to fruition in the Aristotelian notion of form, in which function is contrasted with matter.

Greek philosophy, like Indian philosophy, and most early philosophies, begins with cosmogony: "How did the world begin?" There was a turtle, and then man stood on his back. Or there was a great rainfall, and then man managed somehow to swim or float upon the waters. The cosmic drama becomes relevant for the human drama. We are familiar with this from the first chapter of Genesis. There are many variations on this theme. Later, men came to questions about the nature of knowledge and the nature of goodness, which they tried to solve by some common formula. These were the problems of *human* wisdom (Anthropine Sophia) or a human *kind* of wisdom, contrasted by Socrates with the cosmogony type of thing. When Aristophanes in *The Clouds* represents Socrates as "treading on air and looking at the sun," the picture is to make fun of him who deals with ultimate cosmic issues. To this, of course, Socrates replies, very appropriately, that he was basically interested not in cosmogony, but in human wisdom.

The market place was the first university for the development of such concepts. And as we know from what was said briefly about the school of Epicurus (page 33)—and those with an interest in medical history will think of the school of Hippocrates—a teaching relationship to eager young minds was a primary way in which new ideas were allowed to unfold. It was in teaching that the teacher became aware of what he really believed. The Greek image of the *agora* or market place represents typically a crossroads of eager and often conflicting ideas, as men from other city-states travel in and travel out, and as a group spirit develops. We think of it later on in the thirteenth century as Cambridge University, as it developed around the argumentative monks who stood there on the banks of the river Cam and discussed the nature of salvation.

The market place represents also the crystallization of ideas that were previously formless. We think of Sappho as a great poetess. I doubt whether we should recognize her in the terms Bonnard has developed in his beautiful book on Greek philosophy, as the wise and adroit leader of a school of grace, or we might well say a "charm school." It appears likely that Sappho, being an exceptionally wise and intelligent administrator of that little teaching group, helped to create one of the basic aspects of the Greek conception of beauty, which later appear, for example, in Greek sculpture. That is one of the things that is easily forgotten, in such sharp contrast with what we read in Plato's *Republic,* giving a rather disparaging view of creativity on the part of the female mind. But the Greeks were always going to school, and schools like Sappho's helped in the development of the *beauty* aspect, along with the *goodness* and *truth* aspects, which were so central in Greek thought.

PLATO

Where does Socrates appear in this scheme of education? Of course, he appears in the market place as a former soldier and as a man with mixed and varied contacts, apparently learning the trade of a sculptor and apparently, like all middle-class Greeks—all free men who tried their hands at practical art—rather inclined to disparage the things that could be done with one's hands. People gathered around him like moths around a light, beating their wings and trying to make sense out of what was said by this extraordinarily tough and unyielding, yet infinitely pliant, interrogator, who put hopeless questions to those who struggled with them, and who, in what we call the Socratic method, developed dialectically a sense of *process* rather than of final wisdom sufficient unto itself. He said he was a midwife to assist at the birth of ideas. A very appropriate metaphor, too, in the sense that the idea moves from a potential to an actual form, insofar as the teacher and the students interact. We get that picture brilliantly in most of the Socratic dialogues, and of course, particularly in the *Symposium*—the banquet—in which the very nature of love, as of all positive outgoing response, is seen as capable of self-fulfillment only in an interaction process. I set this up as a foil in contrast to what I want to say about the development of a process psychology, because it is ordinarily assumed that Plato, mediating Socrates' thought, believed in innate ideas, which were, like Athena from the brow of Zeus, suddenly realized in full actuality. In reality, we learn, as we read the Platonic material, a good deal from the byplay, the backstage, what goes on in the wings. We see what looks like a crisp and dogmatic doctrine regarding the ideas born in man, representing the vast difference between the brute and the man; but it actually requires this cultivation, this midwife function, to give an idea birth. As a matter of fact, as we find in the *Republic,* a long and arduous educational process follows, in which the free soul is to be coaxed and nurtured into the kind of freedom that before was only a potentiality.

This man Socrates captured the imagination, not just of Plato, but of a generation of thoughtful souls, and two millennia of devoted followers thereafter. This was the more extraordinary in that he had two strikes against him. In the first place, though a courageous soldier himself in the field, he was associated in the Athenian mind with the catastrophes of the Peloponnesian War. Secondly, his relation of friendship with younger men was subject to various sorts of barbed or amused comment. This was like water off a duck's back as far as Socrates was concerned, who very intensely enjoyed the development of a rich dialogue with all who would come and exchange ideas with him.

We should not think of this picture of Socrates, created by Plato, as a perfect likeness if we noted how Socrates appears through the eyes of *other* people—for example, Xenophon. Xenophon, the first "military correspondent," who "covered" some of the wars of the period, and who in *The Anabasis* delighted in recording the interchange of personalities, was apparently proud of the fact that he had been to school to Socrates. There is no doubt, in fact, that Socrates was *more* than a specialist in giving birth to ideas. He was a wise and strong Athenian that everybody knew as a man. We can make fun of that kind of person if we are an Aristophanes. We do not pick abstract and remote figures for such lampooning.

The point is that there are at least three figures of Socrates: by Plato, by Xenophon, and by Aristophanes. When we look at the Socrates that is given us by Plato, we never really know how much is original material and how much is a dye or a stain developed through an interaction process. And the Plato picture varies enough from early to late in Plato's own writing to make us feel pretty strongly that the cardinal doctrines must have been systematized at least to a very large degree by Plato's own writing. The fact remains, as has been pointed out by historians many times, that it is Socrates rather than Plato who really has caught hold of the affections of mankind. One typically struggles to find a unity in the Platonic doctrine and falls back upon reverence for the personality of the individual Socrates, which often glows more finely than the sheerly intellectual contours that were defined by Plato.

What was it basically that the young men in the market place wanted to discuss? What were the issues? Well, first of all, the issue of *what can be known.* The Sophists (and the word means the wise or those that pretend to be wise) had solved the problem in terms of the unknowability of all ultimate things, whether of cosmogony or of human society or of the individual soul. The group was led by very powerful people. If we read the dialogue of the *Protagoras,* or some of the other dialogues of Plato, we find that their doubt was not trifling doubt. This was a profound soul-searching, in which the effort was to find what can really be known. The contours of this kind of thinking are relatively well-known to us in terms of our more recent tradition. We think of the doubts of Descartes, who doubted and doubted until he finally was sure that it was *he* who doubted, and we think later on of Hume and his arch skepticism, and the Kantian attempt to save some kind of practical knowledge out of a welter of unknowability. This is what the Sophists were specializing in defining—the unknowability of the world—and Socrates is concerned mainly to probe into the nature of doubt itself and to see whether we cannot doubt doubt; to see whether we cannot reach some kind of certainties that ring true within.

Now, of course, to meet these issues at Socrates' level, you had to be able to marshal enough humor, enough wit, enough spice, to be able to meet the spirit of your questioner. This issue, I think, is often forgotten. When you are being lampooned you do not answer with a straight face. And when Socrates is represented by Xenophon as saying, for example, "to meet this argument you might as well shave a lion," he is using an image that will convince the man on the street that this is not a hifalutin cloud-walker, but an everyday man with everyday ridiculous images ready to be tossed off. Socrates gives us, in almost every dialogue, a kind of whimsy. This has led some people to say that the task of Plato was really not to give convincing arguments, but to hold an issue up so that every conceptual possibility could be considered, including the ridiculous, including even the self-contradictory. That at least is the image that is sometimes given of the Socratic teaching: an endless dialogue of question-answering rather than a system of final formulations. It is a common view among philosophers that in Plato we are dealing with a sort of *speculum,* a holding up of a ball to see how it glints in all the different lights. They tell us that we must not expect from Plato a final answer to the question of what is knowable.

But it seems to me that the humor here is the humor of a man who is sure of himself, not of a man who is intellectually "all things to all men." There is no doubt at all, for me, that the primary thrust of the philosophy as a cognitive system is to find something we can be sure of. Because when this is discovered it will give an answer to the ultimate questions about the nature of the real. It will give us some sense that we do make contact with reality in spite of all our self-deceptions. Such an approach, thought Plato, will carry one on to a certainty that there is such a thing as knowledge, a certainty regarding right and wrong, and the basis of an ideal society. Plato's dialogues represent endlessly recurring themes having to do with the possibility that we *can* solve the problems of truth, of ethics, of aesthetics, by a common formula: the good, the true, and the beautiful. This attempt to solve these three ultimate problems with a single formula is what is really at the heart of the Platonic struggle. This had been attempted before, and of course, has been attempted ever since.

But for Plato the solution has to lie along cognitive lines. That is, in an era of doubt, in an era in which the young men are being drawn away by Protagoras and the Sophists, there has to be an intellectually solid solution. Then if this can be made clear—if it can be shown that true knowledge is possible —you can go on from this to find the basis for goodness and the basis for beauty. This, of course, was the task of Plato's Academy, which did gratefully use many ideas that were flowing in through other channels. Plato visited the Pythagoreans (page 10) at a critical point, involving his own thought; he was excited about mathematical approaches, giving a mathematical cosmogony in the *Timaeus,* and writing over the entrance to his own Academy the proposition: "Only mathematicians enter here." At the same time, Plato was certainly familiar with applied mathematics, as shown in the architectural and sculptural rhythms, so precious to the modern student of the formal relations of lengths to heights, to widths, and so forth, in buildings and sculpture. There is no question that the wars of the period and the problem of slavery were agitating and confusing the ethical teacher to the point where *The Republic*—the largest, the most systematic of the dialogues—has to deal constantly with the question of straightening out and ordering the relations of fact to beauty and to right and wrong.

This leads us, of course, to the conception of the Platonic *idea,* which is almost equivalent to what we would call the general or abstract truth as contrasted with the specific or concrete. Things are known to us at two levels: concrete and abstract. The Epicureans had begun to cope with this issue (page 30). For the Platonic Socrates, it is quite clear that there are lower-order types of knowing and higher-order types of knowing. It is obvious that as we grope about, as we use our eyes, ears, fingers, we make contact all the time with a brute type of reality; so do the brutes themselves. But there are types of knowledge that pertain to the generalized realities. In one half-whimsical dialogue a young man is saying, "I can understand, Socrates, how a person could see a table or see a cup, but you're saying that there is an ideal table or a universal table. And table*ness* is something I don't see. You talk about cups and I see a cup, and I see another cup, but the abstract cup that you talk about I'm afraid I don't see." To which Socrates replied: "This is natural, since you have the eyes wherewith to see the table and with which to see the cup, but you do not have the intelligence wherewith to see the cup*ness* and the table*ness*."

I do not believe that Socrates said *exactly* this, any more than I believe that Jesus said exactly what is incorporated in many of the parables, but I think we can get the spirit that the whole thrust of the Platonic effort is to convince us that there is a world of abstractions to which sometimes the mathematician has a key, sometimes the aesthetician, sometimes the moralist. There is something about beauty that is not fully incarnated in any material object that is beautiful. There is something about goodness that is not incorporated in any act, however just or however generous. These ideal realities we can see if this kind of eye is open. That is to say, that if the mind as a process of coming to terms with reality opens itself to the ideal, it makes contact with the ideal. Beyond perceptual knowledge there is ideal knowledge, which is the knowledge of universals or generalized or ideal principles. This came into Western philosophy as the problem of "nominalism and realism." The nominalists say, "But really," as the young man said, "there are only individual cups—there isn't any cupness." But the man who is concerned, like the potter, to create cups, has ideal forms or he could not create individual cups. And this issue marks off the "realist" in the traditional use of the term as the man who can apprehend the transsensory.

Here, I think, no one has a right *ever* to present any abstraction about Plato's ideas, without reading what Plato has to say in the celebrated opening of Book Seven of *The Re-*

public. Here is the image of men who are benighted, literally plunged into night, doom, and darkness because they only perceive at a perceptual level; they do not perceive at a cognitive or ideal level.

> And now, I said, let me show in a figure how far our nature is enlightened or unenlightened:—Behold! human beings living in an underground den, which has a mouth open towards the light and reaching all along the den; here they have been from their childhood, and have their legs and necks chained so that they cannot move, and can only see before them, being prevented by the chains from turning round their heads. Above and behind them a fire is blazing at a distance, and between the fire and the prisoners there is a raised way; and you will see, if you look, a low wall built along the way, like the screen which marionette players have in front of them, over which they show the puppets.
>
> I see.
>
> And do you see, I said, men passing along the wall carrying all sorts of vessels, and statues and figures of animals made of wood and stone and various materials, which appear over the wall? Some of them are talking, others silent.
>
> You have shown me a strange image, and they are strange prisoners.
>
> Like ourselves, I replied; and they see only their own shadows, or the shadows of one another, which the fire throws on the opposite wall of the cave?
>
> True, he said; how could they see anything but the shadows if they were never allowed to move their heads? [1]

This is an appeal to us to move our heads. This is an appeal to recognize that beyond the material order described by Democritus there is an ideal order. As a matter of fact, the number order comes close to giving the basis for the ideal system, which is always more generalized and lies beyond all other systems. If we go on from this to see some of the applications to social life, we realize that this is the beginning of a social philosophy that aspires to be based upon the universal application of the nature of knowledge. I would call this a

[1] Plato, *The Republic* (New York: Charles Scribner's Sons, 1948), p. 273.

form of functionalism. I would say that this is an attempt to describe functions or processes of the mind that are able to apprehend the kind of reality that the more primitive, the biological machinery, does not permit. Moderns have liked to say that gestalt psychology, particularly as so brilliantly developed by Wolfgang Köhler, is an attempt to see the formal, generalized realities of mind, lying beyond all associative processes, all memory processes, all acts of emotion or will. There is the question of the organized and abstract nature of the mind as a mind. We may say, in other words, that the formalism of modern gestalt psychology, looking for abstract principles of cognition, memory, and so on, represents an embodiment of the Platonic *idea*. We will try later on, when we come to the modern period, to see how far that view can be justified.

There would be one way of demonstrating, I think, whether it is true or not that the main thrust of the Platonic teaching is to show the embodiment of the wise and the good in the individual case. It must not be forgotten in the controversy that there has to be an exemplification of the ideal, because it is of the very nature of the ideal to seek, so to speak, to incarnate itself in the particular. And if Plato actually has a doctrine about an ideal man, the ideal must take on the specific form of a knowable, identifiable personality. That would mean that aside from enormous personal devotion to Socrates as a teacher, there would have to be a belief that there is something about human personality that transcends altogether the usual philosophical concerns with particulars. In other words, the supreme exemplification of the Platonic ideal would lie in a human being who was an incarnation of the ideal. Now to test that idea, let us consider the classical and much quoted passage about the death of Socrates that appears at the end of the dialogue of the *Phaedo*.

Socrates had been condemned for two things, for "not worshiping the gods that the city worshiped" and for "corrupting the youth." He had been allowed all sorts of opportunities to escape; he could have been exiled; and he could have made various shuffling concessions. For a person who believed as he believed, it was ridiculous to make such concessions; and death was no penalty anyhow, because there was a kind of reality that transcended death. So this is the scene in the prison after he had been condemned to drink the hemlock. The scene that I am describing notes the beginning of clamor and wailing and sadness, the sense of doom on the part of both the women and the men gathered about. He pleaded, however, for quiet and good cheer:

> . . . When we heard his words we were ashamed, and refrained our tears; and he walked about until, as he said, his legs began to fail, and then he lay on his back, according to the directions, and the man who gave him the poison now and then looked at his feet and legs; and after a while he pressed his foot hard, and asked him if he could feel; and he said, No; and then his leg, and so upwards and upwards, and showed us that he was cold and stiff. And he felt them himself, and said: When the poison reaches the heart, that will be the end. He was beginning to grow cold about the groin, and when he uncovered his face, for he had covered himself up, and said—they were his last words—he said: Crito, I owe a cock to Asclepius; will you remember to pay the debt? The debt shall be paid, said Crito; is there anything else? There was no answer to this question; but in a minute or two a movement was heard, and the attendants uncovered him; his eyes were set, and Crito closed his eyes and mouth.
>
> Such was the end, Echecrates, of our friend; concerning whom I may truly say, that of all the men of his time whom I have known, he was the wisest and justest and best." [2]

This passage answers the question of whether the Platonic ideal is remote from specific and everyday human individuality. It is certainly not experienced as such. On the contrary, the fulfillment of the ideal function appears to lie here in the completeness and expression of human individuality.

[2] Benjamin Jowett (trans.), *The Four Socratic Dialogues of Plato* (Oxford: Clarendon Press, 1903), pp. 273–74.

ARISTOTLE

Now in this extraordinary school, the Academy, presided over by Plato for such a long time, there was a young lad from parts north, a young man who, as they often did in spite of the wars and the chaos, made his way to study in the metropolitan schools. Young Aristotle was apparently, at seventeen years of age, full of eagerness to read and to take notes and make a sort of encyclopaedic system out of what there was to learn; he learned and systematized it all as he went on. He was, for a while, a tutor to Alexander the Great. Unable to keep still, he wandered about, both physically and intellectually. He was constantly breaking into new fields, and organized a biological survey, in which qualified observers gathered specimens and helped him in the organization of a taxonomy of living things. The *Parts of Animals,* for example, is one of the resulting biological treatises. These treatises are evidently notes for his lectures.

But despite his encyclopaedic range of interests, his deepest concern was with first principles. There is a *Metaphysics,* a discussion of methodology following right after his book on *Physics.* There is a great amount of what we would call social science, notably works on economics, politics, and ethics, and there is a very vigorous and profound psychological treatise *On the Soul,* usually known by the Latin title, *De Anima.* Here, for the first time, we have an orderly and systematic psychology. He begins with the fragments which the men of old time have offered us, gives a somewhat argumentative but factually pretty satisfactory account of the early psychologists, and goes on with his own observations and original conception. He produced at least four other books which were concerned with pure or applied psychology.

The fact that he apparently had to "stomp about" rather than sit still, characteristic of the whole personality of this man, led to his school's being called the Walking School: "Peripatetic" means "walking around." He managed somehow to bring in, by one device or another, nearly all the standard knowledge of the era, and had, of course, a typical scholar's obsession with the question of the adequacy of what was known. One rather extraordinary phrase from his *Politics* appealed to me. In connection with the fact that people complain that we do not have knowledge enough to decide various issues, he remarks that the trouble is not that we lack knowledge; for "most things are known." The trouble is that we do not apply our knowledge. It is very curious in terms of our conception today, facing the world of the infinitely large and infinitely small, about which we typically remark "how little we know." From the point of view of the great classical standardizer of knowledge, the problem was to systematize, to be just, to be consistent, and to develop a working system in which we use all that is significant.

Now this brings us into the clear opposition of Aristotle to Plato on very fundamental themes. Plato had managed to create two levels, a level of the ideal in contrast to a level of the concrete. And this meant that there was a sort of cave psychology. That is to say, somehow there is a denial of immediate reality, a denial of the things that seem to be most immediate to most people. Suppose, for example, we take the collections of the animals that Aristotle and his collaborators did so well. We should have to deny the working stuff that comes our way in order to set up, with Plato, an *ideal* scheme. This might make a lot of trouble in terms of development, and particularly in terms of comparison of various living things with one another. Such living things must adapt to their environment, which is a general Greek idea; take Hippocrates, for example, who had taught this in the fifth century B.C. There must be a specific living organism, an organism that is partly adapted and that, in the struggle for existence, loses some things and gains others. We must take seriously the reality of the living stuff that makes its contact with the environment. In other words, the Platonic idea did not seem to Aristotle to help him in a *functional* definition of what living things are doing. He thought that the opposition between the concrete and the ideal could be replaced by quite a different kind of opposition. Aristotle was convinced that reality, always needing to be respected and studied, is the *functional* reality by which the *form* of the living thing is expressed. The term *form* is very close to the term *process,* and not very far from the German word *Gestalt.* This kind of form makes it possible for a potential material entity to *become* something. It makes it possible to transcend the blindness of sheer dumb matter, and take on some qualities that realize its potential function.

I think Aristotle's analogy of the ship, near the beginning of his *Psychology,* is useful here. Is the ship that you see lying in the harbor a real object? Well, what do we mean? How does it differ from the logs of wood that we see when the loggers float these down the stream? Plato would say the ship embodies an idea. That is all right so far. But there is much more than this. Even at this level of the non-living thing, there is a function being carried out. What is that function? That function begins to be real if we talk about the sailor who stands on the deck of the ship. The sailor, in terms of what a sailor has to do, gives meaning to this situation. It can be a real ship, it can move upon the waters, if the sailor sails.

In the same way, if we ask: "What is an eye?" the answer will be that if we are talking about the eye of a statue, a stone eye, we are only talking about a rather spatial arrangement, a geometrical organization. But if we are talking about a functional eye, the eye of a living man or animal, then the function of seeing defines what the eye is. We could go on indefinitely with the geometry or the physiological optics of the eye, but if we did not know what *seeing* is, we should miss the biology and the psychology of the definition. It is the function by which the potentiality of the sheer *stuff* there, the sheer *material,* is organized.

This is where the really interesting psychological problems begin. The soul, as a matter of fact, about which Aristotle is writing, is not an unobservable essence. It is not an idea that has existed before birth and that somehow got into the body. On the contrary, the reality of the process of seeing lies in the fact that two potentialities are meeting: One is the potentiality of the living creature to adapt to its environment by taking in some of its context, some of the realities around it; in other words, it is beginning to perceive. The other is the potentiality on the part of the environment to actualize some aspects of itself in a selective process of interaction with the environment that goes on. The environment is potential, as a stimulus pattern. A man wanders about, lost in the woods. He is in a potential environment, some aspects of which he selects, and they become real to him. A great deal of that environment he does not ever take in. He is not in a physical environment that impresses him with all of what it is; there is a highly selective process. The potentiality of seeing and the potentiality of being seen are brought into functional actuality in the process of visual perception.

This is an attempt to get rid of the dualism of Plato; an attempt to say that if we must have a dualism, there is a dualism of matter and form, in which the matter passes over through the reality of form into an actualization process. There is no perception in the sense of Democritus's little images, the *eidola* (page 25), that are thrown at us, which impinge on the eye. Rather, perceiving—visual perceiving—is a process by which the dumb, inert, and meaningless protoplasmic reaction, we might say, moves functionally into contact with an environment that itself has functional possibilities for nurturing the development of response.

This concept of form makes possible, moreover, an interpersonal kind of process, which we shall find developed much more fully in the *Politics,* in the *Nichomachean Ethics,* and particularly in the *Rhetoric.* Let us look at these studies in *applied* psychology. If we think of Aristotle as a biologist with a theory of form and of adaptation, we shall be impressed, but we shall find a very different kind of Aristotle when we pick up the *Rhetoric,* the extraordinary book in which Aristotle tells the orator how to win his cases in court and in the political arena. We may think of the highly developed system of litigation current in the Greek city-states; we may think of Demosthenes, and of the importance of the public speaker who sways audiences; we may think of the "democratic" scene in which Aristides, for example, was ostracized by citizens who had a grudge against him because he was always being called "the just." We have the fulfillment of the milling-about process in which the orator, swaying demagogically this kind of response, acts as a sort of perpetual restraint or antidote to the higher individualistic ideal to which Plato had earlier pointed.

Aristotle, like Leonardo da Vinci, accepts the everyday conflicts of mankind as a part of reality, and writes vigorously and very impressively indeed on the art of oratory. This is social psychology: A study of the way in which the emotions of the human mass function to guide or becloud or redefine the thought processes. It is just as far from the pure biological definition of perception or memory as it can be. It is the psychology of the market place in the full sense of the term. Most of Aristotle's working psychology that has gotten into modern thought is from the *Rhetoric.* It makes very modern reading to scan the way in which the passions of mankind, particularly those that the orator would sway—fear, pride, rage, shame, self-justification, and so on—are spelled out, and the way in which Aristotle weighs the devices by which, for the sake of material gain or good name or self-justification, people manipulate ideas to have them come out the way they want them to come out.

But it is also in the *Rhetoric* that we find the brilliant discussion of the way in which memories are stored, and the way in which associative processes lead from one to another activity. Thus, the *Rhetoric,* as a discussion of applied psychology of everyday life, leads on back again into a series of studies of the more academic sort, dealing with memory and associated processes and with some aspects of the process of thinking. It is in this connection that we find his extraordinary discussion of the dream. The dream is brought in as one of the types of associative process guided by drives, needs, tensions. This was already an old story, of course, at the time Aristotle took it up. But what he has to say about dreams is brought into relation to the general memory storage system, as we should say today, the way in which ideas leave impressions which then are worked over and reorganized by the sleeping mind, preoccupied with its needs. The following, for example, is often quoted: "The most skilful interpreter of dreams is he who has the faculty of observing resemblances. . . . I mean that dream presentations are analogous to the forms reflected in water . . ."[3]

This Aristotelian system with its concern with drives, with associated patterns, with memories, reaches its highest formal expression in the doctrine of the active reason, which is a special kind of reasoning that escapes from the lower, muddy, turbulent thinking controlled by the orator. It is possible to be more than an animal—it is possible to realize a higher type of creative thinking through the full utilization of the active reason. Here we do have a theory of *levels,* again.

Another of Aristotle's psychological treatises is an extraordinary series of little essays. Again, we know them in terms of the Latin title. They are called the *Parva Naturalia,* the little nature essays. They deal with issues like sex differences, age differences, the nature of the memory processes. There is a beautiful, intriguing discussion of the relation of age to the memory process: The mind, he notes, may be compared to a wax tablet, which is at first very soft and which during the years gradually hardens. The memory of the little child is subject to some limitations because impressions made on the soft material are not firm and cannot last long. Impressions, however, that have been firmly established early in life may be maintained in the brittle period of old age, in which the early memories are well retained, but in which new impressions are very hard to make. There is little, I think, that could be added to this at a descriptive level, with regard to the conception of the gradual reorganization, through the growth process, of the modes of response to environmental stimulation; and it is a beautiful application of the concept of structure and function.

Now the ultimate test of the Aristotelian system, I suppose, is the place that it had in the scientific evolution of mankind.

[3] Richard McKeon (trans.), *The Basic Works of Aristotle* (New York: Random House, 1941), p. 630.

During the Middle Ages, some of the Platonic material was kept alive in the Western Church, but Aristotle was really hardly known in the West. Later on, after the Crusades, and after the greater contact with the Islamic world, Aristotle came into Western thinking on a large scale. By the thirteenth century, his was the dominant form of philosophical thinking. It is very curious that, in spite of their great differences, Plato and Aristotle came to represent almost twin deities in the guidance of Western thinking. Plato, however, offered more in matters of beauty and goodness, with a conception of the cognitive function which is rather arid, whereas the Aristotelian conception, particularly the discussions of logic, of form, of memory and association, and of active reason, did prove to be acceptable and usable.

In Chaucer's *Canterbury Tales,* you may remember that the "Clerk of Oxenford," that is to say, the clergyman with an Oxford background, is represented as making his cheerful way on the pilgrimage, stopping to talk all the time, always preoccupied with the nature of knowledge. In those years, to be an Aristotelian was almost equivalent to being a scholar. "A Clerk ther was of Oxenford also,/ That un-to logik hadde longe y-go." Why? Because he was giving all his attention to Aristotelian philosophy. "For him was lever have at his beddes heed/ Twenty bokes, clad in blak or reed,/ Of Aristotle and his philosophye,/ Than robes riche, or fithele, or gay sautrye." The one great good for the philosopher was this marvelous, *marvelous* system of ideas which so beautifully blended in with Christian theology. From the thirteenth century on, it was possible to utilize with inspiration and with excitement all that had been filtered through both at a theoretical and at a practical level. Plato, yes—but the history of Western ideas will show, I think, that the system of Aristotle had certain basic appeals to the potential scientific development of the West that make the Aristotelian functionalism even more central and even more important than the idealism of Plato. We shall need to say more about Aristotle when we come to the medieval period.

4

Hebrew, Greek, and Roman Components in the Emergence of Catholic Psychology

If we allow a rough and general distinction between secular and religious thought, we may say that we have been dealing mainly with secular ideas. We must attempt at least a limited counterbalance, in terms of religious thought, dealing with some of the same general issues that arose in ancient times. If we look at Dante's *Divine Comedy,* we shall be able to say that despite the use of scientific conceptions of astronomy, the formation of the earth, and the development of life, this is essentially a religious cosmology rather than a scientific cosmology. And for an English-language rendering of the same issues we may say that Milton's *Paradise Lost,* although rich in the seventeenth-century scientific thought to which Milton was exposed, is still a religious cosmology. For those of us in the West, this means essentially an amalgam, or perhaps at best an integration, of Hebrew, Greek, and Roman contributions as they finally crystallized into a new structure in the medieval period, in what we may legitimately call Catholic psychology. A great many massive efforts have been made to tell this story, and I am tempted, where giants have trod, at least to find where their footsteps lie, and to recognize, in the attempt at an emerging religious psychology, something that is at least conceived on a grand scale, and uses the secular material to make its own synthesis. The word *Catholic,* from its Greek derivation, means pertaining to all or to wholeness. And what we will attempt to do is to show how the Hebrew, Greek, and Roman components reappear in their new guise, in Catholic psychology. The word can be spelled with a large *C* or a small one. But at least in the small *c* sense of the term *catholic,* that attempt has to be made.

To begin with the tremendous tradition that had been established in Greek secular thought, we may say, with Gilbert Murray, that the Peloponnesian War did more than destroy specific architectural-sculptural efforts, specific schools, particular documents. There was, as Murray says, "a failure of nerve" with reference to the works of the city-state. City-states had supported local religious efforts as well as local economic, military, and political efforts. The failure of nerve meant that one fell back, perhaps, on that which was locally comforting, looking to the cosmic only insofar as the cosmic might support the local quest for safety and redemption. One might say that the Olympian Pantheon, with its magnificent independence, had nevertheless intervened constantly in human affairs, as it did, for example, in a conspicuous way in the *Iliad* and the *Odyssey.* Athena makes herself visible and her works obvious, and intervention in human affairs in the lives of dominant and successful people is to be taken for granted.

But what about a broken and defensive people? How about city-states that had been almost literally razed to the ground and life demoralized? The picture given by Gilbert Murray is one of human hope for restitution through a Deity or a system of deities, capable of warm and personal relations to mankind. Such closeness to the gods had existed before. The question is whether it can be regained, or salvaged, or even intensified; whether the immortal gods can become more personal. They *had* to be, according to the dictates of human needs. There might be less of the cosmic order and the impersonal, the remote, the rational; but there must be a plea for the ministrations of a loving Deity. Murray's suggestions were in harmony with the conception of a kind of "lost generation" that was so commonly expressed after World War I, as in Hemingway's *The Sun Also Rises.* The conception, then, is that a religious psychology in such an era has to be a psychology of comfort. I will not press the parallel between the post-Peloponnesian War era and the period following World War I. There is perhaps a tendency today to doubt whether failure of nerve and compensatory messages of love do actually express the essence of the "lost generation." But one may certainly say that the various *mystery religions,* which may indeed rightly be regarded as competing with the Olympian gods, offered something strong, warm, and continuous, not only in crisis but over a span of hundreds of years. Even a rational psychology must give the life of impulse, the life of personal meaning, great emphasis, and express it in terms of the everyday realities of passion and dread that are so much a part of life, not only in crisis, but always.

From this point of view we may really ask whether "failure of nerve" does justice to a process that involves a genuine new birth. That is to say, if we think of the period after the collapse of the Greek city-state as a period of growing strength in various respects, as it certainly was, it may be possible to think of the new psychology that slowly came into existence as anchored upon realities rather than illusions. We may say, for example, in Epicurean confidence, that man has only himself to deal with; the gods do not care. Or we may indeed find something genuine in building this psychology upon the desperately real and needed reciprocity of human and divine, or whatever is experienced as having larger cosmic dimensions than that of a suffering and failing human existence.

One may say, then: Was not the failure of nerve one aspect of this failure of a secular psychology, and was there not a place for the ripening of the conception of a psychology that offered greater fulfillment of human destinies and needs than had been possible before? As a matter of fact, if we took a glance for a minute at Oriental psychology, we should find that the periods of ecstasy or of impulsive irrationality are often periods of high intellectual development. So, too, if we look at later Greek history, at what happens after the collapse of Alexander's empire (third century B.C.), we may ask whether there was not, despite the collapse, a fulfillment even at the rational level, which combined with new religious meanings of various sorts. It was not a world going to pieces.

Take, for example, the astronomy of the Alexandrian world, which was a tremendously ingenious, competent, mathematically rich development of ideas that ultimately were seen to have tremendous cosmic meanings; not just stellar meanings, let us say, nor planetary meanings, but cosmic meanings in a larger sense. It was in the Alexandrian world that the Ptolemaic system, the system giving our world a place in a vast order, took shape. And centuries later it was in Dante that the scheme of human life as expressive of Divine purpose was fully realized in this Ptolemaic system. In such expressions as "the love that moves the sun and the other stars," the divine order prevails. That is to say, it was not physical force but love that gave the orbits their necessary contours, in the vast beautiful mathematical system of Alexandrian and therefore of Ptolemaic astronomy. What had been added slowly but steadily, in the years from the Greek city-state through to Dante, was an insistence that the two orders, the mathematical order and the personal order, can be fused, or if you like, that a religious and secular approach can be combined. The religious note was dominant over the secular, but used the secular approach, used what science had accomplished.

THE HEBREW TRADITION

Now if we turn back to that era known as Hellenistic, in which Greek and Hebrew thought began to fuse, we may either think of the loss of the individuality of Greek thought and the loss of the individuality of Hebrew thought; or we may think of the fruition of both. If we think of a figure like Philo of Alexandria, or any of the great integrators in the years just before Christ, we shall have to ask ourselves why we have so confidently assumed that there has to be decadence of both Greek and Hebrew messages in order to get the unified field of human endeavor that we think of as present in the Hellenistic period.

I want to say only a few words—more or less self-evident things—about the Hebrew message as it then stood, let us say fourth or third century B.C., and the continuities the Hebrew message maintains from that time forth. After an early period of tribalism, a period of relative simplicity, there came a strong, clear, theistic definition of a loving and a jealous God. Note the extraordinary way in which this developed into a religion of humanity. The loving father of mankind that we find in Hosea, Amos, and Deutero-Isaiah is different from the Olympian, or any other Greek conception. Individuals are held personally responsible for their transgressions, and personally borne to their father's forgiving arms. Amos and Hosea represent an era of responsibility, justice, and love: "Thou shalt not sell the needy for a pair of shoes." This is a doctrine in which ethical vitality, as well as responsibility to a personal Deity, were taken for granted. These two qualities reached such a pitch that they were often preserved in a rather rigid form, but nevertheless with literal devotion to the tradition all through the Hellenistic period, that is, after encountering the Greek tradition. Certainly any survey, however superficial, of the integration of Hebrew and Greek traditions must emphasize this intense personalism and this intense ethical quality of the relations of man and God. And the "family psychology," as Freud taught us to see the matter, involves the assumption that if the relation to the Deity is sound, the relation to the brothers likewise must be sound, as in any family psychology in which the whole human tradition is rich and strong.

If we cast about for a single phrase to represent what is distinctive in Amos, Hosea, Deutero-Isaiah, and other great prophets, it would be hard to find unless it be the phrase *prophetic love* itself. If we look around for a basic psychological conception, a conception of human nature and its relation to ultimate rather than momentary things, we shall find this in phrases that have been picked up where Hebrew and Greek thought fused in early Christianity. These phrases are parts of the tradition in drama, painting, and music; the great prophetic figures of Michelangelo, for example, or the *Messiah* of Handel, in which there is an attempt to show that man does not realize himself fully through perception and memory and active reason and so on, but through some sort of emotional contact with a figure that he conceives to be his Origin, Source, and Fulfillment. The expression from Deutero-Isaiah is used so magnificently by Handel—"Comfort ye my people"—and the message that "Her iniquity is pardoned" is hard to imagine as part of any *secular* psychology. It is hard to see how the conception of reciprocity with the Ultimate, and the reciprocity with one's fellow man, could be extracted by following the principles of a rational psychology as previously described. The Hebrew component, however, is often forgotten, and needs to be emphasized. The modern student does not have to know all these things, and be "mighty in the scriptures," as was customary in the great days before the existence of the printing press and, certainly, of Xerox! (It is only necessary to have in hand appropriate Xerox copies in order to remind you of things you have heard from the Old Testament, the New Testament, and Dante, and which perhaps need only to be revived and integrated.)

My suggestion, then, is that we try to represent this first message of the Hebrew tradition in terms of *prophetic love,* and show how poorly this would fit, let us say, either the predominant Greek or the predominant Roman ideas in the tradition I have been trying to describe. But then, I did say that the term *Hellenistic* can be regarded as relating to a fusion of Hebrew and Greek ideas, and here we have some beautiful philosophical issues that tend to remind us more and more of what we have gained by modern biblical scholarship. We cannot today think of the four Gospels as four contemporaneous records, but rather as involving the slow and gentle cross-cultural reworking of the ideas of a great tradition, with the Fourth Gospel and the Book of the Revelation certainly much later than the first three gospels and much more saturated with Greek thought, certainly representing modes of thought in which the Hellenistic can be adequately described. Hebrew and Greek, of course, with many other ideas, have been woven together.

We may then ask ourselves about this extraordinary opening phrase in the Fourth Gospel: "In the beginning was the word." The *word*—literal translation of Greek *logos*—is a conception that had already been current for a long time, and that indicated the belief that somehow the rational order and the human process of language funnel one into the other; the "word" can represent a cosmic structure, a design, a plan, a meaning. And now the incredibly bold theological step, which, as I have tried to suggest, is also a simple psychological step, that the historic Jesus is in point of fact "the Word." That is to say, that there is not only divinity in each popular wayside shrine, but divinity in the sense that the rational and orderly, and at the same time, loving personality of a Deity, incarnates itself in the flesh, which is visible, as one looks at the historic Jesus. Now this may be conceptualized in many fashions, varying all the way from a profound center of personal faith to a bit of odd superstition, depending upon different points of view. But psychologically there can be no doubt that this is a kind of psychology that would not have come from the secular developments, in the direction they were taking, for example, in classical Athens. This is the kind of idea which gives man a sort of integrity, a sort of confidence that his emotions have some meaning, that they have some vitality, that they are going somewhere. So we have actually an *incarnation,* which is not the simple and naïve idea of emptying of the body of one kind of nature and the acceptance of another nature, but is actually the infusion of human nature with a divine intent, in which both rationality, as represented in the law books, and love, as represented abundantly in the Fourth Gospel, are fused. The Fourth Gospel is worth rereading in terms of a reconciliation of the rational and the personal, as conceived in this Hellenistic era.

Some would say that the conception of *morality* has been rather lightly treated here, and I would be inclined to agree with this. Some have said in the past, and here and there one still finds the statement, that it was in Zoroastrianism that the conception of moral right and wrong was first made wholly clear and convincing; the idea of the brilliant, divine presence of the beneficent Sun versus the Satanism of darkness and evil. I do not myself fully understand this—why Zoroaster's Ahura-Mazda and Ahriman are introduced so suddenly at this point. After the invading armies of Alexander, there was much communication between Southern Asia and the Western world. But I do think it is important to remember that the need to feel *right* in the presence of the Divine, to feel *decent,* to feel *forgiven,* is a part of the very message we have in the "Comfort ye my people" of Deutero-Isaiah. That is to say, there has to be an interwoven system of relationships between the love impulse and the sense of guilt, which we know from psychoanalysis are so intimately related. To feel guilty is as centrally human as to love. And certainly there is no doubt that during the Hellenistic period the sense of guilt—particularly in this sense of personal darkness which can only be banished by a tremendous light—had actually been suggested by Zoroastrianism even earlier, and was certainly one of the factors that wove itself into the Western tradition.

Now if we state some of these ideas in the context of first-century Christianity, we need something more than a sense of inadequacy, a sense of sin. We need some sort of device by which the soul can be set free of sin and of unbearable loneliness. This requires some sort of a theory of redemption. I would be inclined to lean here on Angus's book on *The Mystery Religions and Christianity,* stressing rather heavily the fact that throughout the Hellenistic world there had to be a process by which the sick soul could be redeemed and made sound again. This idea, then, forces one to some sort of a practical psychology of self-help. How is it going to free one, not only of physical disease, but of the inner sense of emptiness or of evil? These are near-universal human problems. Going to Mecca, the repeating of phrases, or making offerings at a wayside shrine—will all that work also in the case of sin? Well, empirically it just does not. That is to say, whatever the manipulation of words may be, the individual does not feel the confidence that he alone has the power, or even that he can bargain with his Deity and get rid of the intrinsic difficulties that gnaw at his own soul. His own psychology is a crazy-quilt pattern, some parts of which he believes in, and some of which he must reject. But he does not have the power, he does not have the capacity, to reject what he does not like. The issue is *power* to achieve the good, versus *helplessness* in the face of ugliness and evil; it is the issue of the *will.*

This, I think, is another idea that comes into early Christianity, but does *not* come mainly from Greek sources. For the sake of concreteness, think of the ugly little creature, Thersites, in the *Iliad,* who suggested to the warriors that the Trojan War be called off and the ships go back home. He is represented as misshapen, dwarfish, ugly, a hunchback; one cannot imagine such a silly, crazy, rotten, cowardly idea coming from a strong, good, athletic Olympian figure! Thersites is struck across the shoulders and humiliated on the ground that this word of his is an affront to the nobility of human nature. This is another way of saying that evil is *intrinsic*; it is not called "sin," but its *depravity* is intrinsic in certain people. It is not present in other people. We do not have a theory by which a *sick soul,* as William James calls it, can be *made well.*

But such a theory comes into existence; we can watch this conception of renewal of the human soul that is developing during this Hellenistic period and particularly during early Christianity. Sin, a splotch upon the soul, must be externally removed by a symbolic process, but internally there must be a genuine absolution, and a genuine ablution, a purging. Now this process of cleansing had, of course, been taken care of in the mystery religions by a process of identification with the dying god. This was a well-known idea throughout the Mediterranean world. In the mystery religions, the Deity, originally in animal forms but now in a human form, essentially a manlike kind of God, purges the human soul of its sin, of its corruption, of its evil, its dirt, just as the external symbolic use of the water in baptism points inward to a cleansing from sin.

There was a way, then, to become clean. But man could not achieve this alone. Man lacked the power to save himself. We begin to realize, at this point, that the Greeks had never developed a conception of the will. You can read a great deal of Greek psychology and still wonder how the problem of the will was solved. But it was solved in the mystery religions by giving the power of the will, the freedom of choice, to the Deity, and giving oneself a moment of freedom to throw oneself on the mercy of the Deity. That is to say, the will is not something a strong man intrinsically feels to be autonomous in himself. The will is a kind of a derived strength, from the fact that the Deity is free. And by identifying oneself with the Deity, one simultaneously gets rid of *sin* and of *helplessness*. One therefore is made into a new figure.

I shall not use long extracts describing the mystery religions, which would alone be adequate to do justice to this idea. But in this context there is a place for a passage from Paul's letter to the Romans:

> If then I do that which I would not, I consent unto the law that it is good.
>
> Now then it is no more I that do it, but sin that dwelleth in me.
>
> For I know that in me (that is, in my flesh,) dwelleth no good thing: for to will is present with me; but *how* to perform that which is good I find not.
>
> For the good that I would I do not: but the evil which I would not, that I do.
>
> Now if I do that I would not, it is no more I that do it, but sin that dwelleth in me." [1]

[1] Rom. 7: 16–20.

Frederic Myers, in a little booklet entitled "St. Paul," begins:

> Christ, I am Christ's, and let the name suffice you.
> Ay, for me too, he greatly hath sufficed.
> Lo, with no winning words I would entice you,
> Paul has no honor and no friend but Christ." [2]

This is the picture of the identification with the Savior, with the Deity through whom it is possible to find not only restitution, but a new way of life, a sense of enormous freedom. Indeed this is evident in the account, in the Book of the Acts, of the conversion of Paul. Paul, after the period of his conversion, went into the desert, evidently in a struggle for self-actualization, first through the removal of his own blackness and second through the slow restoration of time—processes that are very hard to state in the classical rational terms we find in Epicurus or, for that matter, Aristotle. It seems to me that these are at least emphases that tend to correct the manifest defects in the coherence of previous psychological systems.

But it would not be true to say that Paul here makes a complete break. It is not quite true that this conception of a psychology of the heart was a new venture. Rather, Paul gives fresh emphasis to components that had been missing. In Athens, intellectual center of the world, he is talking to the world. He had already been writing epistles to the brethren in many cities; indeed, he had made warm friends in many cities to which his missionary efforts were directed. But now, in Athens, on Mars' Hill, he could talk to the intellectuals everywhere.

> Then Paul stood in the midst of Mars' hill, and said, Ye men of Athens, I perceive that in all things ye are too superstitious. [Another translation: "ye are greatly religious."]
>
> For as I passed by, and beheld your devotions, I found an altar with this inscription, TO THE UNKNOWN GOD. Whom therefore ye ignorantly worship, him declare I unto you.
>
> God that made the world and all things therein, seeing that he is Lord of heaven and earth, dwelleth not in temples made with hands;

[2] Frederic W. H. Myers, *St. Paul* (1867).

Neither is worshipped with men's hands, as though he needed any thing, seeing he giveth to all life, and breath, and all things;

And hath made of one blood all nations of men for to dwell on all the face of the earth, and hath determined the times before appointed, and the bounds of their habitation;

That they should seek the Lord, if haply they might feel after him, and find him, though he be not far from every one of us:

For in him we live, and move, and have our being; as certain also of your own poets have said, For we are also his offspring." [3]

These last verses are worth keeping in mind with regard to the supposed shock of the message of Christianity in a Hellenistic world. So far is this from being a shock that although there is much grumbling and dissent after Paul finishes, it is taken for granted that the audience will understand that the conception of God living and moving and having his being in human beings, the conception that we are his offspring, has already been abroad in the land. It had been represented through the mystery religions; was represented by the later Greek tradition itself; and was a matter of common expression in poetry and drama. This surely indicates that Christianity had much which it could use.

This part of the message indicates, however, that a dire sense of absolute human helplessness was not dominant in either Paul's or the audience's mind at the time; rather, there was easy access to the Deity; the warm, supportive, continuing presence of the Deity was taken for granted. But this is only part of the story.

WILL AND GRACE

But man was weak and sinful, and *needed* God. Man could not reach the good, alone, by *wishing* for it. This conception of the powerlessness of the *will* throws open another door to a psychology we have not encountered before. Psychology had simply avoided the problem of the will. In these very large terms

[3] Acts 17: 22–28.

I think we can almost pinpoint this: Man first became fully aware of the problem of the will in Paul's formulation. There had been beginnings. But one great new step, a giant step, lay in this attempt to get a description of human nature as seen in terms of impulse, by each person within himself. This had somehow managed not to get the focal position that it has now as we see it. It comes in, not through the professional philosopher or psychologist, if you can use such appellations, but through a prophet and saint, representing both Hebrew and Greek and now the new Christian conception.

It might be argued that the conception of love, which had also been taking shape in the Hebrew prophets I quoted, as well as love in its various other meanings in the Greek literature of the post-classical period, becomes somewhat different when given the anchorage point of the new Hebrew and Christian theology. The various Greek words for *love,* like *eros,* from which we get the term *erotic,* and *agape,* related to more generalized or "sublimated" conceptions, can be translated in a variety of ways. We have the struggle of the translator to render *agape* as we look at another of Paul's celebrated resounding declarations that love is the central meaning of human existence. The word *charity* in Paul's triad of faith, hope, and charity has tended to be dropped out in English usage as designating love, as though implying that the term *charity* has lost its vitality and that a simple rendering of the word *love* would be more appropriate. But here is the King James version, in the hope the reader will keep in mind the question: Where did this idea come from—this idea of love—what are its ancestors and what is its social context in the Pauline world?

> Though I speak with the tongues of men and of angels, and have not charity, I am become as sounding brass, or a tinkling cymbal.
>
> And though I have the gift of prophecy, and understand all mysteries, and all knowledge; and though I have all faith, so that I could remove mountains, and have not charity, I am nothing. . . .

And now abideth faith, hope, charity, these three; but the greatest of these is charity." [4]

It is clear that for Paul the way to personal renewal lies *not* in the will, but in love; and love is something given him by *grace*.

I think we may look upon Catholic psychology for centuries thereafter as struggling with the following issue: How can we build a conception of human nature that provides for rationality, and for the right exercise of the will, but recognizes the power of love? Perhaps we do not have freedom of the will, unless we love. Love sets us free. Here is a tangle of ideas, very difficult to verbalize, that changed the image of a primarily rational psychology and made it a psychology of affect and impulse. We can begin to see, in the formulation of Paul, why Thomas Aquinas, in the thirteenth century, asks how reason is related to the will, and how the will is related to love. Finally, Aquinas asks the question: Which is superior, which is supreme, reason or will? An unsuitable question, we may feel, for any period—but an expression of an era in which there was an attempt to go beyond rationalism in itself and impulsivity in itself.

Returning, however, to Paul, we find ourselves now moving into a psychology of self-control. We noted Paul's distress that the evil he would *not,* he actually did. Throughout Paul's thought and throughout that of the early Christian theologians, the problems of man's inadequacy force an issue similar to that which arose between the Stoics and the Epicureans: Is there actually a device by which man can choose, and perform, the good? Can will defy the intrinsic baseness of what man is? In Homeric times, as we saw, a base man was treated as a base man, and that was the end of it. In mystery religion times, he thinks of himself as struggling to get out of this black cage. In Pauline times, the sinner thinks of himself as overwhelmed by divine goodness as Paul, on the road to Damascus, was overwhelmed. His conversion was not a matter of his will, but due

[4] I Cor. 13: 1–2, 13.

to intervention in which grace then gave him the freedom to will and to accept God's will.

THE ROMAN ATTITUDE

We must now look at the Roman world, for at least a side-light on this conception of the will and of self-control. Along with the Romans' extraordinary mastery of material things, their toughness and objectivity in road-building, bridge-building, aque-duct-building, they had an amazing capacity to think through and codify legal symbols, incredible skill in calling into some sort of practical human order, economic and political, the ways of all sorts of diverse peoples from England, Gaul, and Spain through to the Middle East. The Roman Empire was based on an extraordinary capacity for order.

How did this order differ from Greek order? Greek order was based on beauty. It reverenced the Pythagorean conception, in which all things have their meaning because there is at their heart a primitive rhythm, grace, a capacity to move freely; movements are almost dance steps. The Roman system could establish an empire by the simple device of conquering, with a few thousand men, a group enormously greater, by virtue of the discipline and the order that had been built into them. Now we might be inclined to say that the problem of self-control would not arise among a people like this. No, it would not *arise,* because it is *built so deeply* within them. Self-control is the primary pattern of life. The beloved laurel-crowned poet, Horace, is discoursing with his patron, Maecenas, the way of a noble man: *"Integer vitae, scelerisque purus* (Upright in life, and free of wrong-doing)." Who is this noble man? Is it wis-dom, is it grace, is it love that guides him? No, it is rectitude, the absence of evil-doing. In the same lovely ode, who is it that makes the journeys to the Caucasus—who is it that goes to the faraway River Hydaspes? It is a man free of crime, a man who maintains control, a man free of inner stain.

Exaggeration is easy. In general, though, in no museum of

fine arts could there be any confusion as to which of the faces and forms are Greek, which Roman. Look at the Roman figures, heads, torsos, and try to find the free, the casual, athletic quality of the males, the nymphlike quality of the females. The problem of self-control was solved in a very different way by the Greeks and by the Romans. It was solved in the Hellenistic period by fusing Hebrew prophetism with Greek grace; among the early Christians by saying that it is God that gives grace, and man's problem is simply to will as God wills. But the contrast introduced by the Romans is great, for the Roman *does* arrogate to himself the power of self-control. That is what Roman Stoicism is all about. Listen to Marcus Aurelius, who as a Roman Emperor, and as a Stoic philosopher, speaks to himself: "This Being of mine, whatever it really is, consists of a little flesh, a little breath, and the part which governs . . . Thou wilt find rest from vain fancies if thou doest every act in life as though it were thy last." [5]

This message was carried on to the end of the Roman period, battling by virtue of a relatively limited and scattered system of garrisons against the vast, powerful, disciplined, and effective barbarian forces that came, wave after wave, century after century, the defenders relying always upon the intrinsic power of Roman self-control, rather than turning to divine guidance.

But with the advent of Christianity, and as Christianity became the state religion under Constantine, we may say that the organization and integration of Hebrew, Greek, and Roman thought could be worked through in a stable way.

AUGUSTINE

One of the great integrators was Saint Augustine, an African bishop, a man of profound scholarship, who had already spent decades in the assimilation, utilization, and integration of the

[5] Morris Hickey Morgan (trans.), Marcus Aurelius's *Meditations,* II, 2, 5.

great classical tradition. His thought is an appropriate introduction to a kind of symbolic thinking that I want to stress now. He was acutely aware of the conflict between redeemed man and natural man: between the City of God and the City of Man. But Augustine was explicitly and self-consciously a psychologist as St. Paul and Marcus Aurelius were not; his theology is a *psychological* theology. His joining of the issue of religious necessity and psychological necessity took the form of creating a psychology out of a system of cosmic, or theological, assumptions. Let me illustrate this by reference to the treatise on *The Trinity*. This, we should certainly think, would be a treatise on the Father, Son, and Holy Ghost. But if we look at it, we see that it is nothing of the sort. Augustine is dealing with the *three-fold nature of the mind.* We might almost say that this is a Pythagorean way of thinking, because number three, as a number, predominates. But what Augustine is undertaking to do is to show that the mind in miniature has a cosmic and symbolic structure. This is an early representation of what is called in modern psychology *isomorphism,* in which the human mind takes its own little structure from structures which are vast and eternal (page 174). In discussing the relations of memory to perception and thought, Augustine writes: "Therefore the knowledge and science of many things are contained in two of these three, memory and understanding; but will must be present . . ." [6] That is, with a three-fold structure we look for the three legs of the tripod. We find that memory is fundamental to all psychological operations, and that understanding goes beyond memory very much as active reason goes beyond memory in Aristotle; but *will* must also be present. This is breaking with the Greek tradition and incorporating this central fact, apparently based upon religious experience, that will is fundamental if there is to be any use of memory or of the understanding.

We are so fond of quoting Descartes—who is said to be the

[6] Arthur West Haddan (trans.), St. Augustine's "On the Trinity," in Benjamin Rand (ed.), *The Classical Psychologists* (Boston: Houghton Mifflin, 1912), p. 133.

end of the medieval and the beginning of the modern—because he realized that every step in our thinking begins with *doubt.* So it might amuse the reader—at least it amused me—to note the following discussion in Augustine, over a thousand years before Descartes:

> And one has attempted to establish this, and another to establish that. Yet who ever doubts that he himself lives, and remembers, and understands, and wills, and thinks, and knows, and judges? Seeing that even if he doubts, he lives; if he doubts, he remembers why he doubts; if he doubts, he understands that he doubts; if he doubts, he wishes to be certain; if he doubts, he thinks; if he doubts, he knows that he does not know. . . .[7]

This can also be called the beginning of an introspective psychology, or even of a type of existential psychology that begins with those aspects of the human predicament which bring down upon us the sense of helplessness and the failure of any possibility of really catching hold of the nature of real reality.

We find in Augustine a very good restatement of the issue that I quoted from Paul about the will (page 68). But we also find in Augustine a somewhat clearer description of what in modern terms is called "free will." That is, if I should give the impression that somehow in Catholic theology there was taking shape an idea of the utter helplessness of man, then this statement from Augustine will set the issue right. It is true that some of the passages in the New Testament, notably Paul's Epistle to the Romans, are often quoted as saying that what we ordinarily call "predestination" was dominant in first-century thinking. But there is no doubt at all for Augustine that, in spite of the helplessness and sinfulness of man, *autonomy does exist* in the sense that man is *free to choose* between the way of God and the way of godlessness. And this conception of free will, something that is really built into humanity, is a feature, I think, that is new, that is important, and with which we are still struggling.

[7] *Ibid.*

AQUINAS AND DANTE

Now, if we were asked to find someone to represent the great culmination of these trends, after a long period in which Catholic theology had been working toward a synthesis, certainly most of us would choose Saint Thomas Aquinas. He undertook to integrate Catholic theology with the relatively recently discovered Aristotelian world of thought, but with a great emphasis upon the will. Some, on the other hand, might choose Dante, with his beautiful emphasis upon conscience and therefore his conception of moral responsibility, and at the same time the beautiful recognition of prophetic love, even in the nature of the mechanical universe. The world of the medieval period reached some degree of unification both at a high philosophical level and at the level of average people. Dante's *Divine Comedy* is certainly representative of a world of cognitive and emotional unity, in which man's course is plainly laid out. We need only to read in the *Inferno* the kinds of misdeeds that were never washed out, and in the *Purgatorio* the things that *can* be washed out, and in the *Paradiso* the world of eternal love.

But all this might give the impression that the medieval period succeeded in a full synthesis. And I would be guilty if I left the reader with the idea that we need only to put these parts together like a jigsaw puzzle and that will be the unity known as Catholic theology. Well, there were plenty of people in the thirteenth and fourteenth centuries who thought there was such a thing as a clear complete unity; they came to the lectures that were available to them, and scribbled madly to try to get it all down so that when they went home they would then see it steadily and see it whole. The University of Paris had a very definite formula for handling people who thought they saw how to organize it all:

> Method of Lecturing in the Liberal Arts Prescribed, Paris, December 10, 1355.
>
> In the name of the Lord, amen. Two methods of lecturing

on books in the liberal arts having been tried, the former masters of philosophy uttering their words rapidly so that the mind of the hearer can take them in but the hand cannot keep up with them, the latter speaking slowly until their listeners can catch up with them with the pen; having compared these by diligent examination, the former method is found the better. Wherefore, the consensus of opinion warns us that we imitate it in our lectures. We, therefore, all and each, masters of the faculty of arts, teaching and not teaching, convoked for this specially by the venerable man, master Albert of Bohemia, then rector of the university, at St. Julien-le-Pauvre, have decreed in this wise, that all lecturers, whether masters or scholars of the same faculty, whenever and wherever they chance to lecture on any text ordinarily or cursorily in the same faculty, or to dispute any question concerning it, or anything else by way of exposition, shall observe the former method of lecturing to the best of their ability, so speaking forsooth as if no one was taking notes before them . . ." [8]

[8] Herman Shapiro (ed.), *Medieval Philosophy: Selected Readings from Augustine to Buridan* (New York: The Modern Library, 1964), pp. 250–51.

5

Renaissance Psychology: Hobbes and Descartes

It is customary in the Western world to speak of the centuries after the fall of Rome as the "Dark Ages." The implication of a long period of cultural stagnation, a thousand years of sleep one might say, has been the image perpetuated. Now it is, of course, true that the barbarian invasions destroyed not only physical objects but memories. Though Greek thought was not wholly forgotten, one may say that relatively little Greek thought was remembered after the period of the barbarian invasions, as far as the West was concerned. It is important to remember that many aspects of Western culture were preserved, or quickly revived, by the time of Charlemagne in A.D. 800. Soon there were profound and original contributions, such as Gothic architecture, which far transcended in power and beauty, within its own field, anything achieved in the earlier civilization. But it must be admitted that, as far as *science* is concerned, the Greek message was almost completely forgotten. That is to say, after the tremendous burst of mathematics, astronomy, and even the studies of the human body, for a period at Alexandria, there was a long period in which both physical and biological science was relatively inert.

To make a very complex story very simple, one may say that,

after the period of decline, a rebirth was occurring; by the end of the thirteenth century it was obvious that renewal of Greek thought was occurring at the deepest levels of philosophy, and including psychology. The English monk, Roger Bacon, was appealing for an empirical method, even an experimental method. One finds in this era the beginnings of a rediscovery of Aristotelian thought at its highest in the work of Thomas Aquinas. One finds in the following age of travel and navigation—think of Marco Polo, think of Vasco da Gama, think of Columbus—an accentuation of an act of discovery that had been the essence of the Greek philosophical effort: the conception of discovery, rather than repetition, as the basis of human thought. Consequently, when the Crusades are said to have brought renewed contact with Aristotle, it is important to underscore the broader reality here. It is not only that the crusaders in themselves brought back a great deal; they served also to bring the spirit of inquiry. The West began to make the most of what the Arabs had been able to do, notably in the studies of optics and mathematics, and Aristotle came to the West in this era. One may say the crusaders, the merchants, and the explorers were the scientific acolytes who made possible the grand worship of the investigators themselves. One may say that the Greek spirit and Greek science had been moving West long before the celebrated event in 1453, the fall of Byzantium, in which the Ottoman Turks overran many of the great gates of the East, which, as a matter of fact, they had been threatening for several hundred years.

The westward movement of ideas had begun before 1453, but was accelerated by the physical movement to the West of many of the scholarly personages by whom the Greek contribution was remembered, and by whom a new contribution could be made. One may think then of Petrarch, and of Chaucer in England, as representing a spirit of renewal consonant with much of the most vital in Greek literature. As a matter of course, we find in Chaucer references to Greek mythology and the Greek tradition, as we find them in a heightened scale later on in Shakespeare, using, of course, the standard, widely exploited Plutarch and other sources rich in first-hand contact with Greek events and Greek thought.

So psychology was part of an intellectual renaissance that was moving forward for economic, geographical, military, and a variety of other reasons. Psychology could benefit, too, from the revival of medicine, which became very notable as dissection began to be taken as a matter of course; and the quoting of Galen (which had been the standard method) was eked out by new anatomical and clinical observation. Soon the observation led to new principles, as in the brilliant work of Harvey on the circulation of the blood. So intimate was the relation of psychology to the scientific renaissance that we may rightly say that the founders of modern psychology included Copernicus, Galileo, and Harvey, because it was in this period that the scientific revival was expressed. A convenient date is 1543, for the posthumous appearance of Copernicus's book; and we may think of the Galilean rediscovery, at Padua, of the Platonic mathematical doctrine, together with Galileo's new experiments, as coming a few decades later. This is the period in which we should expect a scientific revival in psychology to occur, and the expectation fits almost perfectly with the reality. Francis Bacon's appeal for experimental method and Harvey's actual utilization of that method are part of the context within which a revived Greek psychology appeared. It was a mathematical era and a mechanical era. Leibnitz, the German, writing in French with a vast conspectus of knowledge at his command, says, referring to the revival of Greek thought: "Their fine ways of explaining nature mechanically charmed me." As a matter of fact mathematics and mechanics, as applied particularly to astronomy, were the main science of the period, rapidly to be followed by the biological and medical investigations encouraged by the *renewed legitimacy* of direct investigation of the body.

Now, when one looks at the picture presented by René Descartes, the French mathematician, one may easily see the sense in the statement occasionally heard, that Descartes was more an appendage to the Middle Ages than he was a harbinger of the Renaissance approach. We have to weave together several components to see the peculiar contribution Descartes was able to make. In the first place, he was one of the profoundest and most original mathematicians in the history of mathematics, the inventor—almost single-handed—of the method of analytical geometry, which with one stroke shows the way in which the geometrical world can be treated as the algebraic world: thus we can transfer a geometrical proposition into an algebraic formulation. This was, of course, very fundamental for the immediate work of Sir Isaac Newton in developing a differential calculus, which, with Leibnitz's development of the integral calculus, offered a fundamental modern mathematical tool. Descartes then had made his mark through the brilliance of his contribution; he was one to be taken seriously in any area in which he ventured.

He is actually quoted most often today in terms of his conception of mind and body. Here it is evident that he is struggling to combine the medieval approach with the modern mechanical approach, which he saw everywhere around him. The much quoted *"dubito, ergo sum"* (I doubt, therefore I am) gives us some basis for philosophical operations. We found in Augustine (page 76) almost the same words. However, the issue, now, with Descartes is to *start empirically,* as Roger Bacon had undertaken to do in the thirteenth century, and find, not in theology or any dogmatic system but in direct observation, the basis for psychological operations, including the understanding of the nature of emotions, memory, reasoning, and thought—a complex of psychological functions that, through the initial empirical approach, are made legitimate subjects of empirical inquiry. In Descartes as a physiologist we also find expressed the integration of mathematical with mechanical ideas. The nerves, as tubes, carry the animal spirits to and from the brain, somewhat as in our modern central switchboard arrangement, which makes possible the rerouting through circuitry of messages from one point to almost any other point in the body. This is often regarded as the beginning of the doctrine of "reflex action."

This conception leads naturally to the over-all description of animal function as automatic and of animals as automata. The "automaton theory"—as William James called it—is essentially the Cartesian idea that living bodies are essentially expressions of mechanical law and mathematical knowledge. Animals therefore obey our command, or behave instinctively, or become inflamed with rage; for in terms of the way they are constituted mechanically, there is no other possible outcome. Much of the traditional material from the history of medicine about the nature of the emotions, as from Galen, for example, is easily assimilated. Descartes had actually done some dissecting. Brett tells us: "Descartes was greatly impressed by the clock-work structures which were to be seen at Nurnberg and elsewhere. The gardens of the aristocracy were adorned with fountains so constructed that the water running in the tubes would move mannikins, play instruments, or even produce sounds like words . . ."[1]

But this point carries us much further. We have started out with a fundamental dualism; for we have looked at the mind as something that can be observed, and yet here we have animals who are behaving effectively although they do not have minds to be observed. The dualism is developed fully and cogently. In *The Passions of the Soul* Descartes tells us that he will treat the passions "after the manner of physics." This makes it possible to define the nature of the reflex act, as used ever since in medical and psychological science: a concept that gradually led to the concept of coordination of instinctive or reflexive acts, in such a way as to give the integrated response that this marvel, the nervous system, is capable of achieving. A good deal of research on the brain was going on, and it was taken as a matter of course that one would push this theory to the point of fully automatizing animal behavior. It would

[1] R. S. Peters (ed.), *Brett's History of Psychology* (abr. ed.; Cambridge, Mass.: MIT Press, 1965), p. 359.

follow also for man, except that with man the problem of rationality arises; except for reason, man can be treated in mechanical terms.

The doctrine of *The Passions of the Soul* differs from Aristotle's celebrated discussion of the emotions in the sense that with Descartes we start with physical principles almost as in Democritus or Lucretius.

To a modern this may appear inconsistent. Descartes aims, however, to apply the same logic to man as to animals. He had started with the assumption that he could work empirically, and we find in man by *direct observation* doubts, thoughts, memories, and so on, that do *not* appear to be of the same substance as the mechanical processes we observe in animals' and man's emotional life. Matter is extended (*res extensa*); soul is *not* extended; it is rational, not a spatial reality. Extension applies to the body, but does not apply to the mind, which we directly observe. Consequently, Descartes can claim full empiricism in denying that automatism holds for man. Man's activity is conceived essentially as it had been in Christian philosophy (whether pre- or post-Aquinas types of philosophy); man's nature was basically separable into two kinds of reality: that which is mental and that which is physical. Note that there was no debate regarding the reality of consciousness, in which affects, feelings, images, and so on are to be discussed. Rather, the essential thing about the higher principle found in man is the capacity for rational thought, and from this follows rational decision. So, as with Aquinas, the will and the active reason are brought close together, and there is no real exercise of the will except in the sense that rational support is offered to a decision. This gives us, however, all that could be asked in terms of a psychophysical dualism. Such dualism we encountered among the Greeks, notably in Plato, and among most of the Christian philosophers. But Descartes laid the foundations for a systematic mechanism and with it a radical dualism.

Now there was going to be an explosion somewhere. Those who were really impressed by the automaton principle could not be satisfied with Descartes' dualism. The mechanical principle by which animals are said to be regulated obviously applies to much of the behavior of mankind, unless having given the rule you decide on a higher rule that constitutes a grand exception. We have in Descartes a beautiful illustration of a man struggling openly and honestly and clearly with a monism and a dualism that do not square and that somehow have got to be forced to square. This required facing details. The following passage from *The Passions of the Soul* shows the extent to which he was willing to go to preserve automatism on the one hand and psychophysical dualism of mind and body on the other.

Article XXXIV

How the soul and the body act one upon the other.

> . . . the minute filaments of our nerves are so distributed throughout all its parts that, on occasion of the different motions which are excited there by means of sensible objects, they open in divers manners the pores of the brain, which causes the animal spirits contained in these cavities to enter in various ways into the muscles, by means of which they can move the limbs in all the different ways of which they are capable, and, also, that all the other causes, which in other ways can set the spirits in motion, have the effect to turn them upon various muscles [keeping all this in mind], let us add here that the little gland which is the principal seat of the soul is so suspended between the cavities which contain the spirits, that it can be affected by them in all the different ways that there are sensible differences in objects; but that it can also be variously affected by the soul, which is of such a nature that it receives as many different impressions—that is to say, that it has as many different perceptions—as there occur different motions in this gland; as also, reciprocally, the machine of the body is so composed that from the simple fact that this gland is variously affected by the soul, or by whatever other cause, it impels the spirits which surround it toward the pores of the brain, which discharge them by means of the nerves upon the muscles, whereby it causes them to move the limbs. . . .[2]

[2] René Descartes, "The Passions of the Soul," in Benjamin Rand (ed.), *The Classical Psychologists* (Boston: Houghton Mifflin, 1912), pp. 176–77.

Now this is a starting point for any subsequent mechanistic philosopher to take to pieces and to elaborate. Actually, it happened that La Mettrie, another student of theology, philosophy, and psychology, developed the resolute conviction that this kind of reconciliation of monism and dualism was simply not possible, and he proceeded with a radical reformulation. I urge the reader to embellish his mind with this charming eighteenth-century literature about human nature. In his *Man a Machine* we find a beautiful analysis, almost an evolutionary analysis, of the modalities of difference between creatures of various sorts of complexity, especially complexity of the nervous system. As we read, we find good reasons given why monkeys are brighter than dogs, why apes are brighter than monkeys, and why people are brighter than apes. And then we find La Mettrie repeatedly posing with great force the question: "Where is the dualism which has been presupposed?" What is its basis? Is there no rationality in the ape? Is there perfect rationality in the man? All the questions that Darwin later on in the last century studied in *The Descent of Man,* a supplement to *The Origin of Species,* are stated beautifully, charmingly, by La Mettrie in 1748.

His essay is laid out in almost cosmic proportions. We encounter a universe, creatively organized and progressively organizing and expressing itself through organic as well as inorganic functions, working through the medium of life in ever more complex and creative process. We note the development of powers that lead into rationality, not as a discontinuity, but as an actual expression of the progressive organization that is going on. On this basis, of course, it is necessary to emphasize mechanisms of learning and, in particular, of the development of symbols. The role of words is given with very much of a modern emphasis as the vehicle of the higher rationality that mankind possesses. Quoting from La Mettrie: "Words, languages, laws, sciences, and the fine arts have come, and by them finally the rough diamond of our mind has been polished." [3]

[3] Julien O. de la Mettrie, *Man a Machine* (La Salle, Ill.: The Open Court Publishing Co., 1961), p. 103.

He goes on immediately to show how the infrahuman primates —monkeys and apes—possess a latent capacity for the development of the symbolic life, and he predicts some of the efforts that have been made in the last few years to reduce this gap by describing symbol formation in infrahuman primates at various levels. It is then La Mettrie, not Descartes, who pushes forward the message that has come down from Democritus, Epicurus, and Lucretius. Though we refer a thousand times to Descartes for once that we refer to La Mettrie, it is La Mettrie who first wrote in an orderly and systematic way (and in charming French) an introduction to the new medical and biological sciences that was capable of bridging the evolutionary gap.

In La Mettrie, the new chemistry is obvious here and there. He draws illustrations from chemistry just as he does from mechanics. This is not the case, so far as I know, of any earlier systematic theories. As a matter of fact, mechanics was the dominant science, but chemistry had made enough progress by the mid-eighteenth century to appear, for example, in the analogy of fire as a chemical process prefiguring a few years later the development of the theory of oxidation. It is worth while also to remember that this was only a short time before Voltaire. We must keep in mind the general growth of an insistent agnosticism, frequently pushed to the point of atheism, as characteristic of the eighteenth century. This was encountered elsewhere in Western Europe, too, certainly to a notable degree in the position taken by Laplace with his *Celestial Mechanics,* which, he said, needed no theological buttressing to offer a mechanically perfect universe, and of course, notably Voltaire, who has been referred to as the French interpreter of Newton's mechanical theory of the universe (minus Newton's personal theology). Voltaire and the whole system of the Enlightenment just before the time of the French Revolution offered elaborations of the machine theory early expressed by La Mettrie.

PSYCHOLOGY IN BRITAIN

Now what was going on in Britain during this period of French mechanism, Cartesian dualism, and the struggle to create monism where dualism had been before? I think we could begin with a reference to Roger Bacon and his belief in an empirical psychology, but we would encounter no high psychological effort until the seventeenth century—until the great intellectual-cultural movement represented by the Elizabethan drama, the King James Version of the Bible, the experiments of Harvey—had paved the way. But it is worth remembering that the British were going everywhere and looking and taking part in everything, exactly as the Greek merchants had made their way to Mesopotamia and brought back ideas that soon expressed the hybridization of Greek thought, with elements from many other sources. We do not find very much science, very much original philosophy actually, until this era. It is the Elizabethan period that constitutes the nursery of the psychology that begins in Britain. It is generally recognized that Francis Bacon can be put first in this story. Bacon was himself a man of great cultivation in the new sciences as well as in the classics. I need not drag in the old controversy as to whether Bacon's *Novum Organum,* with its exposition of inductive method, played a large part in the new era of science, but I want to mention him because of his influence on Thomas Hobbes.

Hobbes, who is our main figure for present consideration, had a period of association with Bacon; he seems to have helped with translations and other tasks that Bacon was interested in, and Hobbes, as a vagrant with no firm anchor anywhere, was glad to be associated with a man who was knowledgeable in the new science that was spreading from Italy and France. Now Thomas Hobbes, born in 1588 and living to be ninety years old, is a good figure to represent what is ordinarily called the empirical spirit in Britain. After his Oxford education Hobbes settled down to odd jobs as a page here, a secretary there, and particularly as a tutor, being apparently quite expert in the classics and able to command respect among Oxford gentlemen generally.

There are three great systems of thought beginning to take shape in the Britain of this period, and Hobbes represents all three of them in a very extraordinary integration. That is the reason why he is important for us. He exposed himself very early to the new science of mechanics, and got very excited about it. He went back to France repeatedly, and, picking up in these visits some real understanding of the new science, began to try to push it into practical application.

This was a period of enormous social confusion, represented by the impact of the Commercial Revolution upon the political system, which meant concretely that the landowners were losing their power with reference to the competition of the merchants. It meant ultimately that dramatic events like the execution of Charles the First, and later, the expulsion of the Stuarts, which are political landmarks, give us a good physical culmination of a struggle against royalty and the landowners, carried out effectively by the larger and smaller merchant powers. This social revolution was very clear to Hobbes. At a time when most of the scholars of the period were simply reading essays on sovereignty that had come down from ancient times, it was obvious to Hobbes that the theory of sovereignty was being rewritten right around him.

It was clear, then, that there was some relation, if you could find it, between the mechanical sciences and the social changes going on. The philosophers of a later age would have said that he sought the basis for the science of the spirit, and found it in the science of natural events. Actually he begins with very crude and petulant definitions of social behavior, in simple mechanical terms. But he does not remain long at this level. In his various contacts he manages to make himself something of an integrator. Galileo, professor of mathematics at Padua, had established the mechanical way of looking at the physical universe, generally as an extension of Plato, and partly an extension of what was going on in the mechanical and astronomical mathematics of the period. Hobbes visited Galileo in 1636, and was electrified by the excitement of seeing the great man at work and talking with him. Characteristic of his petulance and excitement, he began making original observations of his own, which Galileo thought were mistaken—guesses as to how to square the circle—and made himself ridiculous among the mathematicians. But this did not stop him. He had a need to push his nose under the tent—all the tents of the period. He had a *mechanical* and a *social* bias, and now a *psychological* one, which came in fits and starts over a long period. You remember that he had an Oxford education; and in particular, he got an education in Aristotle. This was no longer the truncated Aristotle of a few centuries earlier, but essentially the Aristotle that we now know. Hobbes, who translated portions of Aristotle's works, was particularly interested in the *Rhetoric*. We may recall that Aristotle's *Rhetoric* is far indeed from a study of beautiful phrases; it is a study of human nature in various stress situations. The *Rhetoric* is the study of the ways in which human beings, contending for power over one another, are controlled, particularly by symbols, and therefore it is a marvelous introduction to a science of the emotions. Of course, Hobbes ate it up.

Then he began to ask whether there was not a psychology that transcended the psychology he got out of Aristotle. The theory of the association of ideas had come down in various forms from the Stoics, from the Epicureans; as a matter of fact almost everybody had talked about the association of ideas as a fundamental guide to rational as well as irrational behavior. In the *Rhetoric* Hobbes found an Aristotelian association psychology, encountering the doctrine that the impact of the senses does not die out rapidly, but fades out over a long period, into what may be called a memory image. Images within us, just as the Stoics and Epicureans later said, are late phases of sensory processes; even though not having a theory of brain function, there is a physiological clue here: Impressions do not disappear like a plummet dropping into the water; they are more like the slow disappearance of the wavelet that appears on the lake's surface. In other words, if we understand sensation thoroughly, there is a possibility that we can understand its faded form in memory—even a possibility that we can understand creative thinking, because we may say that the images of sense impressions succeed one another in an order that has been given by the original order of stimulation.

Hobbes has an extraordinarily modern conception of what has to be done to make this idea intelligible and useful. Moreover, he proceeds at the same time to develop an introspective psychology based on watching the way in which his own thoughts took shape. He said in the introduction to his great work, *Leviathan,* that if the reader is in doubt at any point as to the nature of thought, let him "consider, if he also find not the same in himself"—not a question of whether we find it in Galen or Aristotle, but a question of whether we find it in ourselves.

So if we say we have Hobbes properly classified as an introspective psychologist, we miss the fact that he is also, up to the limits of his capacity, a physiological psychologist, trying to push Galileo's mechanics into the understanding of nerve process. And, of course, he has close contact with French thinkers of the period, particularly their work with the Descartes group in Paris, making the most of physiological interpretations of psychological process. We have, then, an association psychology based upon Greek and in particular Aristotelian ideas about imagination: "Imagination is decaying sense." That is, sense impressions that are slowly decaying form the basis of thought.

His association with the royalist-conservative forces led him to think of himself as a target in the increasingly bitter civil wars of the period. He became convinced that his days were numbered if he stayed in England. He went to France, remaining over a decade. In Paris, he continued to observe, to think, to exchange ideas with the Cartesians, and to write, until finally he decided that the trouble signs were not as great, and it would be safe to go back to England. There he completed his general formulation of the nature of man, which is what we must chiefly consider here. This was to be a comprehensive theory to show the relation of man's nature to the great problem that was facing him. Hobbes had himself come to terms with the threat that the situation of the civil wars presented. "Myself and fear were born twins." It was obvious that fear was going to be one of the leitmotivs in his development of a conception of man and society.

In any society where powers are constantly shifting, it is necessary to understand something about the status system, the power system, the system of checks and balances that makes possible the operation of a society, a "leviathan," a huge living system like an animal, in which it is possible to separate out the organs and to show how the magnificent thing somehow keeps itself going. How can it do so? Only by a "contractual" relationship, which is essentially a mechanical arrangement involving the balance of forces. The natural state of man is the state of man before he has made this contractual arrangement with other men, by which a guarantee of mutual protection—in other words, immunity from mutual fear—can be provided. But some one individual must have the power to represent the state. In this period of civil war it is obvious that the king is going to be central. The life of the king is ultimately the key to the freedom of all. There are two states of man: There is the *natural* state of man, living in fear before he has a sovereign upon whom all can converge in this quest for safety. The natural state of man, Hobbes says, before the contract with the sovereign, is "solitary, poor, nasty, brutish and short." Man in this state manages to achieve a better state, lifting himself by his bootstraps to arrange a power system, and to place a sovereign at the top who has the authority to protect all.

But what are the driving forces within mankind that make it possible to function within this system? This is a question of *social motivation,* as it is called in the psychology textbooks today. As Saint Ignatius Loyola had pointed out, man seeks wealth, power, and prestige. You find almost the same formulation in Hobbes. A large part of his book is devoted to the elementary interrelations of the economic or "gain" motive, the nobility or "power" motive, and the status or "glory" motive. There is a long catalogue here of the ways in which the nature of mankind leads to the hierarchical structure that we see.

First, nobility: "Nobility is power, not in all places, but only in those commonwealths, where it has privileges: for in such privileges, consisteth their power."[4] What men aim for is power over one another and immunity against the extravagant power struggle; but nobility is a system of status arrangements that make it possible for one person to achieve greater power than another, and to exercise that power is an expression of his noble station. Next follows a very detailed analysis of the process of "honoring" and "being honored," which we would probably call a *prestige* system.

> To pray to another, for aid of any kind, is *to* HONOUR; because a sign we have an opinion he has power to help; and the more difficult the aid is, the more is the honour.
>
> To obey, is to honour, because no man obeys them, whom they think have no power to help, or hurt them. And consequently to disobey, is to *dishonour*.
>
> To give great gifts to a man, is to honour him; because it is buying of protection, and acknowledging of power. To give little gifts, is to dishonour; because it is but alms, and signifies an opinion of the need of small helps.
>
> To be sedulous in promoting another's good; also to flatter, is to honour; as a sign we seek his protection or aid. To neglect, is to dishonour.
>
> To give way, or place to another, in any commodity, is to honour; being a confession of greater power. To arrogate, is to dishonour.
>
> To show any sign of love, or fear of another, is to honour; for both to love, and to fear, is to value. To contemn, or less to love or fear, than he expects, is to dishonour; for it is undervaluing.[5]

[4] Thomas Hobbes, *Leviathan* (Cleveland: World Publishing Co., 1963), p. 115.

[5] *Ibid.*, p. 116.

This is an anatomy of the process of reciprocity, and suggests what McDougall later called "positive and negative self-feeling" —placing oneself in status, honor, glory terms with regard to earlier persons in the hierarchy. We see why Hobbes himself, sedulous, constantly concerned for status and for protection, believing that fear is the most appropriate reaction, asked if others "find not the same in himself." This is usually treated as a "theory of sovereignty," based upon the psychological system of assumptions about the human beings who demand sovereignty.

All this would be sufficient in itself as a reference to Hobbes's place among political scientists. We may go further. We may call Hobbes one of the classic formulators of the theory of the relation of human nature and the state. However, in this one book, and then in an adjoining treatise called *Human Nature,* Hobbes is interested in a much more detailed picture of the actual inside view of the human mind. A classic is his conception of humor: the honor system leads into the quest for "glory." Glory is the subjective side of power.

> *Sudden glory* is the passion which maketh those *grimaces* called LAUGHTER; and is caused either by some sudden act of their own, that pleaseth them; or by the apprehension of some deformed thing in another, by comparison whereof they suddenly applaud themselves. And it is incident most to them, that are conscious of the fewest abilities in themselves; who are forced to keep themselves in their own favour, by observing the imperfections of other men.[6]

Slapstick comedy is a device for replacing one's sense of humiliation by the "sudden glory" that then breaks out into a paroxysm of expression. Each of the motives has to be anchored at both ends, social and physiological; there are thus the power relations of mankind, and at the other end the psychophysiological aspect, the structures that make us laugh.

We have stressed a mechanical theory of motivation and of association. But there is need for a clear distinction: Are *free*

[6] *Ibid.*, p. 93.

associations the only kind of association? When the question is put this way we immediately see why the Stoics and the Epicureans and the scholastic doctrines all missed an essential point about human thought: namely, the process that *guides* thought. They treated thought processes as unguided, unmotivated. They thought of the free associations as essentially like the beads on a string, or like the rings or reflections in a pool, mechanically related to the preceding and the following. But what about the fact that thought is organized around the needs of the person? How about the fact we just considered with regard to the manifestations of glory, that people are seeking in such a way as to formulate and resolve issues? Hobbes, on the basis of his own reading of Aristotle and on the basis of this analysis of the Commonwealth, says at the very beginning of *Leviathan:* "This train of thoughts, or mental discourse, is of two sorts. The first is *unguided, without design* . . . The second is more constant; as being *regulated* by some desire, and design." Titchener, looking over three hundred years of modern history, quotes this passage from Hobbes. That is one of the few instances in which it is possible to pick out a very fundamental fact of human nature that has simply been ignored. Life in general is subject both to mechanical and to highly motivated central control. This is the central and first issue in Hobbes's formulation. The point at which he transcends the Greek formulation is in his theory of controlled association. (Of course, Hobbes's controlled association was also a *physical* process in the body.)

Perhaps with this emphasis upon three systems—the mechanical, the social, and the psychological—it begins to be clear that we are dealing with a real integrator: In this one book, *Leviathan,* we find the mechanical, the social, the psychological. We find, for example, a very good mid-seventeenth-century discussion of brain function in terms of medical studies, and undertaking to reduce all of the psychological processes that he had been describing, to motions within the brain. A hundred years later this could be done much more adequately by David Hartley (page 109). But Hobbes is available to us, as of 1650, with a definition of the way in which the mechanical serves the psychological, namely by giving us concepts by which to understand brain function. How far this is from Descartes! And it is long before La Mettrie. At the same time Hobbes gives us a conception of the thought process, a conception of social motivation, and a conception of the nature of the political contract by which a society is formed.

This is not the right place to go into the ultimate soundness of any of these concepts—later we will try to look back at Hobbes from the twentieth-century point of view—but all three of these ideas from Hobbes represent areas of major modernization of Western thinking with regard to motivation, the relation of body to mental activity, and the relation of both of these to the social order. Croom Robertson, an expert in this field, has this to say in terms of describing the work of Hobbes: "Hobbes attempted a task which no other adherent of the new mechanical philosophy conceived, nothing less than such a universal construction of human knowledge as would bring society and man within the same principles of scientific explanation as were found applicable to the world of nature." [7]

JOHN LOCKE

Now for reasons it would be fascinating to pursue if we could, it is not Hobbes, but John Locke, with his celebrated *Essay* in 1690, who is ordinarily regarded as giving the modern spirit to a rational and empirical psychology. I hope I have conveyed indirectly some of the reasons why Hobbes was very coolly, indeed bitterly, received, not only by people involved in the political fracas at the time, but by people annoyed by his simple and straightforward mechanism, by his essentially irritating and self-satisfied dogmatism, with no established competence either as a mathematician or as a statesman, making

[7] G. C. Robertson, "Hobbes," in *Encyclopaedia Britannica* (11th ed.), XIII, 552.

himself a sort of universal authority. It must be remembered that a great deal had happened in the forty years between 1650 and 1690; that the Stuarts had been expelled; that the middle class or, more accurately, the merchant groups had become dominant. There was every reason, in the mood of 1690, not to emphasize violence, war, brutality, the meanness that we get from this so-called realistic analysis of Hobbes. People settling down to a long period of mercantile prosperity are eager for a simple, generous, straightforward account of how human beings function in a reasonable way—that is what they want to hear.

Locke tells us he will spell out for us empirically the way in which the human mind actually develops. In the child the mind is white paper, waiting to be written upon. That is almost the medieval expression—*tabula rasa,* or wax tablet, waiting to be written on. He develops this systematic empiricism through hundreds of pages of detailed discussion of the origins of the content of human thought.

> 2. *All ideas come from sensation or reflection.*—Let us then suppose the mind to be, as we say, white paper, void of all characters, without any ideas; how comes it to be furnished? Whence comes it by that vast store, which the busy and boundless fancy of man has painted on it with an almost endless variety? Whence has it all the materials of reason and knowledge? To this I answer, in one word, From *experience.*[8]

He is battling the doctrine of the innate ideas, and is arguing that the mind takes shape on the basis of associations formed by sensory impacts—exactly as in Epicurean theory, as a matter of fact, and with a principle of reflection devoid of the theological implication of the Cartesian formulation. He will not, he says, "meddle with the physical considerations of the mind." He is going to save people from the anxiety and confusion of theological arguments; he is going to deal empirically with the

[8] John Locke, "An Essay Concerning Human Understanding," in Benjamin Rand (ed.), *op. cit.*, p. 234.

fact that the mind, as we watch it work, is made up of sensory material ready, at countless points, to be acted upon by reflection. That is to say, the mind is not made up solely of sensory impressions, as one might conclude, but of sensory impressions reworked and reorganized by the reflective process. He can then go on with the statement of the association of ideas, which is a simple, orderly process. Ideas can be reduced to clusters of sensations, and *sequences* of such clusters. The rationality of man finds itself exemplified in the easy, natural way in which we use reflection upon sensory materials to make creative ideas. Hundreds of pages of discussion follow as to how ideas get started and how they work.

A great deal has been written about the Age of Reason, or about the enhancement of the rationality of man as a result of eighteenth-century thought following John Locke. Note, however, the fundamental difference between the conceptions of rationality that we find today in Hobbes and in Locke. Both can be called supreme rationalists. What we have liked to hear is that our supreme rationality is owing to the simple fact that we can take empirical material into the senses and recombine them, and reflect upon them, in an interesting and practical combination. And naturally it is universal education, free political institutions, a great deal that we revere in terms of the emancipation of man from superstition, that we find in the rationality of man as conceived by Locke. The other rationality, springing from the crude impulses of mankind, but shaped by his capacity for controlled association, gives a practical society based on a power struggle, and a law of live-and-let-live solely because existence is possible on no other basis. This is the crass realism of Thomas Hobbes. Modern man does not like to listen to it. What contributions from Locke's and from Hobbes's ideas the twenty-first century will choose to accept, I wish we could predict.

6

Physiology and Psychology in the Eighteenth Century: David Hartley and the Association Psychology

One of the fascinations of the history of psychology is to see what the different national and cultural traditions make out of the same ancient ideas. The differences between German, French, and British approaches become at times very dramatic.

We turn to Leibnitz. Despite his international scope, we begin to find a specific German tradition taking shape, which I thought I would first emphasize, because we shall have to come back from time to time to ask why it is that the German-speaking tradition is so tremendously rich in the whole three hundred years immediately behind us. If, for example, we compare John Locke and his associationism with that of Leibnitz, we are impressed with two deeply ingrained German proclivities that we will find with us through this whole period of three hundred years, from then to now. First is the notion of the *unity* of mental life as expressed, for example, in the word *monad,* as contrasted with the piecemeal nature of the ideas that thread like beads on a string. Along with unity there is, of course, the concept of *activity*. Many have been impressed with the essentially passive nature of the process of perceiving, through most of the history of psychology. The assumption is that things hit us and make a dent on us, and then later on there is a course of events defined temporally, in the physical world of time, to which we relate the succession of our ideas as things that happened to us. But *activity,* in the sense that the perceiver is there controlling, selecting, guiding, organizing these impressions, was usually ignored. That was one reason why Freud—soaked as he was in association psychology—used as much as he could of this principle of activity, but had to invent a theory of motivation and a more full-bodied theory of activity. With Leibnitz we have the individual, the monad, reflecting to be sure the past and the world outside, but actively cutting a course, so to speak, through the thickness of reality. With Leibnitz, consequently, we have the distinction between essentially unconscious receptive processes and active or dynamic ones. Writing in French, he called the former *petites perceptions;* these are the little impressions that are made upon the margin of our minds, as in our modern *subception* or *subliminal perception.* This is to be contrasted with the highly organized and focused nature of the process of receiving, which is called *apperception.* Though this idea had been toyed with in many ways in the Western world, it was peculiarly a German contribution to emphasize the organized, unified, and creative nature of the mind, carried out by a single monad, an indivisible central unit.

CONDILLAC

I want to offer an extreme contrast: The best statement of a *German* conception of unity is in the *French* written by Leibnitz. The best expression of the English conception of unity is in the *French* of Condillac, a very extraordinary philosopher who loves to push everything to extremes. Let us imagine, he says, a statue, and let us see how the statue will give us all of psychology. We have to endow this statue with sense functions —even Locke has done this for us. Condillac, as a student of Locke, endows the statue with a sense of smell. It has nothing else. It has no memory; it has no affect; it has no will. "If we give the statue a rose to smell," remembering that it is endowed with nothing but olfaction, "to us it is a statue smelling a rose, to itself it is smell of rose." The sensory impression is itself complete. The statue's experience is "smell of rose." There are various qualitative variations within rose odors, and, of course, there are successions of sensations because different things strike the nostrils of the statue at different times. "At the first smell our statue's capacity of feeling is entirely due to the impression which is made upon its sense organ. This is what I call attention." This is not an activity like Leibnitz's apperception. This is an experience of transition. As the statue enjoys or rejects the experience there is a subjective experience that we will have to call *affect,* which is a necessary derivative from the sensation.

> From this moment it begins to enjoy or to suffer. For if the capacity of feeling is confined to a pleasant smell, there is enjoyment; and if it is confined to an unpleasant smell, there is suffering.
>
> But our statue has yet no idea of the different changes it can undergo. Thus it is well without wishing to be better, or ill without wishing to be well. Suffering can no more make it desire a good it does not know than enjoyment can make it fear an ill it does not know.[1]

If we have transitions, comparisons of the earlier and the later, making possible the raw quality of transition, this is *attention.* We cease to attend and then we begin to attend to something else. *Pleasure* and *pain*—that is, the good or the bad qualities—constitute the basis of operations in which there is as yet no world of motive or of impulse. The world of motive and impulse are derived almost geometrically from the fact that *comparisons* are inherent in these olfactory experiences. The statue, as absolutely passive and as absolutely lacking in all the unifying central process, becomes, by virtue of the simple sensory associated principles, more and more like a man. There is a certain whimsey about this. But there is also a great deal

[1] Geraldine Carr (trans.), Condillac's *Treatise on the Sensations* (Los Angeles: Univ. of Southern California School of Philosophy, 1930), pp. 4–5.

of seriousness about it. It had been shown that the mind can be reduced "after the manner of physics" to a few components that, from one point of view, are passive. And the same can be done for all the elaborations of psychology that the Renaissance is going to produce.

BERKELEY

During this same era other derivatives of Locke's ideas were being expressed by the philosophers of Western Europe. By all odds the most important British contribution to the psychology in this era was the discovery of the psychology of three-dimensional space by Bishop George Berkeley, shortly after 1700. How is it that the two-dimensionality of the retina, as things are reflected or projected upon it, can give us the world of *depth?* How is it conceivable that I can see an audience organized in space when actually the photographic impression and the retinal impression would both give simply a two-dimensional projection? This we do by the association principle, but we bring in another modality, namely *touch.* In the infant there is reaching. Then eye-hand coordination develops. Along with touch there are inner impressions that were later called *muscular sensations.* So touching, grasping, reaching, taking hold, build tactual and muscular impressions into a complex combined with the two-dimensionality of the visual impression itself. And the third dimension, the direct and intuitive experience of the third dimension, is given by the integration of modalities. This is therefore association psychology, but it is a struggling effort to enrich the purely photographic function earlier described.

Thus we are introducing law and order in place of chaos. And anyone who defines psychological laws is subject immediately to the challenge of the capricious and tenuous character of all the laws that govern the experience of *analysis.* No one, whether it be Aristotle, or whether it be the Epicureans, or whether it be Hobbes or Locke, succeeded actually in a convincing picture of the active texture of the mind. But Berkeley has gone so far as to say: "I can explain to you our world of space by association psychology alone."

HUME

"How can this be?" asked David Hume, a literary man and a traveler, a Scotchman with a wide variety of esoteric ideas about how to write a real psychology that will make fewer assumptions and *deal immediately with the actual stuff,* the actual behaving stuff of people in society. His *A Treatise of Human Nature* went into one edition after another in the whole Western world because arch skepticism of the sort he represented was exactly in harmony with the spirit of an age that was getting so many dogmatic answers, so many easy solutions, such as those I have described. Actually the problem of humanity is the problem of claiming just enough and not too much. The following is the beginning of Hume's *An Inquiry Concerning Human Understanding*:

> Moral philosophy, or the science of human nature, may be treated after two different manners; each of which has its peculiar merit, and may contribute to the entertainment, instruction, and reformation of mankind. The one considers man chiefly as born for action; and as influenced in his measures by taste and sentiment; pursuing one object, and avoiding another, according to the value which these objects seem to possess, and according to the light in which they present themselves. As virtue, of all objects, is allowed to be the most valuable, this species of philosophers paint her in the most amiable colors; borrowing all helps from poetry and eloquence, and treating their subject in an easy and obvious manner, and such as is best fitted to please the imagination, and engage the affections. . . .
>
> The other species of philosophers consider man in the light of a reasonable rather than an active being, and endeavour to form his understanding more than cultivate his manners. They regard human nature as a subject of speculation; and with a

> narrow scrutiny examine it, in order to find those principles which regulate our understanding, excite our sentiments, and make us approve or blame any particular object, action, or behaviour.[2]

Here is the romantic, the literary, and there is the hard, tough, severe task of seeing what we are actually made of and why we behave as we do. Now it is to this latter task that Hume sets himself. We will find out how far we can dissect and get the raw ingredients of human nature. He finds that all the guides, ancient and modern, are based on this delight in speculation that he has just described, and come inevitably to a pessimism, a skepticism, regarding the possibility of ever really knowing. You can write flamboyantly, you can write the novels of Smollett and Fielding, but you cannot really write a human story that is convincing if you content yourself with intellectual analysis. He takes as his target all the philosophers who found the answers. He takes the claims of association psychology to show us that inspection of our minds really offers us only a meaningless sequence of impressions that follow from previous impact. Take Locke, with his beautiful distinction between sensation and reflection. Where do we come out with reflection? We find that reflection itself is given by the series of impacts upon us, and that there is, in other words, no ultimate rationality to be found.

Take the experiences of causality, which so many philosophers have believed to be ingrained in us as a basic form of experience. In terms of the probability of the sun rising tomorrow, in terms of the probability that a mathematical analysis will come out a particular way, we have nothing to go by except a previous empirical order. Skepticism comes, therefore, as the final arbiter, exactly as it has with some of the Greeks. Skepticism comes suggesting that all psychologies are going to come back to essentially irrational orders or sequences of im-

[2] David Hume, "An Inquiry Concerning Human Understanding," in *Essays and Treatises on Several Subjects* (Basel: J. J. Tourneisen, 1793), III, 1–2.

pressions from the past. This is a way of saying that association psychology becomes skeptical philosophy.

Of course, there was resistance against this, and a reaffirmation of common-sense faith, which was called the "Scottish school," a group of philosophers who based their work upon Sir Isaac Newton's studies of the color spectrum, insisting that there *is* a hard world of experimental findings. Psychology must proceed from this world of experimental findings, and not from the philosopher's heavy self-involved doubt. Hume himself had remarked that all of his doubts disappeared when he was "making merry with his friends." That is to say, if you go back to *action,* and give up your sense of *understanding,* your problems will fly away.

SCIENTIFIC TRENDS

Now a few words about what was happening to the hard-nosed world of science in this era. Recall the tradition that Galileo, in Pisa, had observed that swinging lamp, which lent itself to mathematical analysis, as taken up later on by Sir Isaac Newton in the development of a beautiful discussion of vibratory motion. Then think of Harvey, the extraordinary English physician who went to Padua, where Galileo was professor of mathematics. The intimate relation of mathematics, physics, and medicine could hardly be more beautifully underscored than by the journey of Harvey to Padua in 1608, about twenty years before his publication on the "movements of the heart," which we call the theory of the circulation of the blood. The ancients had known that there is some sort of process moving the blood around, but most of them had inclined to the idea that there were two separate systems, a red blood and a blue blood. Even Harvey himself did not discover the nature of capillary circulation. But he did indicate the way in which the new mechanics of the era applied to medicine. And I want to stress particularly that it was mechanics—not science in a broad sense, but just mechanics, exactly as taught by Democritus.

Harvey, writing in Latin, of course, could not think of any word in Latin to describe what the heart does. He knew that Galileo had worked on pumps. Finally he decided that that would be all right, but there was not any appropriate Latin word, so he said simply that the heart works "cum water pump." That is to say, he would at least say what he meant, and he knew what a water pump was. And he goes to work and describes mechanically this guide to the vital functions.

Consider also the vivid anchorage value of Rembrandt's painting, the *Anatomy Lesson.* Recall the fascinated faces of these very successful Dutch business men, who are not just watching a dead body, but are watching the devices by which the tendons operate, the beautiful way in which the surgical preparation makes possible a post-mortem demonstration of the movement of the fingers. It is the *mechanics* that come first of all, long before pathology and, of course, long before biochemistry can be introduced.

But another important movement in the later seventeenth century, along with the discovery of the use of the microscope, in the Netherlands, is the tremendous development of clinical medicine, again prominently in the Netherlands. From clinical observations powerful clues were given, suggesting what was happening at an ultramicroscopic level, the basis for what was appearing in the visible visual field of the microscope. Chemistry was on its way in. I quoted, from La Mettrie (page 87), the reference to new chemical discoveries, and this becomes evident through the whole course of the eighteenth century as an accelerating phenomenon that caused a basic change in medicine from a mechanical to a life science. There were all sorts of mystical ideas as to what the life principle might be, but actual progress in understanding life was coming not so much from mechanics as from chemistry. It was in France, the center of the exact sciences, in the great world that Descartes had dominated and in which clinical medicine now becomes so strongly fortified, that the process of respiration was so beautifully described by Lavoisier just before the French Revolution.

If we turn now to look across the Channel again, we find that Newton has, of course, been the dominant influence. Mechanics was the new science, dominated by Newton, showing how the world is put together. Alexander Pope, writing just about 1750, and, of course, the touchstone of reality for all thoughtful English readers, put it, as usual, very well: "Nature and Nature's laws lay hid in night:/God said, Let Newton be! and all was light." It was only necessary, then, that the perfect mechanics and the perfect mathematics give shape to an ultramaterial reality, a relentlessly and implacably working force, commanding the understanding of that which lay beyond the direct observation of the world. By general agreement, Voltaire becomes the impresario who brings together the world of science and the world of philosophy and religion, and gives a mechanical definition of knowable reality, just as Laplace is writing on what he called the "system of the world" and *Celestial Mechanics,* not needing theories of divine intervention, angels to push planets around. It is only necessary to understand mechanical realities.

So you can begin to see an intellectual force so great that it is going to pervade every scientific effort, whether in medicine or even ultimately in psychology.

HARTLEY

This carries us on to the medical achievements in the eighteenth century in the English-speaking world, which became so important directly and indirectly for the growth of psychology, even until the time of the evolutionary theory. I want to try to make as real to you as I can the work of David Hartley, an English physician, a country gentleman, a quiet practitioner, a man of urbane habits and wide familiarity with the knowledge of the period, who, of course, like the physician, John Locke, was reading philosophy. David Hartley stumbled, about 1741, upon a volume written by a "Reverend Mr. Gay." The parsons, too, were dabbling in philosophy; they were dabbling in mechanics; they were dabbling in Newtonian mathematics. The Reverend Mr. Gay, about whom practically nothing at all is known, had written a little book describing the principle of association as derived, of course, from Locke, Berkeley, and Hume, and the others who were tossing it about. Mr. Gay decided that the whole course of mental activity is guided by the laws of association. Events come to mind in the order in which their impacts first hit us through the senses. First the lightning flash; then, a few seconds later, the thunder; then the splashing of the torrents of rain around you. Later on, given a stimulus word that brings back the flash of lightning, you will think of the clap of thunder, and of the torrents of water. The order of events given in the mind is the order of events given in the original impact on the senses. That is about all that one can safely say must have been present in Mr. Gay's little essay.

About 1740, or 1741, David Hartley read this little book, and it meant something to him that it did not mean to Mr. Gay. Hartley was soaked in the English tradition, and apparently was virtually unfamiliar with the beginnings of the German tradition. Hartley's view was just about as far as one can get from the Leibnitz view; as we will see, it is more in the direction of the Condillac view. But it had a great deal about it that is highly original, and a great deal that was bound to remake psychology. In the first place, among the immediate predecessors there is Hobbes's notion that sensory and associated phenomena depend on localized processes in the body. This is very tentatively stated by Hobbes. What Hobbes has to say about the location of our associative processes is that they depend on "the brain or heart or some internal substance of the head." He cannot give up; neither can he say exactly what happens. It was only a few years after this that the British physician, Sydenham, began to give a classification of mental disorder, making use somewhat of this "organic" point of view. It was only necessary, however, to push a little further, because the art of *dissection* was advancing—think of Vesalius and his incredible drawings, think of Leonardo da Vinci. We learn of students, just before this time, wandering across the face of Western Europe to find a cadaver because, until this time, they were not available. The rate at which the study of the body had become respectable was philosophically important.

As Hartley studied the brain he saw that it could do more, so to speak, than had been demanded of it. He saw that implicit in the Hobbes type of thinking was the idea that each sensory impact involved *its own place in the brain* (the doctrine afterwards called the theory of cortical localization). This for Hartley meant that there are spots in the brain excited in a certain sequence. He used capital *A, B, C, D,* to indicate the order in which sensory impacts are made in the brain, each exciting a local brain process. Now our problem is: How do associations flow in a certain order? This is easy. We have the original physical excitations, *A, B, C, D;* later on, one of these, *A,* is excited again. Let us say that this is a flash of lightning. This is the brain basis for the sensation itself. Now we will use small letters *b, c, d,* to describe the excitations in the brain, on a smaller scale, that follow as the original events are mentally rearoused in due course, not through fresh stimulation, but through slight movements taking place when *A* is set going again. Small *b, c, d,* which follow are the *brain* processes at a level *less intense* than the original excitement. We therefore run through, in association, the same steps we ran through originally in sensation; the only difference between an image by which we recreate the past and the original stimulus itself is in the degree of intensity. A memory image is a faint sensory impression. Its temporal course, its position in the series, is that which is given by the original sense impression.

A good deal of this is in ancient psychologies. Aristotle wrote: "Imagination is decaying sense." We have the idea that memory images are determined by association and that they follow in place of the original massive sensory impact. But, of course, Aristotle did not have any brain, so to speak, in relation to all this. Aristotle apparently thought with his heart; the brain was concerned with cooling operations and with the secretion of tears. It took medicine, it took dissection, it took functional disentanglement of fibers, and so on, to give the kind of medical science that was available by 1750, when Hartley was producing his theory. What he did was to take the psychology of the associative process and put it on a brain basis.

This still leaves us without a good working model of what is going on physically. But there it was, waiting for Hartley's use: It was Newton's work on the pendulum. Newton, following Galileo and the lamp at Pisa swinging in pendular form (page 11), has given Hartley exactly what he needs; the "white medullary substance of the brain" is obviously capable, Hartley says, of vibratory motion. That is, stimulation sets going *waves.* These waves, going on in each of the appropriate regions, are obviously in communication. If one has a process fading out at *A* and beginning to excite *b,* one establishes a habit within the white matter of the brain, conveying its agitation from one region to the next. The white medullary substance of the brain, vibrating in a particular fashion, sets going the successive trains of movement required for the chains of *association.* The medullary substance, and the nerves proceeding from it, are the immediate instruments of sensation and motion. When any considerable injury is done to the medullary substance of the brain, sensation, voluntary motion, memory, and intellect are either lost or much impaired. If the injury be very great, this extends immediately to the vital motions, for example, those of the heart and the organs of respiration. The medullary substance, then, is plainly acting as the local basis for mental activity—almost, indeed, as the "seat of the soul." It is the basis of consciousness, and it serves its function through vibratory motion, exactly as Newton's theory of the pendulum would require.

The Sensations remain in the Mind for a short time after the sensible Objects are removed.

This is very evident in the sensations impressed on the eye. Thus, to use Sir Isaac Newton's words, "If a burning coal be nimbly moved round in a circle, with gyrations continually repeated, the whole circle will appear like fire; the reason of which is, that the sensation of the coal, in the several places of that circle, remains impressed on the *sensorium* until the coal return again to the same place. . . ." [3]

To the modern psychologist this is "critical flicker fusion." That is, if you give brief sensory contacts, one after another, the impression finally becomes a continuous glow. We thus have recourse to specific identifiable observations from time to time to document the general thesis of the dependence of sensation and perception upon bodily activity.

> *Sensations, by being often repeated, leave certain Vestiges, Types, or Images, of themselves, which may be called, Simple Ideas of Sensation. . . .*[4]

> *Any Sensations* A, B, C, *&c. by being associated with one another a sufficient Number of Times, get such a Power over the corresponding Ideas* a, b, c, *&c. that any one of the Sensations* A, *when impressed alone, shall be able to excite in the Mind,* b, c, *&c. the Ideas of the rest.*[5]

We have thus the beginning of a physiological psychology, integrated with a serious consideration of the way in which sensations are related to images, which extends the ideas of the Reverend Mr. Gay so as to yield a really comprehensive scheme. This means that a psychology based on the study of the body, using current observations available from physics and medicine, can for the first time be taken seriously. This kind of physiological psychology began, in the nineteenth century, to include all psychology.

Now we might well say that Hartley leaves out the problem of affect. No; in Hartley's *Observations,* Part II, in which he attempts to apply his basic principles, he treats the affects, particularly the feelings of pleasure and pain, as sensory input,

[3] David Hartley, "Observations on Man, His Frame, His Duty, and His Expectations," in Benjamin Rand (ed.), *The Classical Psychologists* (Boston: Houghton Mifflin, 1912), p. 317.

[4] *Ibid.,* p. 320.

[5] *Ibid.,* p. 323.

exactly as some modern psychologists do. He shows the distinction between cognitive and affective, between cold, clear knowing processes and the turbulent processes of feeling. Feelings are like sensations, and function, in association, as if they were sensations. Psychologists are still struggling with the question of whether feeling is simply a kind of sensation. It is partly a question of linguistic convenience. We may say that the input of affect is like the input of cognitive information; sensations and affects are only relatively distinguishable, and then only by linguistic *tour de force*. Consequently we cannot accuse Hartley of having missed the affects.

But if we compare him with others of the period, notably with Leibnitz, we may have the feeling that somehow action did not come in very prominently. As a matter of fact, it would be rather a nuisance in Hartley's scheme, if it did. You can argue that since Hartley realizes that behavior *follows from the associative train,* his association psychology is really a *behavior* psychology, or even behaviorism. But this is pushing things very far. In point of fact, Hartley does about what Locke did; namely, to give the primary controlling value in life to the sensations. Sensations come in, stream themselves out in a particular order, and then, insofar as acts have been in the past connected with prior sensations and associations, they follow.

I should like now to consider briefly the "intellectual climate" of this beautifully simple and rational psychology, produced by a gentleman-physician, using the newest contributions from science in an era not yet responding to the turbulence and complexity of the dawning new social order. We are intrigued today by the notion that each psychological system is the result of the character of the system-builder. We can push this quite far. John Dewey was fond of saying that to study intellectual history you must recognize that ideas emerge as and when they do because they are the creative expression of a particular person in a particular era. We can even go so far as to say that time and place and culture are all secondary to the *personal* meaning of an idea. When Hobbes creates a society saturated with the fear of man of other men—*bellum omnium contra omnes*—we may say that the timidity of Thomas Hobbes is the reason. We might go on to say that the gentlemanly psychologies are written by gentlemen and that the esoteric or flamboyant psychologies are written by esoteric or flamboyant people. In this connection E. G. Boring, in his *History of Experimental Psychology,* reproduced for us what David Hartley's son wrote about his father. Our acceptance of this is not based on the pretense that a story written by his son could be fully authentic history. But in terms of Hartley's remarkably urbane and ambitious conception of the whole cognitive life, including memory, thought processes, creative thinking, as reduced to a certain series of events stimulating us mechanically through the sense organs, maybe we should expect a certain kind of man to write such a very cognitive kind of psychology, just as we would think of Nietzsche, with his sufferings and his ambition, to write a psychology limited in cognitive detail but rich in the affect-impulse system. Anyway, this is what Boring gives us from David Hartley's son:

> The philosophical character of Dr. Hartley is delineated in his works. The features of his private and personal character were of the same complexion. It may with peculiar propriety be said of him, that the mind was the man. His thoughts were not immersed in worldly pursuits or contentions, and therefore his life was not eventful or turbulent, but placid and undisturbed by passion or violent ambition. . . . He was an early riser and punctual in the employments of the day; methodical in the order and disposition of his library, papers and writings, as the companions of his thoughts, but without any pedantry, either in these habits, or in any other part of his character. . . . He never conversed with a fellow creature without feeling a wish to do him good . . .[6]

[6] E. G. Boring, *A History of Experimental Psychology* (New York: Appleton-Century-Crofts, 1957), pp. 194–95.

On this Boring comments:

> This is human perfection, and yet perfection seems to be but *l'homme moyen* in greatness. It is not merely that the ordinary man reacts against assured, tolerant, benevolent poise in self-defense (for one could still love Hume after two centuries, but scarcely Hartley). It is more that the driving force that leads to greatness runs to extremes of good and bad, or of truth and error. Some error is the price of much truth, some smallness of much greatness.[7]

And I think we could say that nobody ever saw the orderly way in which an association psychology could be built until he became educated in the physics and physiology of his era, and until, at the same time, he cared more about the order, the logic, the cool grace of the whole picture than he did about the representation of the turmoil, the confusion, the internal contradictions, and above all, the emotional explosiveness of human nature. This is a way of saying that Hartley went as far toward systematic psychology as any orderly, thoughtful, poised, or balanced person in the eighteenth century could go.

It is not surprising, then, that this system of ideas got transplanted, became not only the standard English psychology, but was assimilated with suitable transformations everywhere in Western Europe, and that association psychology up to the era of Freud was still the orderly, the systematic, the scientific psychology of the Western world. It could not have done so without the background of association theory from the Greeks, and it could not have done so without eighteenth-century physiological discoveries.

Now the reader will not be surprised, I think, if he notes the addition of a small codicil to this. One may say that this doctrine is materialistic. *Not in the world.* It took La Mettrie, the idol smasher, to make materialism out of ideas of this kind. No. The mind and the body, Hartley says, are one. You could not have asked more from Spinoza, for whom mind and body expressed one reality. The mind and the body *are* one; no

[7] *Ibid.*

mind without the body. And after we die there is no consciousness—until the last trump, until the day of judgment—when body is restored and mind can again be restored.

This is not a diatribe against the Christian tradition; it is an adaptation to the intellectual climate. It is always fascinating to see the pursuit of a scheme *within a certain frame of reference,* and then the necessity to come to terms with *other* frames of reference. And as a warm, generous, decent, gentlemanly person, with a place in a stable social and religious order, one is not going to find the iconoclastic, violent, antivalues approach that might have been predicted if one were dealing with a revolutionary era.

Hartley carries us on *almost* into that great transformation of society we call the Industrial Revolution. As a matter of fact, his book appeared just before the invention of the "flying shuttle," which is sometimes referred to as ushering in the Industrial Revolution in England. It was the beginning, making it possible for one man to do the work of twenty. Shortly after, the factory system was introduced; then came James Watt with his steam engine. Within fifty years the orderly world based upon land and commerce was plainly beginning to be replaced by another kind of orderly world based upon the application of physical forces, and the science of the period was, of course, channeled copiously into the increasing productivity of this system. This had a terrific and immediate effect upon psychology, one of the most dramatic cases of the principle that psychology is rewritten as the times change. Hartley's gentlemanly country-squire type of psychology had no particular relation to the flying shuttle or to the steam engine.

But Jeremy Bentham's pleasure-pain philosophy was not just a traditional hedonism. It was a doctrine having to do with the economic order. Everyone, according to Bentham, makes calculations regarding his own gain and loss. This is the "felicific" calculus, the calculus of pleasure gains, as applied to the business world, the world of the inventor, capitalist, and the worker, spilling over into a theory of penology. How much punishment do we have to assign to keep people from stealing, in terms of a pleasure-pain theory, which is absolutely associationistic all the way through, bringing the affects into a working relationship to the system? In Jeremy Bentham's scheme everyone is governed by association of pleasures and pains with various courses of action, and the total system, based on each person's private pleasure-pain psychology, operates in the mass to provide "the greatest good of the greatest number." The world is a systematic pleasure-pain system, applicable, on the one hand, to the capitalist who decides to withdraw his capital investment from one area and put it in another, and on the other hand to a worker who tries, if he can, to better his status. The social order is conceived in terms of *The Theory of Morals and of Legislation,* the theory of social behavior as based upon rigorous association of conduct with the pleasure-pain principle. Each act is governed by the anticipated consequences based upon past good or bad consequences of such acts.

Side by side with Jeremy Bentham one must name his close associate, James Mill, a Scotchman trained for the ministry, who could not accept the vigorous Presbyterianism of the period, who made his way to England and set himself up as an editor and free-lancer in literature. He gave much time to the study, *History of British India,* and spent all his *leisure*—it is hard to know how to use this word—with little John Stuart Mill sitting on the opposite side of the table working at his studies. There was no Greek-English lexicon at the time, and believing that Greek was the center of civilization and of education, James Mill supplied his little son with slips of paper containing English and Greek equivalents, so that he learned Greek (as he tells us) so early that he never remembered a time when he could not read it. A little later came Latin, and history, and at thirteen came long walks with his father, talking about political economy. Thus John Stuart Mill got a full education. It was very obvious to James Mill—on the principle that the mind is formed by association—that the boy needed more than facts to be memorized. There was a second principle: if the boy was to have a rich, thoughtful, and creative life he must be taught in terms of *habits* that involve doubting, critical analysis, and original thinking. The father was applying the association principle to character education. A very bold and confident father. How to train character becomes clear: in meticulous detail associate something good with any given idea, and that is the association that will stick in the mind. In other words, you can make the little boy into any kind of human stuff you want. Since, of course, he, the father, in the enlightened era to which he belonged, was *right,* the little boy (as he saw it) would also be *formed right.* John Stuart Mill grew up as the living example, for all time, of association psychology rigorously applied. And it is true that he made an outstanding contribution to those three areas—psychology, logic, and political economy—in which he was trained year after year by his father. He did exactly what his father knew he would do.

There may have been a fly in the ointment—that is for you to decide. When he was just short of twenty years of age, he had his own "failure of nerve." He woke up one day to realize that all his values and preferences in literature and characters in history had all been drummed into him. Suppose these associations were all arbitrary? Suppose that the men he considered as noble were base; and the base were noble? Suppose the things he thought of as the *natural consequences* of acts seemed so only because certain selections of material had been presented to him? Maybe neither his father nor he really encountered *any* reality, but just strings of associations.

But he stumbled upon poetry—notably Wordsworth. He read avidly for several weeks, and found intrinsic delight in Wordsworth, and cured himself of his doubts. It is very interesting to see here a step beyond the gate through which David Hume had passed: Hume had learned to challenge everyday confidence in reality; to John Stuart Mill it was found beyond doubt. What had happened was that the association psychology had been pushed to the point where the lack of concern for the *spontaneous motivating forces* of mankind became painfully evident. Association psychology, however, did not drop out because of this dramatic case. It was still the simplest and the most adequate, and physiologically the best base, among all the theories of the period. Indeed, when Freud confronted psychology half a century later, it was still in vogue.

NATIONAL PSYCHOLOGIES

Now I said earlier I would try to say something about national differences in the psychological world. Take the meaning of the word *science*. The word is very important for all the specific sciences, and with a vengeance for psychology. The word *science*, as the French use it, means *exact science*. It is from Latin, "to know." If you studied science in the late eighteenth century in France, you would be studying mathematics, and physics, and beginning to include chemistry. If you do all these things you are a scientist. A little further east, however, there is the word *Wissenschaft*, which the Germans use. Superficially it may seem to be the same thing, for *wissen* is "to know." But it includes a good deal more. It includes what we might call "familiarity with" or "appreciation of" or "wisdom regarding" all that is knowable.

Wissenschaft in the German university is an utterly different thing from *science* in the French university. Beginning back in 1734 at Göttingen, the Germans established a chair for a professor without a specific subject matter—a professor "without portfolio." Thomas Carlyle had a lovely note on such a chair: *Diogenes Teufelsdrökh* was "professor of things in general" at "the I don't know where university." Such a man *really* is broad, wise, urbane; he *knows*. In the German universities *Wissenschaft* includes more than the exact sciences. If we look at the table of the things that were taught at Göttingen, we would find not only Latin and Greek, but other languages, even Oriental languages. All this went far beyond the traditional faculties of law, medicine, and theology. They had the idea of "general education," and there had to be a professor who was broad enough to get some sort of perspective on all these things. Of course, the cultural sciences —such as Baumgarten's work in aesthetics toward the end of the eighteenth century—must be included. It was, of course, not a science in the French tradition.

Society epitomizes in language what its values are and where it is going. It is natural that from now on psychology in France should be modeled very largely upon mechanical and, later, chemical models. It is very natural that the Germans, with this conception of *Wissenschaft,* would find a place for the "spiritual sciences" or "mind sciences." There is no exact translation of *Geisteswissenschaft,* but through the whole German tradition in the life sciences questions are asked far beyond the physics and chemistry of the cell, or the tissue. It is going to ask questions about the meaning of life. We will have a chance to see why the developments of the more exact types of investigation take different forms in France and in Germany, and why, to such a considerable degree within the German-speaking world, the life sciences have taken the shape that we know. This would apply very much, of course, to gestalt psychology and, of course, very much to psychoanalysis. In the German-speaking tradition, the tradition of *Geisteswissenschaft,* it was so broad as to include the whole world of the things of the spirit.

7

Evolution: Charles Darwin

We have encountered the physician David Hartley and the era of eighteenth-century physical and physiological science. Soon the French became pre-eminent in the physical sciences, but the Germans passed them, and soon went on to new conquests in the biological sciences. In the work of Johannes Müller and of Helmholtz we find German physiology rising to a high pitch. With physiology came a wide array of new psychological discoveries, and the growing conviction that psychological problems were amenable to experimental attack. It was still experimental physiology, but a generous physiology. It had under its wing many of the traditional psychological problems about the nature of the process of perceiving. One might have predicted that the rest of the century would well be spent in the use of the *physiological laboratory* in illuminating one psychological problem after another: the nature of memory, thought, emotion, and will.

Actually, however, history had in its womb a child who could compete with the physiological laboratory in terms of scientific interest, especially in terms of implications for humanity. This was the evolutionary conception that all things grow into something new; that life itself is a succession of new stages and forms; that the higher forms are derived from the simpler; and that humanity itself is the expression of a very long and very complex evolutionary process. The Renaissance spirit of rediscovery of the ancient world, and of fresh delight in the principles of order and rationality, had led on into more and more *developmental thinking,* until the thoughtful man of the eighteenth century had begun to conceive of himself as achieving a great enlightenment, an understanding of his own past. He began to enter upon what Tom Paine, and many of the French and British, regarded truly as an "age of reason." The symbols of such rationality were, of course, eagerly welcomed, especially the orderly beauty of the rationalist astronomy. How far astronomy had moved from Phoebus Apollo driving his chariot across the sky and the cycling planets singing the harmony of the spheres, to the cold and orderly movements of celestial bodies, cold but beautiful, as expressed in Laplace's "system of the world" ! The rationalism of Locke and of Descartes, swelling with the new pride of the advancing sciences, had indeed led to the habit of thinking of the eighteenth century as the age of intellectual triumph.

Yet as early as the middle of the eighteenth century many signs of a new and very different kind of stirring appeared. As men traveled they began to find a new *delight* and a new beauty in the world. Heroic couplets changed rapidly into romantic expressions. The troubled young Swiss, J. J. Rousseau, began to protest the dry, mechanical, and authoritative spirit in education, and to insist on setting free the young mind, encouraging it to explore, and giving it for nourishment all that it delighted to discover and to devour. Robert Burns, scornful of discipline and authority, wrote: "A man's a man for a' that!" As Wordsworth was turning to the radiant beauty of lake and stream, the new romanticism began to rock Germany in a movement of "storm and stress," intimately expressed in the great music of the early nineteenth century.

Not so much a *cause* of this as a parallel expression of it, the earth sciences, and especially the life sciences, began suddenly to make strides. The development of the microscope, and the development of interest in field explorations and the gathering of specimens, were accompanied by a sense of growth, a need to see in nature the constant reawakening to newer and higher forms of expression. Both in sober laboratory devotion to careful observation, and in the literary heights of a "philosophy of nature" that sought spiritual meanings in every life principle revealed in animal or plant, we soon find ourselves among a host of *theories of evolution.*

The radical conception of the dynamics of the development of species came in a context of the new and profound emphasis upon the struggles, the successes and failures of life, the feelings and impulses that went with fears and hates and strivings. Lamarck taught an evolutionary system based upon such strivings, and the inheritance of new forms derived from them. *Impulse* came before *thought;* thoughts indeed had arisen out of the very tissues of impulse. Impulse may be the raw struggle for air, water, food, or mate, or it may take on the form of an increasing struggle to master a complex environment—to learn, to understand, to control. The modern psychology that we try now to portray is modern not only in the sense that it finds a place for man's evolutionary past, but more especially because it finds a place for a life of struggle, feeling, impulse, and action. It is not only as important as thought, but historically precedes and, in a deep sense, always preconditions and underlies the higher phenomena of mind. We make a real break, then, as we turn to the evolutionary psychologies of the latter half of the nineteenth century and of our own twentieth century.

TRANSMUTATION OF SPECIES

The primary problem for the biologist was the *transmutation of species,* the capacity of species to develop from other species, rather than arising independently once and for all, as in the creation story in the Book of Genesis. The problem had been recognized, but not solved, by the ancients. As with Lucretius, the new evolutionary doctrines seem to lend themselves to poetic form. Buffon, in the mid-eighteenth century, speculated poetically about evolution; and at the beginning of the nineteenth century Erasmus Darwin, grandfather of Charles Darwin, made a similar bold stroke in a poem entitled "Zoonomia." French and British biologists argued, unconvincingly, pro and con, many of them seeing how an evolutionary principle would clarify their subject matter.

With the vast accumulation of knowledge about forms of animals and plants spread over the earth and in the air and under the sea, and with rapidly increasing skills in the discovery and interpretation of fossil remains, it began to appear, by the second quarter of the nineteenth century, that the cardinal question for biology was to find an empirically justified and rationally coherent theory of the derivation of one species from another. There was need for more evidence. But the matter could not be settled solely by the sheer accumulation of more and more massive evidence on the part of the collectors and the dissectors, the interpreters and the debaters. The great Cuvier, founder of comparative anatomy, rejected the evolutionary principle simply because there was not enough evidence. In his utterances, honoring the glory of the life sciences, he still could not see how the study of life could be *unified*. At the same time, Cuvier gives us a vivid picture of the *romantic* spirit of the biology of the era. In one of his addresses we read:

> The study of animals presents difficulties which only great zeal can surmount; we have to subject them to torments in order to appreciate their physical powers; their innermost energies only reveal themselves to the dissecting-knife—only by living among corpses can we discover them. Among them we find the same spectacle as in the world, whatever moralists may say: they are hardly less wicked or less unhappy than we are; the arrogance of the strong, the meanness of the weak, vile rapacity, short pleasures bought by great efforts—death brought on by long suffering—that is the rule among animals as much as among men. With plants existence is not surrounded by pain—no sad

> image tarnishes their splendour before our eyes, nothing reminds us of our passions, our cares, our misfortunes—love is there without jealousy, beauty without vanity, force without tyranny, death without anguish—nothing resembles human nature.[1]

There had to be poetic perception. But there had to be more. There had to be, at the same time, interpretation of the life processes; the enunciation of a principle by which the interrelations of species could be conceptualized.

CHARLES DARWIN'S BIOLOGICAL BEGINNINGS

We see the story unfolding in the life of Charles Darwin. I read from his own autobiography:

> By the time I went to day-school my taste for natural history, and more especially for collecting, was well developed. I tried to make out the names of plants, and collected all sorts of things, shells, seals, franks, coins, and minerals. The passion for collecting which leads a man to be a systematic naturalist, a virtuoso, or a miser, was very strong in me, and was clearly innate, as none of my sisters or brother ever had this taste.
>
> One little event during this year has fixed itself very firmly in my mind, and I hope that it has done so from my conscience having been afterwards sorely troubled by it; it is curious as showing that apparently I was interested at this early age in the variability of plants! I told another little boy (I believe it was Leighton, who afterwards became a well-known lichenologist and botanist), that I could produce variously coloured polyanthuses and primroses by watering them with certain coloured fluids, which was of course a monstrous fable . . .[2]
>
> With respect to science, I continued collecting minerals with much zeal, but quite unscientifically—all that I cared about was a new-named mineral, and I hardly attempted to classify them. I must have observed insects with some little care. for when ten years old (1819) I went for three weeks to Plas

[1] Georges Cuvier, "Éloges historiques," in J. T. Merz, *A History of European Thought in the Nineteenth Century.* (3rd ed.; Edinburgh: William Blackwood, 1907), I, 127–28.

[2] Francis Darwin (ed.), *The Autobiography of Charles Darwin and Selected Letters* (New York: Dover Publications, 1959), p. 6.

Edwards on the sea-coast in Wales, I was very much interested and surprised at seeing a large black and scarlet Hemipterous insect, many moths (Zygœna), and a Cicindela, which are not found in Shropshire. I almost made up my mind to begin collecting all the insects which I could find dead, for on consulting my sister, I concluded that it was not right to kill insects for the sake of making a collection. From reading White's *Selborne,* I took much pleasure in watching the habits of birds, and even made notes on the subject. In my simplicity, I remember wondering why every gentleman did not become an ornithologist. . . .[3]

On returning home from my short geological tour in North Wales, I found a letter from Henslow, informing me that Captain Fitz-Roy was willing to give up part of his own cabin to any young man who would volunteer to go with him without pay as naturalist to the voyage of the *Beagle.* I have given, as I believe, in my MS. Journal an account of all the circumstances which then occurred; I will here only say that I was instantly eager to accept the offer, but my father strongly objected, adding the words, fortunate for me, "If you can find any man of common-sense who advises you to go I will give my consent." So I wrote that evening and refused the offer. On the next morning I went to Maer to be ready for September 1st, and whilst out shooting, my uncle sent for me, offering to drive me over to Shrewsbury and talk with my father, as my uncle thought it would be wise in me to accept the offer. My father always maintained that [my uncle] was one of the most sensible men in the world, and he at once consented in the kindest manner. I had been rather extravagant at Cambridge, and to console my father, said, "that I should be deuced clever to spend more than my allowance whilst on board the *Beagle*;" but he answered with a smile, "But they tell me you are very clever."

Next day I started for Cambridge to see Henslow, and thence to London to see Fitz-Roy, and all was soon arranged. Afterwards, on becoming very intimate with Fitz-Roy, I heard that I had run a very narrow risk of being rejected on account of the shape of my nose! He was an ardent disciple of Lavater, and was convinced that he could judge of a man's character by the outline of his features; and he doubted whether any one with my nose could possess sufficient energy and determination

[3] *Ibid.,* pp. 10–11.

for the voyage. But I think he was afterwards well satisfied that my nose had spoken falsely. . . .[4]

The voyage of the *Beagle* has been by far the most important event in my life, and has determined my whole career . . . I have always felt that I owe to the voyage the first real training or education of my mind; I was led to attend closely to several branches of natural history, and thus my powers of observation were improved, though they were always fairly developed. . . .[5]

During some part of the day I wrote my Journal, and took much pains in describing carefully and vividly all that I had seen; and this was good practice. . . .[6]

The above various special studies were, however, of no importance compared with the habit of energetic industry and of concentrated attention to whatever I was engaged in, which I then acquired. Everything about which I thought or read was made to bear directly on what I had seen or was likely to see; and this habit of mind was continued during the five years of the voyage. I feel sure that it was this training which has enabled me to do whatever I have done in science.[7]

Another extraordinary event of great timeliness was Darwin's lighting upon Thomas Malthus's *Essay on Population.* It was in the first years of the Industrial Revolution, with fantastic new wealth and abject misery of millions of industrial laborers—men, women, and children—that the clergyman Thomas Malthus had noted the high birth rate and the high death rate of British industrial workers, and wrote an essay pointing to the inexorable fate that would have to reduce the number by war, or by starvation and disease. What Malthus saw in human life, Darwin had begun to see in animals and plants. These are Darwin's words:

In October 1838, that is, fifteen months after I had begun my systematic enquiry, I happened to read for amusement Malthus on *Population,* and being well prepared to appreciate

[4] *Ibid.,* pp. 26–27. [5] *Ibid.,* p. 28. [6] *Ibid.,* p. 29.
[7] *Ibid.,* p. 29.

the struggle for existence which everywhere goes on from long-continued observation of the habits of animals and plants, it at once struck me that under these circumstances favourable variations would tend to be preserved and unfavourable ones to be destroyed. The result of this would be the formation of new species. Here, then, I had at last got a theory by which to work; but I was so anxious to avoid prejudice, that I determined not for some time to write even the briefest sketch of it. . . .[8]

But at that time I overlooked one problem of great importance; and it is astonishing to me, except on the principle of Columbus and his egg, how I could have overlooked it and its solution. This problem is the tendency in organic beings descended from the same stock to diverge in character as they become modified. That they have diverged greatly is obvious from the manner in which species of all kinds can be classed under genera, genera under families, families under sub-orders, and so forth; and I can remember the very spot in the road, whilst in my carriage, when to my joy the solution occurred to me; and this was long after I had come to Down. The solution, as I believe, is that the modified offspring of all dominant and increasing forms tend to become adapted to many and highly diversified places in the economy of nature. . . .[9]

In September 1858 I set to work by the strong advice of Lyell and Hooker to prepare a volume on the transmutation of species, but was often interrupted by ill-health, and short visits to Dr. Lane's delightful hydropathic establishment at Moor Park. I abstracted the MS. begun on a much larger scale in 1856, and completed the volume on the same reduced scale. It cost me thirteen months and ten days' hard labour. It was published under the title of the *Origin of Species,* in November 1859. Though considerably added to and corrected in the later editions, it has remained substantially the same book.[10]

One of the extraordinary coincidences of history is that a young Englishman, Alfred Russell Wallace, after reading Malthus, and falling ill in Malaya, hit upon this idea of natural selection and, as he recovered, wrote it down and sent it to

[8] *Ibid.,* pp. 42–43. [9] *Ibid.,* p. 43. [10] *Ibid.,* p. 44.

Darwin. Imagine the problem for Darwin: receiving the essence of his own theory, written not after twenty years, but after a three-week period, and as far as he could see, with identically the same dynamics. Lyell, the evolutionary geologist who had already seen the stages of the development of the strata of the earth, and the meaning of fossils within this evolutionary scheme, read both Wallace's and Darwin's materials, and told Darwin to go ahead and present this to the Linnaean Society at the same time that Alfred Russell Wallace's paper would be read. The two were therefore presented at the same time, and Darwin's book appeared two months after that presentation.

The biologists, of course, saw that the work—the definitive demonstration by Darwin—should receive the primary acclaim, and so it did.

The essence of Darwin's theory, as summarized by T. H. Huxley, with a little rephrasing, can be stated in three logical steps. First, a pair of statements: (1) There are more offspring than parents. It is true almost universally, of plants and of animals, that the progeny far outnumber the parental stock. But side by side with this is the fact that (2) the total number of individuals, species by species, as observed, for example, in England in the neighborhood of Darwin's own home, tends to be stationary. How can there be more offspring than parents, but the total number remain stationary? The reply is given in the phrase "struggle for existence."

Now if there is struggle for existence, and at the same time *variation,* among the offspring, then we come to an inexorable second step: "survival of the fittest." This phrase has been regarded as the essence of the competitive definition of the evolutionary process.

But this still does not give us the transmutation of species. To be sure, the "fittest" within a particular environment are those that succeed in terms of that particular type of competition, and the death of the unfit will result in some adaptation of the remainder to the nature of the situation. But suppose the situations *change,* and the descendants who are appropriately adapted in *one* environment move to another, where they are no longer well adapted. Now the type that would have failed in the *first* environment became adapted and dominant in the second environment. Thus "survival of the fittest," together with "change in environment," gives us the third step, "transmutation of species."

This approach was corroborated by noticing in the Galapagos Islands, for example, that tidewater animals are different from those further inland, though manifestly similar to them; different *niches* have been found for descendants from the same stock. T. H. Huxley offers us an interesting image for the understanding of this simple three-step logic, with emphasis upon competition of each form of life for a place meeting its own needs, and not just in terms that G. G. Simpson has called "adaptive radiation." A species finds its way to a niche that is appropriate to it by the process of eliminating from its own number those that are unfit for adaptation in the environment. We come to the issue of the interrelations between species, which are all adapted to the physical environment, but which have to battle it out (as hosts, parasites, and so on) with regard to the new adaptive possibility.

I will take some liberties with Huxley's image: There is a large barrel that we want to fill. We fill it with apples. It is full. No; it is not full, because we can now fill it with pebbles. It is now full. But is it? We can now fill it with sand. Finally, it is not full, because we can still fill it with water. We may think of nature's balance as involving the interdependence of species. Many of the issues that cannot be settled simply by the adaptation to the physical environment are settled by adaptation to other forms of life that have made their way by the same general principles.

The impact of Darwin's *Origin of Species* was immediate and resounding. Herbert Spencer's theory of evolution had already become known during the 'fifties. Spencer had said that stars, earth, and life were all products of a gradual process of differentiation from a primitive undifferentiated whole. Changes in the earth, and the evidence from fossil remains, the forms that must have lived long ago, excited attention. In all this, however, evolution had remained a matter of talk, a matter of opinion, something on which serious people could argue inconclusively. Darwin's paper before the Linnaean Society of 1858 had offered something more. It offered a structured system buttressed heavily on a wide range of solid facts. The fifteen hundred copies of the new book available in the retail book stores were exhausted on the day of publication. Right and left the excitement rose. Bishop Wilberforce thought it was disgraceful to be descended from monkeys. It was none other than the great empire-builder, Disraeli, who said, in 1864: "Is man an ape or an angel? I, my lord, I am on the side of the angels. I repudiate with indignation and abhorrence those new fangled theories." The great Harvard zoologist, Agassiz, teacher of William James, died without accepting Darwin's evidence.

But the pressure of more and more facts, and clearer and clearer theory, closed in upon the reluctant and the doubting, and by the end of the century most biologists, and indeed most thoughtful persons, had begun not only to take in stride the evolutionary principle, the principle of the transmutation of species, as a new cardinal foundation for the life sciences, but to see the implications for human life, and in particular for human psychology.

Charles Darwin himself in *The Descent of Man* went on to show that infrahuman mammals are not necessarily as "dumm" as they seem, nor man, in relation to infrahuman mammals, as bright. The transitional forms of behavior between infrahuman animal learning and human learning were shown to have implications for the animal character of at least much of the human mind.

Perhaps the constitution of the human mind can be understood in the light of this long development through ages of adaptation. While Immanuel Kant thought of constitutional limits in man's capacity to know reality, Darwin represented the view that the limits are given by the biological level of the species. William James was to make this the cardinal principle for the understanding of the broad dimensions of human existence (page 154). James's relativism and pragmatism are on the one hand based upon skepticism regarding all absolutes, but on the other hand premised specifically upon the recognition that what the mind, the heart, the feelings, the will can be, must be seen in terms of development from earlier and simpler structures. In the romantic phrase of Emerson: "And striving to be man, the worm/ Mounts through all the spires of form." Such an evolutionism was not pessimistic; it was not a derogation of human dignity. On the contrary, it accepted man's status as the finest end-product of evolution, and was going to present an unceasing upward continuation along the lines defined in this same majestic Emersonian spiral of growth.

I am going to read the concluding paragraph of Darwin's 1871 *Descent of Man*:

> Man may be excused for feeling some pride at having risen, though not through his own exertions, to the very summit of the organic scale; and the fact of his having thus risen, instead of having been aboriginally placed there, may give him hope for a still higher destiny in the distant future. But we are not here concerned with hopes or fears, only with the truth as far as our reason permits us to discover it; and I have given the evidence to the best of my ability. We must, however, acknowledge, as it seems to me, that man with all his noble qualities, with sympathy which feels for the most debased, with benevolence which extends not only to other men but to the humblest living creature, with his god-like intellect which has penetrated into the movements and constitution of the solar system—with all these exalted powers—Man still bears in his bodily frame the indelible stamp of his lowly origin.[11]

Charles Darwin was not only the founder of a new biology and necessarily a new psychology. He was very specifically and

[11] Charles Darwin, *The Origin of Species by Means of Natural Selection or the Preservation of Favored Races in the Struggle for Life* and *The Descent of Man and Selection in Relation to Sex* (New York: The Modern Library [n.d.]), p. 920.

very effectively an observer and an interpreter of human and of animal powers and functions. His best-known psychological contribution is his celebrated *The Expression of the Emotions in Man and Animals*. This is an attempt to view in large perspective the development of primitive instinctive tendencies that aid in the survival of the animal possessing them. Take, for example, the biting and clawing that go with successful attack, the behavior repertories of those that survive and pass through moments of danger rather than being overwhelmed. The action patterns are inborn, and those in whom their inborn quality is poorly defined are constantly being eliminated, while the more effective in attack, or in defense, tend to be preserved. But let us suppose that the situation does not actually demand full use of teeth and claws. Suppose that one can defend one's food by baring the teeth and snarling. Or suppose indeed that one can preserve one's own identity by scaring off those who offer such threats. We can see how the incomplete or truncated expression of primitive rage may easily survive with an adaptive value, and how a wide variety of emotional expressions may be explained as residual expressions similar, except in degree, to the overt movements of attack or defense. Some of the emotions may be essentially expressions of overflow of excitement; but here, too, they would have a background derived from the stirred-up state of the organism, which is regularly present among strains that have been successful in the struggle for existence. Here again I would like to give you Darwin's own words. The following is from *The Expression of Emotions*.

> . . . The three Principles are as follows.
>
> I. *The principle of serviceable associated Habits.*—Certain complex actions are of direct or indirect service under certain states of the mind, in order to relieve or gratify certain sensations, desires, &c.; and whenever the same state of mind is induced, however feebly, there is a tendency through the force of habit and association for the same movements to be performed, though they may not then be of the least use. Some actions ordinarily associated through habit with certain states of the mind may be partially repressed through the will, and in such

cases the muscles which are least under the separate control of the will are the most liable still to act, causing movements which we recognize as expressive. In certain other cases the checking of one habitual movement requires other slight movements; and these are likewise expressive.

II. *The principle of Antithesis.*—Certain states of the mind lead to certain habitual actions, which are of service, as under our first principle. Now when a directly opposite state of mind is induced, there is a strong and involuntary tendency to the performance of movements of a directly opposite nature, though these are of no use; and such movements are in some cases highly expressive.[12]

One thinks here immediately of moving *out* and moving *back,* as in Kurt Goldstein's system, or one thinks of *flexor* versus *extensor* systems, as in Sherrington. Physiology has picked up this idea and elaborated it in many ways.

III. *The principle of actions due to the constitution of the Nervous System, independently from the first of the Will, and independently to a certain extent of Habit.*—When the sensorium is strongly excited, nerve-force is generated in excess, and is transmitted in certain definite directions, depending on the connection of the nerve-cells, and partly on habit: or the supply of nerve-force may, as it appears, be interrupted. Effects are thus produced which we recognize as expressive. This third principle may, for the sake of brevity, be called that of the direct action of the nervous system.[13]

This has come also to be known more recently as a "surplus energy" theory of action, and especially of play; many of the theories of play in child and adult life are derivatives of this third type of "expressive energy" principle.

Darwin was, of course, broadly concerned with the inheritance of action patterns, whether related to emotion on the one hand or to conation and impulse on the other, as seen in the experimental and naturalistic study of instinct throughout the phylo-

[12] Charles Darwin, *The Expression of the Emotions in Man and Animals* (Chicago: Univ. of Chicago Press, 1965), p. 28.
[13] *Ibid.*, p. 29.

genetic series. A celebrated example is Fabre's study of the sand wasp, which stings its prey near the great nerve center, so that the prey remains paralyzed and immobile, capable of giving sustenance to the growing sand wasps of the next generation. After decades of controversy, such ideas of inherited action patterns, with vivid documentation, are again closely studied in many quarters and are to be seen, for example, in a Walt Disney film.

But it was not only in insects that such inherited functions were observed in Darwin's time, and greatly emphasized as expressions of evolution. Lloyd Morgan intrigued a whole generation of psychologists by his observations of the manner in which the moor hen dives when startled, and with his discussion of the innate neuromuscular structure that makes this "perfect" behavior possible in an inexperienced bird. This never-ending question of innate behavior patterns and the question of whether they could really be simply *early-learned* behavior is one on which Dr. Joseph Kovach is now at work in our Menninger laboratories in Topeka.

Soon more and more aspects of psychology, more clearly anchored on the physiological life of man, began to be affected. In time it became evident that there was just nothing in the psychological view of man that was not going to be influenced by the evolutionary principle in one way or another. One might, with Aristotle and with Descartes, lift out a certain group of functions, "active reason," for example, from the context within which the rest of the living system is judged. One might seek to define an intellectual principle that is not derived from an evolutionary background. There are philosophers who still defend such a position. This special exemption, however, creates problems; and these must be faced at the level of the severest and most exacting demands that philosophers impose on one another. These are not, we believe, the kinds of issues that can be fully debated back and forth in a presentation of modern psychology. It would be nearer to the truth to say that, in the hundred years since the *Origin of Species,* psychology has been moving toward a generalized and fundamental evolutionism.

Darwin's retrospective view of his work in science as a whole is expressed in the following words:

> Therefore, my success as a man of science, whatever this may have amounted to, has been determined, as far as I can judge, by complex and diversified mental qualities and conditions. Of these, the most important have been—the love of science—unbounded patience in long reflecting over any subject—industry in observing and collecting facts—and a fair share of invention as well as of common-sense. With such moderate abilities as I possess, it is truly surprising that I should have influenced to a considerable extent the belief of scientific men on some important points.[14]

And now the last paragraph of the *Origin of Species:*

> It is interesting to contemplate a tangled bank, clothed with many plants of many kinds, with birds singing on the bushes, with various insects flitting about, and with worms crawling through the damp earth, and to reflect that these elaborately constructed forms, so different from each other, and dependent upon each other in so complex a manner, have all been produced by laws acting around us. These laws, taken in the largest sense, being Growth with Reproduction; Inheritance which is almost implied by reproduction; Variability from the indirect and direct action of the conditions of life, and from use and disuse: a Ratio of Increase so high as to lead to a Struggle for Life, and as a consequence to Natural Selection, entailing Divergence of Character and the Extinction of less-improved forms. Thus, from the war of nature, from famine and death, the most exalted object which we are capable of conceiving, namely, the production of the higher animals, directly follows. There is grandeur in this view of life, with its several powers, having been originally breathed by the Creator into a few forms or into one; and that, whilst this planet has gone cycling on according to the fixed law of gravity, from so simple a beginning endless forms most beautiful and most wonderful have been, and are being evolved.[15]

[14] Francis Darwin (ed.), *op. cit.,* p. 58.
[15] Charles Darwin, *The Origin of Species* . . . , pp. 373–74.

For a long time Darwin maintained a central position in the world of science. Before the era of Einstein no one questioned that he was *the* scientist par excellence of modern times.

FRANCIS GALTON

Darwin's evolutionary doctrine not only offered a rational developmental order for all life processes, including mind itself; it pointed everywhere to the individual differences, the variations, person by person, that make up so much of the life of the more advanced species. It was mainly through Darwinism that *individuality* came into psychology. As it happened, it was a first cousin of Charles Darwin, Francis Galton, who saw a whole system of evolutionary psychology based upon individuality. At first sight his facility in devising new methods may make us think of him as a consummate gadgeteer, or tinkerer, a man intrigued by little practical immediate devices that he manipulated, rearranged, patched up, and made into a new pattern; a sort of Benjamin Franklin, we might say, who invents a Franklin stove, draws a spark from a thunderstorm, while he creates the homely wisdom of *Poor Richard's Almanac.* We have several such practical tinkering psychologists in our notebook. Some are great psychologists. Others are not. But all, insofar as we care for the world of mechanics and invention, or for *Better Homes and Gardens,* offering improvements in the way of drawing a court or laying linoleum, make psychology come to life as a series of processes to be realistically observed, taken apart and put together again in terms of some practical objective. But in time perspective, we recognize here the first great psychological student of individuality, and the first great deviser of *methods* for the study of individuality.

Galton wanted to know, for example, what goes on in the "mind's eye" in the world of visual images. He prepared a questionnaire to ask people how they visualized the breakfast table as they had sat down to it that day, and devised a method of scaling the vividness of images from 0 to 100. For there were indeed people who denied that they had any mental pictures whatever; some had them faintly, some more strongly. Some insisted that the images were truly hallucinatory in form; they could be scaled at 100, the image being indistinguishable in intensity from the actual sight of the object. He compared images in the visual field with those in the auditory and other fields. He managed to convince a large portion of his colleagues that painters, scientists, inventors, mathematicians, actually carried around in their experience images of various sorts. He showed the apparent weakening of imagery as a product of training in abstract subjects such as mathematics. But he showed that one could carry out effective activity even without needing images in the fine arts; there were painters in the Royal Academy of Fine Arts who admitted to no visual images at all. He showed that the world of images was rich and complex, but above all accessible. It was the accessibility, the practicality, the effort to get materials out where they could be observed, that intrigued him the most.

Quantitative method regularly goes with this posture of the inventor. Thus he decided that all observations could take the form "greater than," "equal to," or "less than." All right, he thought, we will learn to use this method in the measurement of British noses. He made himself a little paper cross-shaped figure with one long arm and three short ones. He hid this in his coat and attached a little pricking instrument to his thumb, and when, as he walked along the Strand, he saw a man whose nose was plainly longer than that of the average he had in mind, he would prick the right arm of the cross. When he saw a man whose nose was shorter than the norm, he would prick the left arm, and for a man whose nose was about standard size, would prick the middle arm. Before long he had gathered enough material to determine whether the norm he had chosen was valid. If it was set excessively high, most estimates would indicate short noses. On the other hand, he could set a norm that would allow approximately equal numbers above and below. The noses have been forgotten, but norms and measurements came riding in, so to speak, upon them. When once we work out a method of this sort we can compare noses of different populations. And what is vastly more important, we can develop a simple, quantitative method by which all data can be ranked or ordered in terms of one, two, three. Today the public-opinion pollster may want to know, in a time of financial crisis, how people feel about the business situation, and he may class people as more optimistic, less optimistic, or about the average level of optimism. He may systematically measure shifts in the direction of optimism or pessimism as he repeats his measures. In the same way, estimates of the competence of students or teachers may be set up.

Galton went on to study the associations between words. He put words on slips of paper hidden under books, and later, after a lapse of time to permit him to forget, used a stopwatch to measure how long it took for words to occur to him in association with those suddenly presented. This was the beginning of the association test, and one of the beginnings of the measurement of the speed of mental processes. Naturally enough, Galton went on to devise a method of *correlation,* to show the relative dependence of one group of measurements upon another. If, for example, within a particular population, walking the sidewalks of the Strand, the long-nosed men tended to have mustaches, he could devise a method of showing the degree of connection between the two. Or he could even go on to refine measures, and to compare ability in engineering with scores on mathematics tests. Correlation coefficients go back to Galton, too, and he took time off to develop fingerprinting and composite photography, and other Franklin-like practical techniques.

All this is the psychology of the man of action who is also a man of thought—a lover of things, a lover of manipulation, and a lover of results. We may compare all these with the kinds of sensory and intellectual satisfactions that we have already considered in earlier psychologies. If, however, there is such a thing as rich and exuberant delight in sheer things to see, handle, and use, Galton is the perfect exemplification of it. You can well write the psychology of a psychologist if you start with the empirical material of what he produced, looking to find his love of the task—in other words, the motivation driving him, the form of the skill he used in fulfilling the task, and the nature of the systematic product that is the personal psychology the man produced. Psychology springs from all that is in human beings, whether at a deeper or less profound level, whether scattered or unified, or whether highly integrated, as in the work of Darwin, or grubby, molelike, particularistic, anchored on immediate reality, as in the case of Galton.

I would like, in closing, to deal with the character of the extended family of the early evolutionists. We may choose five figures to serve as symbols for the great transition to evolutionary psychology. First, Charles Darwin as naturalist, recluse, ruthless self-critic, modest philosopher, of hopes and failures, creativeness, and the tragedy of defeated individual and race. Second, Francis Galton, tinkerer and inventor, the first psychological individualist, preoccupied eternally with the problem of the assessment of individuality in all its forms. Third, from across the Channel in Germany, Friedrich Nietzsche, the nervous, lonely, blind, bitter, grandiose, and prophetic lover of beauty and of spontaneity, who in his solitude dreamed magnificent dreams of the natural man who becomes more than the now-conceivable man—becomes a superman. Fourth, William James, the far-roaming psychological and philosophical genius, who built a new psychology upon evolutionary biology, medicine, the arts, and the new cosmic evolutionary conception. Fifth, Sigmund Freud, the research biologist turned physician and psychiatrist, who saw the broad sweep of the deeper impulse life and its vast implications for the entire spectrum of human expression through mind, heart, and will, creating almost single-handed a psychological system, with the biology of instinct expressed through all the tissues of the body. These are all members of the spiritual family of the evolutionist, Charles Darwin.

8

William James: The Stream of Thought

❦

American explorations into the ways of the mind during the colonial period and until the mid-nineteenth century were largely reflections of British, and to some degree French and German, influences, claiming no great autonomy nor any high-towering originality. Romanticists and transcendentalists, notably Thomas Carlyle, made their huge impact upon our own Emerson, and the discovery of the philosophical issues of ancient Persia and India were channeled through Schopenhauer and Nietzsche to Walt Whitman and Emily Dickinson. Mariners in Indian ports brought back fragments of the fabulous East, and the whalers and clipper ships of Massachusetts helped a little to make East and West aware of one another.

The more orderly thoughts about thoughts, the cognitive psychology, the modes of formulating the way in which the thinker's mind operates, were being richly investigated in Britain and France in the eighteenth century, and more profoundly, and at times more romantically, by the German philosophers of the era. A deposit of all this was left upon our American shores in the Nineteenth Century by those who crossed the Atlantic—the young Americans going for their education in Britain; wandering literary figures like Dickens and Rosetti, who came our way; and a long line of artists, sculptors, architects, poets, whom Van Wyck Brooks has vividly described in *The Dream of Arcadia.* The young American with an idea or a creative impulse was often warmly received in the Florence, the Rome, the Paris, or the London of the period. But still there was no real American philosophy of mind, or any working conception of what an American psychology might be. There was the mystical and prophetic Bronson Alcott, father of Louisa May Alcott, with his curious and highly original philosophy of nature, with his modern conception that a humane person will hesitate to put an earthworm upon a hook at least until he has contemplated whether earthworms experience pain. There was the extraordinary yen for a new religious experience, as evidenced by the growth of the Latter Day Saints, modern spiritualism, the new church of Swedenborg, Mrs. Eddy and Christian Science, and several other vigorous young conceptions of the place of the mind in God's universe. American psychology, in the contemporary sense of the term, did not exist.

There was not even much response to the new British psychology of the nineteenth century, so rich in its evolutionary conceptions as developed by Herbert Spencer and soon to be immortally defined by Charles Darwin in the *Origin of Species.* There was some familiarity with John Stuart Mill's study of logic and scientific method. Above all, America derived inspiration from the Scottish school of philosophy, which opposed the materialistic dissection of the mind into associative bits, and appealed to that direct "common sense," that direct confrontation of reality which we all seem to find when we discover in ourselves the ability to perceive, to remember, to think logically, and to reach realistic conclusions, refusing to accept any doctrines that "belittle the dignity of man." The Scottish school comported well with Calvinistic rigor, a tough-minded facing of the wilderness and the frontier, the harsh problems of slavery, the rapidly advancing wave of industrialism, and the need for something simple and believable while one mastered both Indians and the soil. The Scottish school was the elder brother among a fraternity of young psychologies from abroad, striving each and all to dominate the American scene.

Immense was the transition from the middle to the end of the century. First came the enormous impact of Darwin. A personal example: a New England minister, who happened to be a great-grandfather of mine, read an Amherst professor's volume, *Genesis and Geology,* and saw how geological and biological evolution could be viewed as expressing God's plan for the world. The theme of evolution as an expression of God's scheme, as contrasted with the expression of an impersonal and fortuitous concourse of atoms, danced and staggered through the theologies and philosophies of the rest of the century.

Second among the forces making a new American psychology was the travel of young American scholars to German universities. James McKeen Cattell, first of the troop, arrived at Leipzig to study experimental psychology with Wundt in 1880. He rapidly mastered the new experimental techniques, contributed to the quantitative study of individual differences in the speed of action and thought, made pioneer studies in psychophysics, in reading, and in the process of judgment. Then, needing to know more about an evolution-oriented study of individual differences, he crossed the English Channel and worked for a short time with Francis Galton in the South Kensington Museum in London. Evolution meant writing a psychology in terms of individual differences, and in particular showing how individual differences could be measured. It was Cattell who brought back Francis Galton's message to the Americans.

JAMES AS EVOLUTIONIST

But the great link between the old and the new psychologies was William James. His grandfather, William James of Albany, New York, had made a fortune with which his five children could secure independence for life. One of the five, Henry James, the father of our William James and of Henry James, the novelist, made extraordinary use of this endowment. An accident added tragedy, but also color and direction. A vigorous lad, he tried to stamp out a bonfire and suffered severe burns, with the result that a series of amputations on his leg had to follow. He thus had a second reason for relative isolation from the hurly-burly of the business world. He was, however, a seeker, one who sought by all the routes of philosophy, and above all the new approaches to religion, to find a personal, cosmic meaning that could be intellectually respected and fully incorporated in life. This led to an interest in countless new doctrines, but complete espousal of none. When it was guessed that he was a Swedenborgian, he made it clear that he could not think of committing himself to such a system. When asked what he wanted done about his epitaph, he suggested: "Here lies a man, who has thought all his life that the ceremonies attending birth, marriage, and death were all damned nonsense." Everywhere the family circle, as we know the picture from Henry James, the novelist, and especially from the correspondence of William James with his father and with many others, was one of vigorous and continual intellectual interchange, seeking and enjoying the quest, never really finding, never really content with the result. The letters of William James to the family also breathe winsome affection and devotion. "Beloved Sweetlington," he begins a letter to his sister.

One feels the intensity of his internationalism, his cosmopolitanism, in all his writings. Two impressions are sure to emerge from every account of James's travels to European centers of learning, particularly the new laboratories of psychology: first, his titanic effort to understand, to assimilate, and to judge as fairly as he could the meaning of the new science; and second, the warmth, the personal touch, the burgeoning friendships with men like the musician-experimentalist Stumpf, of Berlin, and the clinical experimentalist Flournoy, of Geneva.

The sons, William and Henry, born respectively in 1842 and 1844, were, from the first, cosmopolitan, roaming with the family to France, Switzerland, Germany, and Britain, mastering the languages, hearing the music, spending days in the museums, absorbing the cultural riches. William James loved the world of visual representation so much that he planned for some years to become a painter. But he loved medicine, too, and philosophy.

His strength was limited. In 1861, back in the United States, he found himself at the age of nineteen in a land entering upon civil war. But he was grossly disqualified on physical grounds from bearing arms. As a matter of fact, even college studies proved to be exhausting. His chemistry professor tells how he would have to lie down in the midst of an experiment. He went on and, despite delays, completed his medical training, in 1869. He went on a fish-collecting expedition to the Amazon with the great Swiss-American naturalist, Louis Agassiz, came back again exhausted and nearly broken; settled into another round of European studies; went on devouring German, French, British medicine, philosophy, and psychology.

Suddenly, as by an act of God, he found himself appointed in 1872 to teach anatomy and physiology to Harvard undergraduates at $600 a year. This small post, around which he organized a small psychological laboratory, gave him a background from which to write his first serious psychological publications, articles in the journal *Mind* in 1876 and thereafter.

His words in a letter to President Eliot are prophetic of his developing world outlook:

> Of course my deepest interest will as ever lie with the most general problems. But as my strongest moral and intellectual craving is for some stable reality to lean upon, and as a professed philosopher pledges himself publicly never to have done with doubt on these subjects, but every day to be ready to criticize afresh and call in question the grounds of his faith of the day before, I fear the constant sense of instability generated by this attitude would be more than the voluntary faith I can keep going is sufficient to neutralize. . . . That gets reality for us in which we place our responsibility, and the concrete facts in which a biologist's responsibilities lie form a fixed basis from which to aspire as much as he pleases to the mastery of the universal questions when the gallant mood is on him; and a basis, too, upon which he can passively float, and tide over times

> of weakness and depression, trusting all the while blindly in the beneficence of nature's forces and the return of high opportunities. A "philosopher" has publicly renounced the privilege of trusting *blindly,* which every simple man owns as a right—and my sight is not always clear enough for such constant duty.[1]

He was already concerned in those years with the implications of the evolutionary theory for the understanding of mind and its biological contexts, and the implications for religion. "Reflex Action and Theism" is a typical title. Side by side with this came an attempt to get away from all the absolute idealism and dogmatic generalities of the era, and to find in the empirical method the raw, grubby confrontation of reality, something immediately given as real, solid, and convincing by which man may live. Evolutionism provided the setting, a context in which specific empirical facts might have meaning.

There was, however, a third psychology to be had for the asking, one supplementing both the evolutionary approach and the new experimental approach. This was the study of psychopathology, coming rapidly into articulate form in France. German studies of mental disease had been held in high esteem in the middle of the century, but slowly the spectacular studies of hysteria by the great Charcot in Paris, and by the provincial medical hypnotist, Liebeault, and his successor, Bernheim, in Nancy, gave France a great position in the study of nervous disorder and, by implication, in the study of personality, from which such disorders may spring. It is not accidental that Sigmund Freud went both to Paris and to Nancy in the 'eighties, as he began his struggle to understand the psychology of hysteria. It was not accidental that the great French physician, Ribot, gave major emphasis to *Diseases of Memory* and *Diseases of Personality*. William James's addiction to the French psychological approach is evident. When it came to the discipline of the medical man and philosopher looking for personality studies he could use, there was much here that he could lift into his

[1] In Ralph Barton Perry, *The Thought and Character of William James* (Boston: Little, Brown, 1935), I, 343.

Principles of Psychology, and surround with the flow of luminous understanding and eager interpretation.

THE STRUGGLE FOR HEALTH

We have already mentioned the illness that James knew in the early years, and that resulted, for example, in the suffering during his years at Harvard. During the trips to Germany we find him frequently suffering from unbearable backaches, eye aches, headaches. In the midst of one of these crises, he obtained dramatic support from reading the French philosopher, Renouvier, a philosophical descendant of Kant. Renouvier had given a central philosophical importance to the *will.* James's letters tell how upon reading Renouvier he saw how he could, by an act of will, live as a well man. The human being, drawn down by illness and discouragement, can, by his own creative and voluntary effort, make himself well; suddenly, and with great force, Renouvier swept aside James's doubts and a good part of his illness. We find in the testimony of his father and brother that he underwent an impressive change. This was one of the formative factors in predetermining his celebrated doctrine of the "will to believe," according to which a belief, and action upon the belief, may bring into existence a reality which cannot otherwise be. This was likewise the basis of James's struggle to defend the mind healers, as a case was brought against them by orthodox medicine in the Boston Statehouse. What do we really know, he seems to say, about the ultimate sources of health and disease? Healers cannot pass your scientific examinations, it is true; but can we orthodox medical men "minister to a mind diseased"? Let us draw strength from restorative forces, whatever they are, as best we may.

THE PRINCIPLES OF PSYCHOLOGY

Settled at Harvard in the mid-'seventies, happily married, rapidly coming into recognition as a medical man interested in philosophy, getting a series of basic articles published, signing a contract with Henry Holt in 1878 for the *Principles of Psychology*—which was to take twelve years to write—James settled down into one of his great creative periods. It is easy to tell from the chapter headings of the *Principles of Psychology* something of the capacity, the range, the depth, and the sensitivity of the many acts of discovery that mark that period. Turning over and over again the problem of unity and complexity, and the relation of mind and body, he argued at times for essentially an associationist's viewpoint, at times for a highly integrated oneness of each psychological act. He gave instinct and habit formation a large place, and at the same time looked for cognitive acts of profundity and range, and for the ultimate pinnacle of the life of the mind in the process of the will. He is at the same time evolutionist and mystic, lover of the raw, crude, vague, confused, intellectually unrespectable. At the other end of the spectrum, he is an aspirant to the sharpest clarity and the highest order that mind can achieve. Consistency in ultimate outlook one should not expect to find in the *Principles,* even were one to regard it as the creation of a single year. The chapters represent different angles, different phases, different recurring themes evident in twelve years of a great man's life. They must be read as profound literature, often factually correct, modern in spirit, but far more important than either, always challenging, guiding, preparing us for new discoveries.

Selection here from so great a work may appear arbitrary. My choice is guided first by what are generally considered the classics, such as his chapters on habit, on the emotions, on the will. But I am guided in some part by the capacity the chapters have to show James as evolutionist, and as a herald of the modern spirit of challenge, doubt, and reaffirmation. First, a brief passage from the chapter on "Habit":

> Habit is thus the enormous fly-wheel of society, its most precious conservative agent. It alone is what keeps us all within the bounds of ordinance . . . It keeps different social strata from mixing. Already at the age of twenty-five you see the pro-

fessional mannerism settling down on the young commercial traveller, on the young doctor, on the young minister, on the young counsellor-at-law. You see the little lines of cleavage running through the character, the tricks of thought, the prejudices, the ways of the 'shop' . . . in most of us, by the age of thirty, the character has set like plaster, and will never soften again.

If the period between twenty and thirty is the critical one in the formation of intellectual and professional habits, the period below twenty is more important still for the fixing of *personal* habits, properly so called, such as vocalization and pronunciation, gesture, motion, and address. . . .[2]

The great thing, then, in all education, is to *make our nervous system our ally instead of our enemy.* It is to fund and capitalize our acquisitions, and live at ease upon the interest of the fund. *For this we must make automatic and habitual, as early as possible, as many useful actions as we can* . . .[3]

In the acquisition of new habits or the leaving off of old ones,

. . . we must take care to *launch ourselves with as strong and decided an initiative as possible.* Accumulate all the possible circumstances which shall re-enforce the right motives; put yourself assiduously in conditions that encourage the new way; make engagements incompatible with the old . . .[4]

. . . *Never suffer an exception to occur till the new habit is securely rooted in your life.*[5]

"THE STREAM OF THOUGHT"

When we riffle through the pages to see what James has to say about the process of thinking, this firm structure of habit is all but forgotten. James looks on the thought processes as an expression of man's capacity to meet life's requirements. The

[2] William James, *The Principles of Psychology* (New York: Dover, 1950), I, 121–22.
[3] *Ibid.*, p. 122. [4] *Ibid.*, pp. 122–23. [5] *Ibid.*, p. 123.

primary emphasis is upon the empirical view as to the nature of thought processes; that is, thought is to be confronted as we encounter it, and if any analysis of it is to be made let the analysis be made empirically by investigating what it is made of and how the parts fit together. The view is functionalist in the sense in which the term came into psychology later, as a way of describing what function is served by each activity; ultimately, what each function expresses by way of adaptation to life's requirements. This can be gleaned also from many other chapters in James's *Principles,* such as the concluding chapter on "Necessary Truths and the Effects of Experience," in which we learn that self-evident truth is that which *has to appear* self-evident to creatures that have evolved as we have evolved. Many of his philosophic writings, notably those leading into the doctrine of pragmatism, go even further in defining truth as relative to our tasks and our modes of meeting them.

In the pages, however, that reveal James's conception of thought, one will find much more. In fact, one will find a rich, philosophically oriented conception deeply grounded in Greek and Renaissance philosophy, reminiscent at times of Descartes and Hume, and certainly of the warring idealisms and associationisms of the nineteenth century. With all the wealth offered here, perhaps the cardinal point to stress is the fullness and the functional character of the act of thought, the impossibility of breaking it into small shining pieces, the need to recognize the dark, obscure recesses of the mind, the "transitive states" that do not stand still to be looked at.

For James there are five basic characteristics of thought:

1) Every thought tends to be part of a personal consciousness.

2) Within each personal consciousness thought is always changing.

3) Within each personal consciousness thought is sensibly continuous.

4) It always appears to deal with objects independent of itself.

5) It is interested in some parts of these objects to the exclusion of others . . .[6]

1) Thought tends to Personal Form.

When I say *every thought is part of a personal consciousness,* 'personal consciousness' is one of the terms in question. . . .[7]

In this room—this lecture-room, say—there are a multitude of thoughts, yours and mine, some of which cohere mutually, and some not. They are as little each-for-itself and reciprocally independent as they are all-belonging-together. They are neither: no one of them is separate, but each belongs with certain others and with none beside. My thought belongs with my other thoughts, and your thought with your other thoughts. Whether anywhere in the room there be a mere thought, which is nobody's thought, we have no means of ascertaining . . .[8]

Passing to the third proposition:

3) Within each personal consciousness, thought is sensibly continuous. . . .[9]

. . . the broken edges of the sentient life may meet and merge over the gap, much as the feelings of space of the opposite margins of the 'blind spot' meet and merge . . . Such consciousness as this, whatever it be for the onlooking psychologist, is for itself unbroken. . . .[10]

When Paul and Peter wake up in the same bed, and recognize that they have been asleep, each one of them mentally reaches back and makes connection with but *one* of the two streams of thought which were broken by the sleeping hours. As the current of an electrode buried in the ground unerringly finds its way to its own similarly buried mate, across no matter how much intervening earth; so Peter's present instantly finds out Peter's past, and never by mistake knits itself on to that of Paul. . . .[11]

Consciousness, then, does not appear to itself chopped up in bits. Such words as 'chain' or 'train' do not describe it fitly as it presents itself in the first instance. It is nothing jointed; it flows. A 'river' or a 'stream' are the metaphors by which it is most naturally described. . . .[12]

[6] *Ibid.,* p. 225. [7] *Ibid.* [8] *Ibid.,* pp. 225–26. [9] *Ibid.,* p. 237.
[10] *Ibid.,* pp. 237–38. [11] *Ibid.,* p. 238. [12] *Ibid.,* p. 239.

. . . Like a bird's life, it seems to be made of an alternation of flights and perchings. The rhythm of language expresses this, where every thought is expressed in a sentence, and every sentence closed by a period. The resting-places are usually occupied by sensorial imaginations of some sort, whose peculiarity is that they can be held before the mind for an indefinite time, and contemplated without changing; the places of flight are filled with thoughts of relations, static or dynamic, that for the most part obtain between the matters contemplated in the periods of comparative rest.

Let us call the resting-places the 'substantive parts,' and the places of flight the 'transitive parts,' of the stream of thought.[13]

James goes on then to discuss the restoration of a place of dignity for the transitive, the shapeless, and the indefinite. This, of course, is the first expression, in so many words, of what came later to be called the "stream of consciousness type of writing," as exemplified for instance in Gertrude Stein, one of James's students at Harvard. This kind of thought also illustrates what is sometimes referred to as "anti-intellectualism" on the part of James; somehow we feel that he *preferred* the shadowy to the sharply formed. Perhaps the best known of all James, the phrase "blooming, buzzing confusion," used to describe the consciousness of the newborn child, seemed to many of his readers to express relish in the indefinite. From this point of view one finds James going very far indeed to protest against the traditional atomism of psychology, and to prepare the way for the various types of holistic and even inchoate psychology that have been taken for granted today. Again a quotation:

. . . Let anyone try to cut a thought across in the middle and get a look at its section . . . The rush of the thought is so headlong that it almost always brings us up at the conclusion before we can arrest it. Or if our purpose is nimble enough and we do arrest it, it ceases forthwith to be itself. As a snowflake crystal caught in the warm hand is no longer a crystal but a drop, so, instead of catching the feeling of relation moving to

[13] *Ibid.*, p. 243.

its term, we find we have caught some substantive thing, usually the last word we were pronouncing, statically taken, and with its function, tendency, and particular meaning in the sentence quite evaporated. The attempt at introspective analysis in these cases is in fact like seizing a spinning top to catch its motion, or trying to turn up the gas quickly enough to see how the darkness looks.[14]

I skip now to the fifth of James's characteristics of thought:

> 5) *It is always interested more in one part of its object than in another, and welcomes and rejects, or chooses, all the while it thinks.*
>
> The phenomena of selective attention and of deliberative will are of course patent examples of this choosing activity. But few of us are aware how incessantly it is at work in operations not ordinarily called by these names. Accentuation and Emphasis are present in every perception we have.[15]

Yes! A few years ago Charles Solley and I were struggling with some problems in the "conditioning of attention." We found ourselves blocked by the lack of a clear definition of the relation of attention to will. But we simply had not done our "homework." For, in fact, long stretches in James's chapters on "Attention," "Association," and "Will" are devoted to his development of the conception that the ultimate decisions in life are made by pulling from the margin of consciousness into the center some little fleeting sensation or idea; the act of will is utimately a process of selecting within the floating materials always available; what is thus *selected* passes on into action. We can bridge over immediately from a relatively simple biological conception of attention to the most complex—if I may say so—metaphysical questions of the nature of self determination.

> Looking back, then, over this review, we see that the mind is at every stage a theatre of simultaneous possibilities. Consciousness consists in the comparison of these with each other,

[14] *Ibid.*, p. 244. [15] *Ibid.*, p. 284.

the selection of some, and the suppression of the rest by the reinforcing and inhibiting agency of attention.[16]

"THE EMOTIONS"

We turn now to the most quoted of all of James's many psychological theories, the one that relates to the emotions. Evolutionary theory had placed a heavy emphasis upon instinct and emotion, the feeling tones, the affects, the expressions of mood and sentiment that interact with and complicate the cognitive life, and color the quality of action. In contrast to the prevailing psychological hedonism, the pleasure-pain theory that characterized the association psychology from Hobbes to John Stuart Mill, the French and the Germans had had much to say about the *impulse life*. The physiological discoveries of the nineteenth century had expressed themselves in psychology and psychiatry by continually drawing attention to the bodily upheavals that underlie men's thoughts and decisions. All of this made its impression on James as he voraciously read through the new medical psychology that was taking shape from Britain to Italy, and as he strove to grasp the implications of evolutionary theory. One might, in these new terms, underscore what the living organism must do through its mobilization of energies and its impulsive decision-making in the confrontation of crises. As we saw, Darwin had already described the emotions as powerful tools in the organism's repertory for dealing with danger. Just as James had sought a functional definition of thought, in keeping with evolutionary assumptions, so he sought a functional view of emotions.

The theory is rooted in the physiological response to crisis. The bodily upheaval in fear or rage or grief constantly sends messages to the brain, and emotion is simply the subjective expression of this particular biological function of energy mobilization. As we might say today, emotion is the input from the

[16] *Ibid.*, p. 288.

vital organs and the muscles. This theory (not unlike that of Descartes' follower, Malebranche, and James's contemporary, the Danish physiologist, Lange) instantly became an international bone of interest and contention everywhere. James had succeeded in rounding out the line of Darwin's thought. He made emotions an expression of adaptation to the environment, each emotion having a character dependent upon the nature of the adaptation made at the time. No modern presentation of what is permanently important in psychology could possibly omit James's treatment of the emotions.

James writes:

> . . . As emotions are described in novels, they interest us, for we are made to share them. We have grown acquainted with the concrete objects and emergencies which call them forth, and any knowing touch of introspection which may grace the page meets with a quick and feeling response. Confessedly literary works of aphoristic philosophy also flash lights into our emotional life, and give us a fitful delight. But as far as "scientific psychology" of the emotions goes, I may have been surfeited by too much reading of classic works on the subject, but I should as lief read verbal descriptions of the shapes of the rocks on a New Hampshire farm as toil through them again. They give one nowhere a central point of view, or a deductive or generative principle. They distinguish and refine and specify *in infinitum* without ever getting on to another logical level. Whereas the beauty of all truly scientific work is to get to ever deeper levels. Is there no way out from this level of individual description in the case of the emotions? I believe there is a way out . . .[17]
>
> Our natural way of thinking about these coarser emotions is that the mental perception of some fact excites the mental affection called the emotion, and that this latter state of mind gives rise to the bodily expression. My theory, on the contrary, is that *the bodily changes follow directly the perception of the exciting fact, and that our feeling of the same changes as they occur* IS *the emotion.* Common-sense says, we lose our fortune, are sorry and weep; we meet a bear, are frightened and run; we are insulted by a rival, are angry and strike. The hypothesis

[17] *Ibid.*, II, 448–49.

here to be defended says that this order of sequence is incorrect, that the one mental state is not immediately induced by the other, that the bodily manifestations must first be interposed between, and that the more rational statement is that we feel sorry because we cry, angry because we strike, afraid because we tremble, and not that we cry, strike, or tremble, because we are sorry, angry, or fearful, as the case may be. Without the bodily states following on the perception, the latter would be purely cognitive in form, pale, colorless, destitute of emotional warmth. We might then see the bear, and judge it best to run, receive the insult and deem it right to strike, but we should not actually *feel* afraid or angry. . . .[18]

I now proceed to urge the vital point of my whole theory, which is this: *If we fancy some strong emotion, and then try to abstract from our consciousness of it all the feelings of its bodily symptoms, we find we have nothing left behind* . . .[19]

. . . What kind of an emotion of fear would be left if the feeling neither of quickened heart-beats nor of shallow breathing, neither of trembling lips nor of weakened limbs, neither of goose-flesh nor of visceral stirrings, were present, it is quite impossible for me to think. Can one fancy the state of rage and picture no ebullition in the chest, no flushing of the face, no dilatation of the nostrils, no clenching of the teeth, no impulse to vigorous action, but in their stead limp muscles, calm breathing, and a placid face?[20]

"THE WILL"

To turn now to the will. James is obviously in conflict as he tries to present an evolutionary and naturalistic conception of the will as an integrated response, and as he likewise tries to do justice to complicated intellectual, aesthetic, and spiritual values among which choices must be made. The chapter is extraordinarily rich, notably in its head-on confrontation of the difficulties man faces in resolving conflicts that move him in different directions. We cannot, he feels, rule out the possibility of truly self-initiated acts, ordinarily called acts of free will, in

[18] *Ibid.*, pp. 449–50. [19] *Ibid.*, p. 451. [20] *Ibid.*, p. 452.

which, as James says, "we ourselves incline the beam." He realizes, however, as few but the philosopher can realize, the intricate complexities involved in the attempt to make uncaused action central in so important a function, or in saying that we ourselves are the cause of action, overlooking or slighting the historical chain of events through which the concept "we ourselves" becomes a name for the evolutionary, the hereditary, the personal growth factors and the situational factors, both inside and outside us, all patently important to the decision that takes place.

James, however, undertakes an empirical attack upon this problem by defining the following:

FIVE TYPES OF DECISION

Turning now to the form of the decision itself . . . The first may be called *the reasonable type*. . . . the arguments for and against a given course seem gradually and almost insensibly to settle themselves in the mind and to end by leaving a clear balance in favor of one alternative, which alternative we then adopt without effort or constraint. . . . As soon, however, as we see our way to a familiar classification, we are at ease again. *In action as in reasoning, then, the great thing is the quest of the right conception.* The concrete dilemmas do not come to us with labels gummed upon their backs. We may name them by many names. . . . A 'reasonable' character is one who has a store of stable and worthy ends, and who does not decide about an action till he has calmly ascertained whether it be ministerial or detrimental to any one of these.

In the next two types of decision, the final fiat occurs before the evidence is all 'in.' It often happens that no paramount and authoritative reason for either course will come. Either seems a case of a Good, and there is no umpire as to which good should yield its place to the other. We grow tired of long hesitation and inconclusiveness, and the hour may come when we feel that even a bad decision is better than no decision at all. Under these conditions it will often happen that some accidental circumstance, supervening at a particular movement upon our mental weariness, will upset the balance in the direction of one of the alternatives, to which then we feel ourselves committed, although an opposite accident at the same time might have produced the opposite result.

In the *second type* of case our feeling is to a certain extent that of letting ourselves drift with a certain indifferent acquiescence in a direction accidentally determined *from without,* with the conviction that, after all, we might as well stand by this course as by the other . . .[21]

In the third type the determination seems equally accidental, but it comes from within, and not from without. It often happens, when the absence of imperative principle is perplexing and suspense distracting, that we find ourselves acting, as it were, automatically, and as if by a spontaneous discharge of our nerves, in the direction of one of the horns of the dilemma. But so exciting is this sense of motion after our intolerable pent-up state, that we eagerly throw ourselves into it. 'Forward now!' we inwardly cry, 'though the heavens fall.' This reckless and exultant espousal of an energy so little premeditated by us that we feel rather like passive spectators cheering on the display of some extraneous force than like voluntary agents, is a type of decision too abrupt and tumultuous to occur often in humdrum and cool-blooded natures. But it is probably frequent in persons of strong emotional endowment and unstable or vacillating character. And in men of the world-shaking type, the Napoleons, Luthers, etc., in whom tenacious passion combines with ebullient activity, when by any chance the passion's outlet has been dammed by scruples or apprehensions, the resolution is probably often of this catastrophic kind. The flood breaks quite unexpectedly through the dam. . . .[22]

There is a *fourth form of decision,* which often ends deliberation as suddenly as the third form does. It comes when, in consequence of some outer experience or some inexplicable inward change, *we suddenly pass from the easy and careless to the sober and strenuous mood,* or possibly the other way. The whole scale of values of our motives and impulses then undergoes a change like that which a change of the observer's level produces on a view. The most sobering possible agents are objects of grief and fear. When one of these affects us, all 'light fantastic' notions lose their motive power, all solemn ones find theirs multiplied many-fold. The consequence is an instant abandonment of the more trivial projects with which we had been dallying, and an instant practical acceptance of the more grim and earnest alternative which till then could not extort our mind's consent. All those 'changes of heart,' 'awakenings of conscience,' etc., which make new men of so many of us, may be classed under this head. The

[21] *Ibid.,* pp. 531–32. [22] *Ibid.,* pp. 532–33.

character abruptly rises to another 'level,' and deliberation comes to an immediate end.

In the *fifth and final type* of decision, the feeling that the evidence is all in, and that reason has balanced the books, may be either present or absent. But in either case we feel, in deciding, as if we ourselves by our own wilful act inclined the beam; in the former case by adding our living effort to the weight of the logical reason which, taken alone, seems powerless to make the act discharge; in the latter by a kind of creative contribution of something instead of a reason which does a reason's work. The slow dead heave of the will that is felt in these instances makes of them a class altogether different subjectively from all the three preceding classes.[23]

Here are two evaluations of the *Principles of Psychology*: both by William James. In a letter to Henry James early in the year 1890, he writes: "With that work, your *Tragic Muse,* and . . . my *Psychology,* all appearing in it, the year 1890 will be known as the great epochal year in American literature." [24] Pure spoof. On May 9, 1890, he turned over to his publisher, Henry Holt, the manuscript of the *Principles,* with this comment: ". . . a loathsome, distended, tumefied, bloated, dropsical mass, testifying to nothing but two facts: *1st,* that there is no such thing as a *science* of psychology, and *2nd,* that W. J. is an incapable." [25] This was the act of triumph capping the long years of preparation.

He was enormously gratified by the oceans of appreciation and praise that the book brought him. But he had turned a corner. Very shortly thereafter James withdrew from professional psychology, as embodied, for example, in the laboratory. He had referred to it as a "nasty little science"; he had referred to it as "brass instrument psychology," and with reference to its German origin he said that it could only be cultivated in a nation whose inhabitants were incapable of being bored. In

[23] *Ibid.,* pp. 533–34.
[24] In Gay Wilson Allen, *William James: A Biography* (New York: The Viking Press, 1967), p. 295.
[25] In Ralph Barton Perry, *op. cit.,* II, 48.

1897 he transferred to the department of philosophy, and until his death thirteen years later his major contributions, with one exception, are in the field of philosophy.

"THE VARIETIES"

There is, however, beginning with 1899, a period in his life of very special importance to those interested in him as a human being. He had gone to the Adirondacks because even at the summer home in Chocorua, New Hampshire, he could not be alone and be quiet—there were always too many guests. That summer, climbing in the Adirondacks, he lost his way, overstrained his heart, and turned out later to have angina pectoris. He had been appointed by the Gifford Lecture Foundation in Scotland to give the lectures on "natural religion." There seemed plenty of time to prepare them, and in the fall of 1899 he and Mrs. James set sail with the intention of going to Switzerland for rest and a year of bookish preparation for the lectures. As the ship put out to sea, James suddenly discovered that he was ill. He made the passage abroad in his stateroom, and was taken by his wife for a long period of incarceration in hotels and pensions, with a blackout in the room because he could not stand normal light. Unable to read, unable to pay attention, he was in utter despair as to what he was going to do about these Gifford Lectures. However, after several months of this he began to gain a little strength, and then he received word from President Eliot of Harvard that he could have another year. He finally made the pace, got going, reorganized, and finally in 1901 produced the very extraordinary double series of lectures that we know as the *Varieties of Religious Experience*. This was "natural religion" in a very full sense, an attempt to consider the facts, the meanings, the implications, that a naturalism, complete in all perspectives of which man is capable, could offer in scientific terms.

He begins with an extraordinary lecture entitled "Religion and Neurology," in which we are reminded that the world of *values* cannot be directly predicted from the *factual* world, and that many a person like George Fox, the founder of the Society of Friends, could be a very sick man but capable of a tremendous religious experience, with much solid and social utility, too. James then goes on to a comparison of two religious types, which he calls the "healthy-minded" and the "sick soul." The religion of the healthy-minded, of course, is just what he had defended in the Boston Statehouse, debating with the medical men; it spoke of the natural goodness of human existence. He understood it, he empathized with it; but after he had had his fill, he turned to the sick soul. He himself represents the sick soul in many of its aspects. He had suffered through black hours, had failed to find peace. In "the dark night of the soul" there may be some vague glimmerings of an expectation of return; but the sufferer often meets the absolute nadir, the absolute bottom point of the human capacity to endure. The sick soul reaches out desperately for meanings in religion for which the healthy-minded has no comprehension. And religion may have, in such terms, fuller meaning. After a very full consideration of the two types, somewhat like Milton's "L'Allegro" and "Il Penseroso," he comes to the issue of which is sounder, the view of the healthy-minded person or the person with a sick soul.

In our perspective as impartial onlookers, what are we to say of the issue raised by the healthy-minded and the sick soul? It seems to James:

> . . . The method of averting one's attention from evil, and living simply in the light of good is splendid as long as it will work. It will work with many persons; it will work far more generally than most of us are ready to suppose; and within the sphere of its successful operation there is nothing to be said against it as a religious solution. But it breaks down impotently as soon as melancholy comes; and even though one be quite free from melancholy one's self, there is no doubt that healthy-mindedness is inadequate as a philosophical doctrine, because the evil facts which it refuses

positively to account for are a genuine portion of reality; and they may after all be the best key to life's significance, and possibly the only openers of our eyes to the deepest levels of truth.[26]

From this James passes to a consideration of the process of conversion so widespread in the evangelical religious organizations of the day; and then to a series of lectures on mysticism, in which the conclusion is maintained that there are real "windows into reality" other than those which are given by the intellectual approach. There are altered states of consciousness, states of depersonalization and of ecstasy, which are perhaps modes of responding to realities that are not within the scope of the ordered science we know today.

It has been current to compare James's interest in the mystic's use of such "windows" with his interest in psychical research. I think this is historically a little out of perspective. James wrote a study on the planchette, an early form of automatic-involuntary communication, all as early as 1869, the year he graduated from the Harvard Medical School. He knew a good deal about the newly developing spiritualistic churches, which had started in the United States in 1848. After hearing about mediums who, according to the reports, could say things that they could not possibly have learned through any normal channel, and when his wife, after a series of sittings with Mrs. Leonora Piper, came back saying that things were mentioned that simply nobody else knew, he was convinced that the matter was worth study. He gave much time that winter to finding out what kind of a person Mrs. Piper was. The James family became intimately acquainted with her over the years, and took her to their summer place in Chocorua, New Hampshire.

James knew, in a very detailed way, what the phenomena were to which people referred in discussions of mediumship, particularly those phenomena he interpreted as solid evidence of a telepathic interchange not only between sitter and medium,

[26] William James, *The Varieties of Religious Experience* (New York: Longmans, Green, 1919), p. 163.

but among other persons at greater distances. When he finally summarized his outlook on what all this meant to him as a psychologist, he expressed it in a essay on "What Psychical Research Has Accomplished," to which he later made numerous additions. It is a vigorous statement to the effect that there is a kind of knowing, without use of the sense organs, to which science must pay attention. He kept a balanced interest in this field throughout his life, visited many other unusual persons, and studied very carefully the report of a clairvoyant vision regarding a suicide, which he wrote up with elaborate documentation of the facts.[27] After his friend Richard Hodgson, professional investigator of Mrs. Piper's phenomena, died in 1905, the question naturally arose as to whether the deceased Hodgson would be able to communicate, through Mrs. Piper, with a living sitter; and James devoted about one hundred pages to a critical analysis of "Mrs. Piper's Hodgson Control," that is, the communicating consciousness offering itself as Richard Hodgson while Mrs. Piper was in deep trance. Psychical research was a very large and solid part of James's work as a psychologist; not simply a bizarre excursion into the unknown, but very serious business as far as James was concerned. It was directly related to his attitude as a seeker; his belief that everything for which there is any evidence at all must be examined critically; the belief that the world is bigger than we know. This was related to what he called *pluralism,* the conviction that the world is made up of many more or less unrelated parts.

Just after his book on the *Pluralistic Universe* came *Pragmatism.* This represents a further development of the evolutionary viewpoint that had been expressed in the *Principles,* the belief that truth can be defined only in terms of the consequences that flow from a belief, expressed in the operations that make contact with a knowable reality.

James died in 1910. Immediately after his death his unfinished

[27] William James, "A Case of Clairvoyance," in *Proceedings, the American Society for Psychical Research,* I, Part 2 (1907), 220 ff.

lectures and essays appeared in various forms, of which I particularly want to refer to one entitled *Essays in Radical Empiricism,* because there is no phrase more ingeniously effective to describe James than *radical empiricism.* Skepticism about abstractions, ardent belief that the empiric, the person digging immediately into reality, has a legitimate hope of transcending the generalizations usually available, was his firm conviction.

But William James's impact, and his place in American life became so great, his stature became so evident everywhere, at Harvard and every place that he made a contact, that it all began to obscure his specific psychological contributions. In fact, James is mostly known as a vigorous explorer of new intellectual and social frontiers, rather than as a technical worker in psychology; and certainly one would have to say that, except for the chapter on emotions and the chapter on habit, the actual specific contributions found in the *Principles* are usually left for those with a special preoccupation with a special problem on which James had worked.

I would want therefore to stress that it is James as a man who completely transcends James as a psychologist. I will conclude with a passage from Ralph Barton Perry's two-volume study, *The Thought and Character of William James,* the most adequate over-all interpretation of James that we have. These are Perry's words:

> He always left the impression that there was more; that he knew there was more; and that the more to come might, for all one knew, throw a very different light on the matters under discussion. He respected his universe too much to believe that he could carry it under his own hat. These saving doubts arose from the same source as his tolerance and respect for his fellow man. The universe, like one's neighbor, is never fully disclosed to outward view, and the last word must be a consent that the other should be itself.[28]

[28] Ralph Barton Perry, *op. cit.,* II, 704.

9

Max Wertheimer: Gestalt Psychology

Max Wertheimer comes back very vividly to me, with his handlebar mustaches and his snapping blue eyes. A tiny little man, who thought so majestically that you wondered whether every thought was not cosmic in its implications, he stood for that great philosophic and scientific tradition in Germany which belongs to the eighteenth and nineteenth centuries, signalized most of all by Goethe. He did indeed share with Goethe the attempt to transcend the analytic method that had dominated French and British thinking. The essence of the naturalistic philosophy, as Goethe had put it, is to grasp that "Nature is neither kernel nor shell; She is everything at once." He embodied the attempt to get *total meanings* and then to find derivative meanings or components, or aspects; or, as the Germans like to say, to work *von oben* (from above), to go down from roof to cellar, rather than beginning at the bottom and building up.

It is this expressed message of wholeness that I want to stress. For Wertheimer there was religious intensity to be found in this conception of nature. One of his friends referred to him, with his little black skullcap, as a "Rabbi of Prague"; he seemed to me a religious, as well as a scientific, teacher.

The background for Wertheimer's Gestalt psychology lay in

the central issue of nineteenth century philosophy of science, namely, the effort to derive wholes from parts; to see totalities as expressions of atoms, particulars, fine details; the belief that things are somehow *made of their parts.* Reduction of wholes to parts seemed to be the main task of science. But there were countermovements. Under the thrust of the romantic movement, philosophy had tended towards holism anyway. The "philosophy of nature," dominant in the early nineteenth century, and the early versions of evolutionary theory prior to Darwin—and of course, the thrust of Schopenhauer and later of Nietzsche—will remind us how firmly the philosophical mold had been structured in terms of the derivation of meanings from *contexts,* always looking for larger contexts. In the later nineteenth century "field theory" in physics, in contrast to atomic theory, involved the *interdependence* of component aspects of a system.

GESTALTQUALITÄT

As far as psychology is concerned, it is ordinarily agreed that a paper by von Ehrenfels in the early 'nineties set the stage. The paper is on "form quality," *Gestaltqualität.* Von Ehrenfels said that ordinarily we think of music as consisting of tones and sequences of tones in the form of chords. However atonal or even arhythmic music may be, one thinks of it as made up of ingredient parts. One learns to put one's finger at the right point on the string, and to handle the bow in such a way as to produce a sequence that has been prepared by the composer. From such a point of view, as we proceed with a study of musical notation, we satisfy ourselves that music consists of structures reducible to component parts. In fact, how are we going to study music or any art form without a theory of elements or parts? Suppose we look at it as von Ehrenfels did. He notes that as a song is sung none of the individual tones is identical with any of the tones heard before. The song is recognizable although none of its parts, in terms of its formal attributes of pitch, loudness, tone quality, etc., is the same. Von Ehrenfels goes on to argue that the whole conception of parts and wholes as the basis for recognition of a whole is wrong. Music consists largely of organized wholes that are almost disembodied from specific physical tones as far as specific quality is concerned. We recognize each melody though it is played on different instruments. There is thus a factor of *form-quality* that ought to be added to the previously recognized components in musical expression.

GELB AND GOLDSTEIN

But what von Ehrenfels was doing was *still* an atomistic effort. He was saying that music has its elements, but the factor of form quality is separate beyond and above the separate tone components. The problem was capable of a much more radical solution. The basic problem is to start with the whole and only incidentally pick up various components that can be identified. Perhaps the best single experimental study to illustrate the early Gestalt theories that took shape was not any of the studies by Wertheimer, but studies done by Gelb and Goldstein in World War I with brain-injured men: men who had lost a portion of the visual field through deep, penetrating wounds of the head. The fovea, or region of clear vision, is also an organizing center around which up and down, right and left are defined. However, if that portion of the brain that is functionally effective in mediating messages from the fovea is shot away, the patient still possesses organized form perception to some degree. How in the world can he do this? He organizes in a new way. He organizes around what they called a "pseudo-fovea." That is to say, the need for organization is so great that some part of the retina ordinarily not capable of giving well-organized foveal vision will operate in this way.

This reminds us of a considerable range of experiments in biology. Take Wilson's work on the cell: you take a sponge; smash it, destroy its structure; reduce it to a formless mass;

centrifuge it; and let it stand. The material reorganizes itself in the form of the original and specific sponge with which the biologist began. There are, then, inherent organizing values that have been identified both in physics and in biology.

Another important background factor for Gestalt theory is that of *phenomenology,* the doctrine that the first experienced reality appears as an unanalyzed whole rather than as a pattern of component elements. Only when a certain attitude toward elements is taken can they have the importance that has been classically assigned to them. The first reality is the wave of experience, not actually very different from the "stream of consciousness."

THE WÜRZBURG SCHOOL

Now the immediate psychological background for Wertheimer's thinking was the introspective study of the thought process going on at Würzburg University. This was initially a study of the way in which judgments and decisions are made and action tendencies maintained. Introspective protocols were demanded after a decision had been made, or a brief thought process had run its course. One of the later investigations, for example, asked their experimental subjects quite difficult questions, questions that would typically take several seconds to comprehend and formulate in terms of an answer. Suppose we take one of the questions that was asked in 1907: "Was the Pythagorean Theorem known to the Middle Ages?" We have most of the requisite material for an answer because we dealt with Pythagoras and learned a little about what happened during the medieval period, and consequently we realize that this is not a question to which a rote answer can be given. Let us figure out all we can as to the comprehension of the Pythagorean principles in view of the state of philosophy and psychology in the medieval period. "Was the Pythagorean Theorem known to the Middle Ages?" After a man has struggled with this for eighteen or twenty seconds and given a brief answer, perhaps a qualified "yes," he is asked to define the steps through which he went, to define the thought process as it emerged.

Now it turned out from these studies that people did not report primarily in terms of sensations, images, feelings, the standard materials of an introspective psychology as we have encountered it in John Locke's sensationism and Herbart's idea-system, etc. On the contrary, people reported that they had *ideas,* they had *concepts,* they had *thoughts.* Contents were often not further analyzable. The "yes" to the question may be a categorical and certain answer; but it is not made up of the summation of feelings of strain and relaxation, of pleasantness and unpleasantness, as we come to the answer. On the contrary, it is a thought, and is not further capable of dissection.

At the same time, Alfred Binet, the founder of intelligence tests and many other new devices, asked his little girls the questions, after they had gone through a similar process: "What went through your mind?" *"Pensées,"* they said, thoughts. "No sensations, no images?" "No, just thoughts." They were completely free of the great German philosophical tradition, but they came up with the same reply that Karl Bühler came up with in Würzburg.

THE PERCEPTION OF MOTION

Now the Würzburg school, with its study of thoughts, is the immediate background for the 1912 beginning of Gestalt psychology, as such, the work of Max Wertheimer. Wertheimer was making a study of the perception of motion. Motion pictures already existed, but he used a very simple device known as a stroboscope, an instrument that makes it possible to project light on the retina in various ways. If we project a horizontal line after a vertical line at the right time interval, we can get the line to *fall over.* The vertical line falls over and becomes a horizontal line; although no track of light is passing across the retina, there is a full-fledged perception of motion. Does this imply that our perception of a moving and fluid world is a series of sensations that have been put together by association, by brain processes? It does not imply anything of the sort. If we choose the time relations appropriately, we will find just what the time interval must be in order to get the perception of motion. Experimentally, we get two independent and stationary presentations, one before the other; *or* we get the perception of motion; *or* with a very short time interval the two lines appear simultaneously, both stationary.

It occurred to Wertheimer that the perception of motion is not a compound of sensations of position, but a *form* of response. Looking at it physiologically, we can say that there are "cross processes" in the brain. And we know that there are actually plenty of fibers reaching from one region of the brain to another. (William James had heavily stressed this in his theory of association.) There had been plenty of theories of ways in which elements are put together; but what we are doing now with Wertheimer is to say that the ingredient materials—the succession of sense impressions—simply do not exist. On the contrary, there is a single comprehensive attack upon the problem presented to be judged in which (quite aside from volition or rational considerations) he perceives motion. This was in line with various principles of form that had been discovered and that, you may recall, were present in the early Greeks and were very strongly present in Plato. The Galilean tradition had defined in mathematical terms the forms and structures that could be found in nature.

Wertheimer decided to refer to the integrated forms by the ordinary everyday German word that means form: *Gestalt.* I do not know why English-speaking readers and discussants of these ideas feel there is supposed to be something mysterious about this. Perhaps the concept of form is actually just as troublesome, and as beautiful. Look at Lancelot Whyte's beautiful book on *Aspects of Form*. Perhaps there is the same resentment of the concept of form in the English-speaking world; and perhaps our resistance is doubled because we do not like to be forced to use a German word when we think our English word is adequate. But the fact is that the German word is a very simple and universally recognized term, exactly as you have it in *Erlkönig: mich reitzt deine schöne Gestalt*—thy beautiful form charms me. And this can be applied exactly in the same way to musical or literary or scientific or any other type of form. It seems to me entirely appropriate to the job to be done. Wertheimer called this *Gestalt psychology.*

KOFFKA AND KÖHLER

Wertheimer immediately saw a wide variety of implications in the Gestalt approach. After World War I he was at the University of Berlin, and with him were two men who served as subjects in his original 1912 experiments at Frankfurt am Main, in which the perception of motion was studied. There was Kurt Koffka, who especially concerned himself with problems of the development of form as an expression of life, and who therefore made the growth process subject, literally, to a formal analysis; growth and learning are not to be conceived as the accretion of parts, but rather as the slow reorganization into a new pattern. There was Wolfgang Köhler, who saw the relation of this psychological form to the physical form appearing in electromagnetic fields, soap films, and many other sorts of physical forms. During the war Köhler had had the good luck to be marooned in the Canary Islands, where there was an anthropoid ape colony available for research. In *The Mentality of Apes*—the German title means literally "Intelligence tests on anthropoid apes"—he published his celebrated studies of problem solving. The hungry chimpanzee, seeing no way of obtaining a distant banana, might suddenly *re-see* the whole situation: a blanket lying in a corner of the animal's cage would be seen as an instrument that, when grabbed by the corner, could be used to knock down the banana and rake it in. This was defined by Köhler in terms of *insight* into the situation. Animal learning was currently conceived rather largely in terms of sheer "trial and error." Köhler's reports served to advertise magnificently the phenomenon of insight—or response conceived in terms of response to form. Immediately after World War I, as Köhler lectured in the United States, a lively controversy arose as to whether psychology really required any principle of insight, or whether the behavior was really trial and error based on earlier experience with the blanket. The pros and cons, and a lively stream of new experimental studies, made Gestalt psychology a rallying point for controversy regarding "higher" and "lower" kinds of learning processes. Gestalt psychology was developing side by side with J. B. Watson's behaviorism, which had been formulated, by a curious accident, in the same year (1912) in which Wertheimer's studies of the perception of motion were reported. The idea was plainly important. Koffka and Köhler gave Gestalt psychology a prominent place, partly by their logic, partly by their charm and vigor.

In 1933, with the rise of Hitler to power, a number of the outstanding psychologists in Germany, including Max Wertheimer, had to flee, and arrangements were rapidly made for academic positions for the more distinguished members of the community. Wertheimer was invited in 1933 to the New School for Social Research in New York. Here he had a chance to lecture to audiences generally representative of the German university audiences to which he had been talking before. By that time the idea had taken hold, and had begun to penetrate into most of the sophisticated thought of the period in the social sciences, philosophy, and education; and while a certain amount of technical psychological experimentation went on, I would rather emphasize the broad impact of this way of thinking, this whole-part redefinition, this definition of psychology in terms of the primary explanatory value of formal or whole relationships.

PRÄGNANZ

I may illustrate from a few terms, which again, like the term *Gestalt* itself, are sometimes felt to be rather untranslatable. We take first the term, *Prägnanz,* which is the tendency of any structure to take on the most complete or developed form possible, which usually will mean the most nearly ideal form of which it is capable. This will mean that in response to brief exposure of almost any irregular curvilinear figure, we tend to see a circle. There is a natural tendency of any form to assume the simplest or, in an everyday sense, the *best* form possible. This, of course, is very close indeed to the Platonic tradition. *Prägnanz* has been the subject of a considerable amount of experimentation. Take a rather childish, but I think effective, study with a red cross on a gray cardboard field. In this situation we see, after twenty seconds or so exposure, the complementary color, green, along the edges of the red cross. But suppose we cut a small notch into the right arm of the cross. What color will the cardboard have *within* that notch? Though by color contrast it should be green, we say immediately and correctly: "It has got to be a part of the cross." This region is so firmly a part of the cross that it will be seen as partaking of the color of the cross.

This principle, illustrated here, is called "membership character." We experience it constantly. In a sunset each patch of color is seen as its total context requires. If we look at a particular color through a reduction screen, a little peephole, it will not be identical with what we see in a free situation. As Turner taught us for once and forever, colors are functions of complex articulated wholes; and you see, in all the attributes of color—in terms of hue, brightness, saturation, and the various complexities of color experience—to a considerable degree what the situation requires. When Turner made up for himself that marvelous set of ochres which he used to produce the paintings now in the Tate Museum, what he was looking for was something that in a particular *context* would look a particular way.

He was not mechanically *juxtaposing* the various ochres and pigments. He was thinking in terms of what the massive impact of the whole thing would be. What Gestalt psychology has done is to make the principle glow, or sing, instead of hiding furtively in a corner in psychology in unsuccessful competition with finer and larger realities.

Of course, this principle applies to temporal phenomena just as much as to spatial phenomena. We noted this in the case of von Ehrenfels's observations on melodic sequences; each tone will do what has to be done in terms of the melodic context that has been supplied. The principle will apply in poetry and in the dance. It will apply in the thought processes; here it will appear in a process that Wertheimer called *recentering*. In productive thinking, we do not pull the various parts of a thought apart and stick them together in a new way. What we primarily do is to find a new center, almost like the fovea in ordinary vision. What we will do at a conceptual level is to anchor upon some central and fundamental issue, and everything else will act in relation to the center, dominated by the role of the center and by the new activities that have been set going by the new center. The principle of membership character is evident here. Similarly, in figure-and-ground studies, as developed by Rubin in Copenhagen, the question of which will stand out as figure in a complex field will depend largely on the specific membership character enjoyed by each component in the total.

Perhaps the most important idea, for this kind of analysis, is the concept of anchoring (*Verankerungspunkt*; the French sometimes call it *point de repère*). In a baffling situation we hold on to something that has a potentially central place in our experience, something of which we can say: "My heart is in it." All the various things that are peripheral to it, which we would not ordinarily care about, become colored by the fact that the heart is in it. Primary reinforcement, secondary reinforcement, and all the conceptual gadgetry of the learning process, are seen in terms of the derivative value which the components take on within a new cluster, a new rearrangement.

Finally, in our search for key terms, giving us a map for the comprehensive picture of Gestalt psychology, the most grandiose that can be used is *isomorphism,* which relates to *identity of form.* If we are going to use form in this comprehensive way we would expect that the observer in a certain sense takes on the same form as the stimulating situation. One person may, for example, take on the same gestures, the same stance, as the person with whom he is talking, or identify outwardly and inwardly with the religious or philosophical brothers of his own thought. There will be in the responding individual not just a *copy* of the complex world as the Epicureans had it, but the same world. Köhler's work suggests that stimulus pattern, sense organ response, and brain response are all of the same form.

This idea had very broad implications, which had already been appearing in contemporary philosophy. Another curious accident: It was in the year 1912 that E. B. Holt, Harvard and Princeton philosopher, developed the idea that the brain, in response to the environment, is actually responding to the same *rhythm pattern* that the external environment presents. The brain is not *copying* it. No, because the very same rhythm pattern, in all its complexities, impinges on the sense organs, goes through the afferent paths, gets to the cortex, and causes motor and glandular responses in the person. It maintains literally the same form. Think of sympathetic vibration, holding the piano key down and singing to the wire. It is not that the wire "imitates" a pitch that we impose upon it; the pitch is the same, stated mathematically. What is happening, then, when the wire picks up what we sing to it, is *isomorphic*. It is all one piece.

RATIONALITY

From this point of view the philosophical case is elaborated that man *apprehends reality* in a literal sense, not in the sense of the so-called "correspondence theory of truth" (that man makes up a very good substitute for the cosmic order), but that the cosmic order invades him; the cosmic order produces *itself*

—not a replica of itself, but truly itself—in the responding individual. If we ask "*Where* is Gestalt?"—is it in the environment or is it in the person—the Gestaltist may become very restless and unhappy. If we say that Gestalt is something that we impose upon an essentially formless external world, he will be equally distressed. If we imply that the world is highly ordered, and that all that a person does is to respond like putty, to accept the din, the pressure of the environment, the momentary environmental form, he will decry your blindness. If we say that the individual, through an evolutionary process, has so developed that with all the tissues and systems and articulations of the various parts of his body, he becomes the harp upon which the tune is played—which has been played by many other forces upon many people—he will beam. But this is vigorously realistic in Plato's sense. Plato belittled the possibility of knowing in any really serious sense the raw, sensory, fragmentary materials that impinge upon us, emphasizing the fact that formal relationships, generalizations, principles of value and truth, are actually apprehended, because man is so made that he is capable of grasping the formal unity of the world.

Now this has, of course, led to the more ambitious developments within Gestalt theory, which at their highest peak insist upon the rationality of man and upon the possibility of a sort of mutual encompassing of man and world. This would seem to suggest a basic antithesis not only between Wertheimer and association psychology, but between Wertheimer and Freud. Freud is sometimes regarded as the great elaborator and defender of the principle of human irrationality. With his place for secondary process thinking notwithstanding, Freud's may be regarded as emphasizing a basically id-centered function. From an evolutionary point of view, as we talk about the drives of mankind, we may talk wistfully about the ways in which a limited type of muting or control of the great drive forces may be achieved.

But this is not Freud's own emphasis. He says, rather, "Where id was, there shall ego be." The analyst works, to be sure, toward the most rational principle possible, but is skeptical as to any total victory—whereas, of course, the total victory is exactly what the Gestalt psychology craves. It maintains vigorously that one must and can achieve rationality *because it is human to be rational.* We can even say that to a considerable extent experimental mice and rats, and certainly experimental anthropoid apes, are capable of rationality of a sort. But the most fulfilling and the most completely human operations are those that represent the perfection involved in seeing, knowing, remembering, thinking, confronting what is really *there,* transcending the limitations of petty and willful and senseless fact by reference to a structure that begins by being human and ends by being cosmic.

It is interesting, in the same vein, to take a glance at the Soviet psychology of recent years with reference to this issue. Our aim, says Smirnov, for example, in the school system and in the revision of curricula, is to achieve the *highest possible level of rationality.* Man cannot remake the world if he is a robot, if he is manipulated in the manner of the classical Pavlov dog-type experiment. Such experiments are legitimate entryways into the larger and more meaningful world, but mankind is capable of a rationality that involves the actual apprehension of real difficulties in order to transcend them.

At the same time there is, of course, always in American thought, as we saw in the case of William James, this belief that there is something more than blind habit; that the irrationalities can all be combed out. Indeed, in all modern psychology we would expect that there would be a place for a family of psychological operations, representing high orders, middle orders, low orders. We should indeed find a system, a hierarchy. In an ordered system there will be units, and subunits, modes of articulation, just as there will be in a symphony or a drama or an epic. Further critical experiments are regarded as helpful, but not definitive.

PERSONALITY

The final task is one of completing the logic of the system. We must say a few words about the branching out of this mode of thought to apply to a number of subdivisions of the field of psychology. Let us begin with Wertheimer's own little home-made experiments, of which he did a great many. He was intrigued, for example, with the question of the recognition of the individual. How do we recognize a friend of ours walking at a distance—from his gait alone? We recognize people's voices; we recognize the style of a painter or composer. So Wertheimer would call together a group of his friends for a Sunday evening and play the piano to them. "Who am I playing?" "Well, *that's* Herr Schmidt, and that's Fräulein Engel." There was no doubt who was being represented. These first studies were not very sophisticated. But soon other investigators looked at expressive behavior, to see whether individuals actually presented this kind of recognizable totality. Rudolf Arnheim took the problem of response to whole versus mutilated expression. He compared whole pages of handwriting with bits of handwriting, to see whether certain traits were identifiable from a fragment. He came to the conclusion that while recognition of totality was possible, the recognition of parts was poor.

Better known are the studies of Werner Wolff. Wolff worked with photographs of the profile and the full face to find out under what conditions one can recognize people one knew, or even one's self. There was much failure to recognize one's own profile. In Wolff's experiments one notes a beginning of a rapprochement with psychoanalysis, in the sense that materials which are disliked, unacceptable, appear to be protests, defenses, meaningful in terms of one's self-image. One has a picture of one's self, and when confronted by a total pattern one can find a way to reject this. One can manage to do worse than "chance expectation" in the identifying of one's own expression. Philip Holzman's recent work here in recognition of one's own tape-recorded voice is very much in the same vein. There is, in other words, a rapprochement between the psychoanalytic theory of defense structures and Gestalt theory as it relates to the process of recognition.

ALLPORT AND VERNON

But by far the largest systematic investigations of this area of personality Gestalt are those done by Allport and Vernon at Harvard, at about the same period in which Wertheimer was establishing himself on our shores. These experiments had to do with the way in which total patterns of gesture, walking, handwriting, and ways of perceiving and judging visual materials, expressed the total personality of the individual. There was, for example, the *area factor,* the sheer degree of a man's tendency to fill up space, to need more space for writing—even with one's foot!—and to overestimate the size of a dollar bill. The measures of this area factor in each individual were substantially correlated; as Allport and Vernon said, they "corresponded." But in addition to these simple correlation studies, there were ingenious concepts showing how individual behaviors were "congruent" (e.g., having similar aims); the different expressive movements hung together, and by blind matching could be shown to be correctly matched at much better than a chance level. Handwriting experts, working with whole scripts, did quite respectably well in matching descriptive personality sketches against individual scripts.

Most of this recognition work launched by Wertheimer is dramatic, but is still awaiting sophistication. The electrifying philosophical conception of wholeness, and the glimpse of *isomorphic* realities, has gotten ahead of the detailed verification. The same is true of the parallel movement of Kurt Lewin, which is unfortunately outside the scope of the present lectures; Lewin conceptualized, in terms of *field theory,* the "life space" in which the individual views and responds to objects organized around him in terms of his values, the wants and aversions that characterize his life. Field-theoretical studies of the life space of the individual are a rich, derivative expression of the Gestalt movement; methodologically the study of a Gestalt is quite different from a study of the life space.

UNRESOLVED PHILOSOPHICAL ISSUES

As issues stand now, I think it fair to say that Gestalt psychology has managed to reassert much that had been felt, and sometimes expressed, in Greek philosophy, notably in Plato. Many of the issues I have tried to spell out are demanding a fuller philosophical and scientific analysis. I will suggest where I think we stand with regard to this very bold philosophical demand for a new conception of the whole-part relationship.

First, I want to meet a common objection. It is often said, by psychologists and by others, that Gestalt psychology is an attack upon analysis or upon atomism. Now this is unfortunately not true at all. Gestalt psychology does not handle atoms quite in the way that this statement would seem to imply. What the Gestalt psychology does is to insist that the atoms—or parts—be found and put to work in the situation itself, not implying that the part *within* a whole is the *same* part that we find outside in its own self-sufficiency. For example, it does not deny that we can study a little patch of color for its intrinsic interest; but it says that the phenomenal analysis, the analysis *in situ* is no longer the same thing as the dismembering process by which we pick up the little components, go off with them, make laboratory studies of the separate components, and try to put them together again as a whole. It is not analysis that is being objected to; it is not atomism; it is not elementarism. It is rather the assumption that the elements provide the phenomena dealt with in psychological laws. Gestalt psychology says that the forms are there all the time, whether we recognize them or not; in responding to them, we become to some degree *isomorphic* with the forms that are present.

Now this can be compared by a modern philosopher both

with Plato and with Aristotle. I have already suggested that Gestalt psychology used Plato's mathematical approach. Recall also that the Aristotelian principle of form gives meaning to formless, meaningless matter; matter, in conjunction with form, yields a meaningful and articulate whole. This alone would not give Gestalt psychology. But it offers promise in terms of formal principles that can be developed. One may think here of Korzybski's "non-Aristotelian" approach and other forms of Gestalt *logic*.

Then, of course, there is Gestalt *science* in a very much broader sense than could be properly spelled out from the psychological examples that I have given. Its foundation had been laid by a "field theory" in physics, which had been used, as we have seen, by Kurt Lewin. In the early years of this century an extraordinary embryologist by the name of Spemann began to develop field theory in embryology, in which he undertook to show that in the growth of an organ we have to understand the whole organism; indeed we have to understand the maternal and the infantile organisms, with all their biochemical interactions, before we can understand the steps by which a recentering or reorganization of the embryo can occur. This field-theory principle has likewise invaded the field of genetics; formal principles of genetics have become heavily saturated with Gestalt thinking.

There is, of course, a countermovement today, with the Watson and Crick approach, the DNA-RNA analysis that again shows the conceptual power of classical elementarism or atomism. I bring up these issues to show that they are by no means dead issues as Gestalt psychology has formulated them. There is today certainly a Gestalt *aesthetics,* in terms of the critique led by Arnheim, a beautiful use of elements of the sort that I have described. The study of color, form, shadow, movement, grouping, all the classical data that the art critics have been talking about, are brought into relation to very sophisticated definition of Gestalt principles as they apply to the painter as well as to the individual painting. Then there is Gestalt *ethics,* which is beginning to make its way into the region we used to describe in terms of relativistic ethics. But, of course, it looks for universal principles, verifiable laws, which respect all the local contexts. Gestalt ethics emphasizes patterned or organized systems of ethical principles which are isomorphic through all the particular ethical systems found operative at specific times and places.

It is natural to ask whether Wertheimer's system of thought gave rise to the whole modern way of thinking in which fields, systems, modes of organization, are held to have logical priority over specific events. This is too much to claim. It would be more nearly correct to say that Wertheimer's Gestalt psychology is one of the many forms of modern thought tending in this direction, in the study of life and even in the study of large cosmic wholes.

10

Sigmund Freud: Psychoanalysis

Erik Erikson, at Harvard to take up his post instructing undergraduate students into the mysteries of psychoanalysis, was asked by President Pusey to come over and meet the staff. The expression that President Pusey used to introduce Erikson was an epitome of much that we are trying to say: "Gentlemen, I introduce you to Erik Erikson, who represents to us Sigmund Freud. Sigmund Freud has changed the image of man."

A word first about the history of medical psychology preceding the work of Freud, with special reference to the conscious and the unconscious, and then an essentially biographical sketch of Freud's intellectual history.

Aristotle made the distinction between *having* an idea and *observing* that idea. As a matter of fact, unless we observe the idea, merely having it will not necessarily make much difference. There is a marginal sphere of events not clearly conscious. When Renaissance psychology revived Aristotle and worked him through, Leibnitz made the distinction between perceptions and *little* perceptions: perceptions so little that they do not ordinarily influence the course of thought. From then on, German psychology became obsessed with this conception of the difference between *focal* and *marginal* psychology (cf. James above, page 152). Focal events patently precede thoughts and decisions; marginal events are of importance in such a system only insofar as they can move toward the center. Herbart discussed the integrative role of apperception (page 12); German psychology thereafter pursued this process by which faint marginal impressions somehow move into the center of awareness and begin to predetermine the course of action. It seems to me that these are background factors most important to emphasize if we are to make sense out of what Freud did.

There were in fact many discussions of unconscious or subconscious ideas during the nineteenth century. But none of them had an answer to the question: What pushed the marginal event into the center? So that in fact the dynamic interpretation, as we would call it today, was almost entirely wanting. Freud in his own *Autobiographical Study* notes the work of the French psychiatrist, Pierre Janet, who had said that ideas may come together through "psychic tension" and may fall apart again. True, says Freud, an important contribution. But the issue is the dynamics of that process by which events move to the center and move away again. The medical science of the period prejudged most of these issues by looking for mechanical interruptions of the flow of consciousness. The prevailing "positivistic" psychology—a hard-nosed, tough, no-nonsense-about-it kind of psychology—usually forgot to include the process by which impulses and thoughts pass from a conscious to an unconscious state, some of them in their peripheral condition continuing to influence thought and to make trouble.

It must nevertheless be remembered that in this respect medical thought was not homogeneous. The great Charcot, for example, whom we think of in terms of his demonstrations on nervous sufferers at the Bicêtre Hospital, undertook to show medical audiences *how ideas could influence behavior*. Having induced, by hypnotic technique, a paralysis of an arm, he would then say to the patient, "That's going away—*ça passe,*" and the paralysis would immediately disappear. The idea had caused the paralysis and the idea could now remove it. This can, by a verbal sleight of hand, be restated in such a way as to be integrated with the positivistic or mechanistic psychologies of the period. But the trick was complicated. Charcot did not take the step one might think of today as a normal step to take, namely, to describe ideas themselves in a dynamic language that would make them physiologically capable of producing changes in symptom patterns.

I stress these things mainly to admit, on the one hand, the reality of much thinking that dealt with marginal, noncentral components in human experience, which, if we like, we can call precursors to the idea of the unconscious; and, on the other hand, the dawning recognition that an idea can in a genuine sense have medical and behavioral significance. But at that point I want to stop. Because it seems to me that these were only fragments that were a long way from giving the new synthesis of dynamic components, which we think of as so central in modern psychological and psychiatric work.

Now my main theme will be to try to spell out a series of episodes in Freud's life. I find convenient the Shakespearean image of the seven ages or seven stages in the life of man, and I will try, after a few preliminary words, to define seven ages of Sigmund Freud as representing definite steps in his movement toward that broad philosophical position that we associate with the last decades of his life.

We can say very little about his childhood, or even his youth, for a variety of reasons that are clear if we look at Ernest Jones's biography. Freud made it very plain that he attached no importance to his own life except insofar as it is expressed in psychoanalysis. He was apparently nettled by the inquisitiveness of would-be biographers. He destroyed great masses of documentary material, and did it so very competently that relatively little is known about many critical issues regarding his early years. We see him as a bright, busy, aggressive, and highly competent playmate and student. We see him in the university years, determined to do something big, clear, and strong; we find a rather solemn and rather sage approach to the challenging issues in medicine; we find him pursuing philosophy and history and the cultural sciences, as well as the natural sciences. We find an attempt toward breadth. But we get no intimation of where he was going. In the German university world, of course, you elect relatively early where you are going professionally. We think of the *gymnasium* (pre-university school) and the medical curriculum as nevertheless comprising an orientation toward all of nineteenth-century thought. A good deal of Freud's library was salvaged at the time of his leaving Vienna shortly before his death, and we know from his notes and letters how very wide a range of philosophical interests characterized him.

He became first of all a biologist, an experimental embryologist. The first stage in his life was one of using his medical training for basic scientific research. He rejected the opportunities for medical practice, and for several years worked on problems of pure science—the embryology of the eel, for example—problems in which a broad evolutionary viewpoint constantly reappears. The philosophy of medicine at this period involved the same contrast of ideas that was mentioned above with regard to Charcot. On the one hand, the tough-minded investigator must renounce all interpretations of life phenomena that are not directly given by physics and chemistry. Mechanistic philosophy means that we confront the ugly reality of disease with an inescapable bludgeoning fist; we forget all this nonsense about ideas, feelings, cultural values. We take the human individual in terms of the biophysics and the biochemistry of his body. Among the medical men of the period there was almost a ceremonial oath to be taken against the so-called "philosophy of nature," which looked always for transcendent or spiritual meanings going beyond physical events. On the other hand, there was the patent fact that Vienna was full of "nervous" sufferers who were not taken care of by any existing technique. There was a thriving practice for the "nerve doctor" (*Nervenartzt*), who would bring to bear the best of the new physiotherapy, hydrotherapy, heliotherapy, all of the devices to which William James was subjected when he had his terrible backaches and eye aches. Physical medicine was sometimes thought to effect cures by means of "suggestion." Yes, says Freud, I would indeed have attributed the cures to suggestion "if I had in fact seen any cures."

1. "NERVE DOCTOR"

The issue plainly called for some sort of facing of the diagnostic and therapeutic problems of those people who turned to the "nerve doctor." After considerable hesitation, Freud associated himself with a medical hypnotist, Dr. Josef Breuer, who was familiar with problems of this sort. Then, becoming convinced that he needed to know more about hypnosis, Freud went to Paris in 1885, attended the lectures and demonstrations of Charcot, and came back to Vienna; then he went off again, this time to Nancy in Eastern France, celebrated as the center of suggestive therapeutics in which both deep-sleeping hypnosis and also lighter-waking hypnosis were extensively and very brilliantly used by Dr. Bernheim. Freud took this seriously—indeed, so seriously that he translated Bernheim's book on hypnotic treatment into German. He again associated himself with Breuer.

During this period Freud was fulfilling his role as nerve doctor by an eclectic utilization of various ideas and techniques, and not hesitating to make use of the more psychological skills, particularly the hypnotic techniques as he saw them being carried out. Some of the hypnotic cures proved to be unstable, the patients getting sick again. But there were other reasons for caution. There were patients with open and obvious heterosexual response to the doctor; a patient might fall in love with the doctor. This gradually appeared to Breuer to be something that a sound male physician should avoid. Freud's idea was quite different; he felt that medicine must follow the leads, regardless of their consequences, dealing with the pathology that appeared in the hypnotic treatment and trying to find out by all possible means what was occupying a frightened or disturbed soul. He saw, as Charcot's patients had shown him, people with rigidities and paralyses that no one could explain, but that could sometimes be removed more and more effectively as one studied the ideas that the patients began to express regarding the fears in which they were involved. He saw over and over again in Vienna the kind of thing that he had seen in Nancy, namely the skillful utilization of suggestion. But obviously there were many things that were not being squarely faced, and it occurred to him that it might be possible to let the patients tell more fully what came to mind. It was conceivable that if the patient made an effort to bring back something that was vaguely out there in the periphery of his mind, the idea might be related to disturbing reminiscences that he was not facing.

Here the celebrated experiments carried out at Nancy by Dr. Bernheim are always worth remembering. The patient is told in a deep hypnosis that in response to a signal, after he wakes up, he will pick up an umbrella that is standing in the corner of the room and put it over his head. At the signal the patient *does* put the umbrella up. The doctor says: "But why do you put up the umbrella indoors?" The patient immediately produces a good reason: "I wanted to be sure it was my own." "I wanted to see the monogram inside." "I thought it had a hole in it, and I wanted to check a minute before I went out." There are always reasons. But they are not the real reasons; action is following upon an unconscious idea. The completion of the experiment is to say to the patient: "Yes, that is a reason, but it is not the real reason. Why did you put the umbrella up?" To which the patient will reply: "Oh, because you told me to." In other words, under pressure there is recovery of the material.

2. DREAMER AND REALIST

Naturally it is not too difficult to pursue somewhat more fully the notion that the patient has far more to say than he ordinarily divulges. Perhaps along with his fears of the original situation that is bothering him comes the fear of the very situation that would occur if he divulged something of this type in the presence of the doctor. The ability of the patient, when asked, to give the *real* reason for his behavior is the root of the idea of "free association," which at first had been grafted onto the hypnotic technique, but which could be separated from it. It was possible for the patient in a relaxed state, usually lying down, usually on the couch as developed in early practice, to start from literally anything and sooner or later recount the basis of his distress. Freud discovered that it was relatively easy and effective to start from the materials brought by the patient relating to his own recent thoughts, or particularly his own recent dreams.

It is necessary to dig a little bit into Freud's actual account of dream analysis to get the kind of loosening process that brought Freud so much precious material. One can listen endlessly and get only the jumble that one finds in the older psychiatric texts. One can find, in other words, all sorts of "disorders of thought" in the recounting of dream content or almost anything else. But it is necessary to follow a "basic rule," in which the patient, lying there, obviously starting from his own worries, his own symptoms, his own relative or absolute amnesias or paralyses, gives ideas that then tumble into a long trough, affording some preliminary guess as to what kind of peripheral material is working itself into the central focus and why it is doing so.

One could refer to this period in contrast to the nerve-doctor period in Freud's life as the dreamer period, or as the realist period, or as the combination of dreamer and realist. It is obviously necessary to dream along with the dreamer! It is necessary to find one's way into what Freud called the *primary process* thinking of the dreamer, the deep primitive impulses that lie beneath the dream façade—usually a façade of decipherable symbols representing his imperious wishes. At the same time it is always necessary to stand back with a certain perspective, and to watch the "secondary process" thinking, the "reality-testing" process, by which the patient postpones the satisfaction of wishes and comes to terms with reality as well as he can.

While each person who studies Freud will come out with his own schematizing of what is central, important, and probably permanently valuable, I think that the conception of "primary process" is one in which the sharpest and clearest break with all traditional psychology is most fully developed. The thought process, as it had been described by most psychologies for 2,500 years, was still essentially based on sensory components that are arranged in accordance with past associations—for the most part contiguity associations. Rabbits remind us of forests, or of guns; skies remind us of rain or tornados. Issues that have been together in experience bring one another back. Is that all that is involved? No; Plato, Aristotle, and many others had had a place for rational purposivism—"design," as Hobbes called it. But the conception that "design" is provided by deep human needs had somehow been lacking.[1] Even in the case of Herbart, for whom there is some sort of a push that takes the peripheral material and brings it somehow into the center, there is no place for the radical reconstruction that is involved in saying: *thought is not a series of contiguity linkages in which one component ties to another because of past experience alone; it is primarily determined by the drive state of the individual.* And this drive state proves to be very complex and comprehensive, involving the whole of the individual's biological being. The essential thing that Freud is doing is to find a new, dynamic,

[1] Nietzsche is the great exception. It is positively painful to have to leave out Nietzsche. Freud said he would not read Nietzsche because their thought was too much alike!

biological, evolutionary source for the stream of conscious activity; to replace or at least to transcend very greatly the contiguity factors, the associationist factors that had previously been emphasized.

I think one might say then that in being a dreamer, dreaming along with the patient and getting the feelings of primary process—that is, drive-directed process—Freud is also capable of transcending this actively in terms of using secondary process, that is, rational and orderly drive-transcending or drive-delaying types of activity. In doing this he becomes essentially a symbolist, overwhelmed constantly by the richness of the language of symbolism, by which the recounted dream or other fantasy suggests to the thoughtful observer the drive-determined dynamics that lie a little beyond the center of his own vision. The dreamer and realist has to become a symbolist. And symbols have to become quite central to the issue.

The Oedipus theme, for example: Why is the story of Oedipus, meeting and slaying his father near Delphi, so central in the psychoanalytic scheme? Because the detachment and the realism that must simultaneously be carried out require the poetic techniques of the symbolist, the dramatist, even the archeologist.

3. MYTHOLOGIST

The mythologist becomes, as it were, the individual who sees most deeply how a universal human preoccupation, which cannot really be fully faced, can transcend the literalism of language and find for itself a secondary type of elaboration, and then can manage to lead back again to a more observable context presented by the raw clinical material itself. I would say, then, that just as the "nerve doctor" passes to the "dreamer and realist," so the interpreter of dreams who sees what may lie beyond the symbols is forced to become a myth-maker or a myth-user, and that here we have literally an "open sesame" to the whole field of folklore of literature and of social expression. This system of symbols will apply not only to language, it will apply to gesture, gait, posture, vocal expression, the arts; the entire realm of human expressiveness would be seen as conveying a message regarding the drives operative at the time and the accretions or residues that past drive-determined activity has left behind within the organism.

4. REDEFINER OF LIFE

Now when we once embark on a theme as big as the role of symbols in the world of communication, we have left psychiatry for a while. We continue to be biologists, and continue to be students of the cultural sciences, but we need a larger canvas on which to work. And as I describe the fourth age of Freud, as I see it, as "the redefiner of life," I stress the fact that it is something about the nature of the life process that Freud is trying to communicate. In contrast with most of the psychiatry of the period, which is concerned with psychopathology, and of course, if possible, with physiological disorder or biochemical disorder, one can understand the Freud of the first decade of this century as seeking an explosive new conception and moving toward a tremendous climax.

The years just before World War I were years of climax. It is impossible to understand this period without recognizing that for thirty years Freud had been wrestling with basic biological issues. Long after his death his earlier gropings became clearer in a speculative piece (1895) on a *Project for a Scientific Psychology,* with a radical system of physiological assumptions (rather than psychological assumptions) regarding the course of mental life. Likewise there has been published an extraordinary series of letters, which he exchanged with a physician friend of his (Fliess) and in which he played very seriously with a physicalistic, almost a positivistic, way of looking at the psychological functions of mankind. Freud was trying to find a way of defining (in terms of the diameter of the neural axis-cylinder) some sort of quantitative predictor as to what can be remembered and used. He came to the natural conclusion—one reason why his findings were not published—that the physiological material was not adequate and that the theory was not really coherent.

Another study of this period, *Totem and Taboo,* offered an attempt to crack some of the "insoluble" problems of the social sciences, particularly the relation of individual drives to the family structure and to the larger community structure. He undertook to tie the biology of the child's response to the parent of the same and of the opposite sex to the dream theory he had worked out, to the Oedipus theme, and to the broader question of stability: How it is that society, amidst the endless complications of economic and political change, maintains certain basic human attitudes? What is the relation of biology to the sociocultural reality?

Freud as biologist is also concerned with that perennial question of evolution, the relation of individual growth to racial growth. The German biologist Haeckel had proposed (Haeckel's biogenetic law) that the individual's embryology, embryonic growth, and for that matter his growth for many years on beyond birth, is a sort of recapitulation of the course through which the species had passed. Freud was, of course, exposed to much thinking of this sort. And he had to come to terms with the question: How can I relate my evolutionary outlook to the specific problems of neurotic disturbances, the inarticulate conflicts and fears, of both adults and children? If we have, in the Oedipus theme, the heterosexual response of the very immature individual to the parent of the opposite sex, how are we going to deal with the question of the evolutionary background as the child passes through a series of psychosexual stages, from an infantile type of sexuality, through intermediate stages, to adult heterosexual patterns?

It is not so often remembered that Freud was working with neuroses in childhood in the early 'nineties. Freud was concerned, for example, with the fact that some of his child patients were scared to death in connection with guilt and possible reprisal associated with sexuality of various types and forms. It was obvious to Freud that the biological basis had to be seen and that the developmental pattern had to be seen, and that somehow one had to come to terms with the fact that the child is spelling out some of the problems of family psychology while still a tiny infant, in the period before we generally begin to recognize the nature of sexual development. This theory led on into one of the dominant papers of the first decade of the century, the *Three Contributions to the Theory of Sex,* in which we are given a picture of the early developmental sequence, considered biologically and psychologically, of adult sexuality. But the *Three Contributions* is an attempt to bring together at a scientific level of interpretation issues that are fraught with very deep hopes, fears, identifications and confusions. So that parallel to the relatively emotion-free papers of the period, like the one on *Wit* and the one on the *Psychopathology of Everyday Life,* we do find Freud's thought profoundly concerned with reference to basic biological issues.

It seems to me, then, that by the end of the first decade of the present century Freud had built a system that was *drive-centered* (drives being conceived in evolutionary terms) with the nature of the *sexual predeterminations* of life, with a theory of *symbols* that made it possible to see how impulses and ideas not acceptable to the central awareness were nevertheless playing a large part in life. He was preparing for a period in which he would more sharply analyze the nature of these central control functions, through which perception, memory, and thought are given a coherent order; through which secondary process activity, accepting the delays inevitable in impulse gratification, tries to build a temporal order with meaningful relationships to society's demand, and in which the problems of impulse control and the problems of orderly space-time structuring through the executive functions of life are brought coherently together.

5. EGO-BUILDER

All these are problems of the person as a person, rather than of impulses as such; beginning perhaps with Freud's paper on *Narcissism* (1912), they have become known as problems in "psychoanalytic ego psychology." Just what is "ego psychology"? Freud was, of course, writing in German, and we must point out some inevitable misunderstandings that we have in the English-speaking world with reference to what Freud was actually saying. Freud had no idea of talking about an *ego*. An *ego* is a Latin word. It is a word full of sophisticated and even befuddling associations from philosophy. It has a large number of moralistic implications. A person has "too much ego" or is "egotistical." At the simple, vernacular level at which he functioned, Freud would never say such a thing. In German one speaks of *"das ich"*—the *I,* the first person singular. Later on it became necessary for Freud to describe the *impersonal* aspect of life, the raw impulse; the uncontrolled; that which is essentially like water under pressure. He looked around for a word, and decided to use the everyday German word for *it: "es."* Along comes the translator, who says: "Well, now, the *'it';* that's not English." So he discovers the Latin neuter pronoun *id,* which means "that thing over there that I am pointing to," and so he proceeds to persuade us that Freud wrote a book on *The Ego and the Id,* when Freud in fact wrote a book on *The I and the It.*

Now to come back to the nature of the reconstruction that was going on in psychoanalysis. Freud had been dealing with a series of very real, omnipresent, important functions having to do with the confronting of reality, the inhibition of impulses, the maintenance of executive functions, and he achieved an answer: these all are ego functions. Of course, the ego had been present even in the beginnings of psychoanalysis, because the ego had been contrasted with unconscious strivings. But the orderly development of a theory about the *I* is another story, and it took a long time. As I noted, one may start with the paper on *Narcissism.* Freud was beginning to work his way through to a more mature conception of the ego—say from 1912 until 1926. To describe the Freud of this period, I am going to use the phrase, "the ego-builder"—or, perhaps, "the builder of the I." The period comprises a series of papers in which Freud defines the instinctual response of child to parent, then brings the parent within his own body, then identifies—becomes one with—the parent through these processes of incorporation and identification. The control processes exercised by parents, by which impulses that get out of hand are held in their place, or are manipulated in various ways, lead to various compromise functions, and become internalized; this exerts an autonomous regulating effect upon conduct.

Let us take Freud's use of the story of Echo and Narcissus. This exquisite story in Ovid's *Metamorphoses* describes how the youth hears a voice he cannot identify; wandering in the woods near a pool, he seeks the source of the voice, looks into the pool, and sees himself. He falls in love with his own image. This is the way in which the symbolist asks us to confront the stark, crude story of human vanity or self-preoccupation. We lift the everyday, galling reality of our own self-love into the distance that a myth creates for us. "Narcissism," then, becomes a name for the process by which one invests the self with passionate love, and launches upon a lifelong and deeply built-in preoccupation with all that represents oneself.

The second paper in this series, *Group Psychology and Analysis of the Ego,* goes on to describe the problem of interpersonal dependence—the affective ties binding members of groups to one another and to their leader. Since we have learned to think in terms of symbols, it is natural to see the leader of the group as a father surrogate, and to expect in the interaction between follower and leader much of what we saw in the little boy's response to his father, involving a curious, dynamic mixture of love and fear, with consequent hate. We find a fraternal bond between the various members of the group. From this we have a new view of the nature of crowd action, and of states and cultural systems as provided with basic energies similar to those that one finds in the individual psychosexual development.

Then comes—we have now gone through the period of World War I—*The Ego and the Id,* in which we are introduced in an orderly fashion to the interrelations between the ego and the instinctual life. It is obvious that the ego cannot be equated with consciousness. It begins to be clear that many of the acts by which the individual defends himself against guilt, for example, are carried out unconsciously, so that the ego is quite literally partly unconscious and partly preconscious. What happens dynamically now is that the ego becomes a completely different entity from what it was earlier. It is a system of energies, dynamically related to the alien id, and operating at conscious, preconscious, and unconscious levels. It gets all its energy from the id, but turns against the id, or like horse and rider, stays in control insofar as the id agrees.

Here is another incredible translation trick that we must face. Freud speaks of energies being *invested* in objects. The translator disagrees, and in place of *investment* comes the word *cathexis* (taking hold). For Freud, an energy may occupy, or be invested in, an object or a region. An object cathexis, including a cathexis upon the I, can be dynamically important without implying that the energies at any time become irreversibly invested in one object; there is some flexibility allowing for changes in receiving and utilizing tremendous investment within the total energy system of the person.

In the same volume, and in a later volume, *Inhibitions, Symptoms and Anxiety,* we now have need for a still further definition of the nature of the ego. It is very clear that in some cases the ego is being attacked by something. The ego feels overpowered. One sees, for example, in some melancholics, and in many aging persons, the feeling of being overwhelmed with unworthiness or inadequacy. Not only is life "no good," but

"I am a great sinner; I have myself destroyed whatever used to be good in myself, and even in the world." It becomes necessary to say that the ego is the object or the butt of this crude joke; there must be something else within the individual that is attacking the ego. Well, surely, if we go back to the early Oedipus theme and follow its tortuous development, we find that there has been identification with the parent in his *disciplinary role* and not only in a love relationship. There has to be some name to define the process by which a part of the I has become a "beyond or *over* I," *"über-ich"* in German, *"super-ego"* in Latin. This represents a process by which the ego has been divided into an ego in the narrow sense, the I of everyday life, and the *conscience* system or control system, the superego in which identification with the parents has made possible a control *within,* acting as a control upon the control. The poor ego is sometimes caught in the crossfire between the intensity of the impulses coming from the id and from the control system known as the superego. But the identification with the parents has incorporated within the child not only a terrorizing disciplinary system or conscience, but also the parental love as the child experienced it—the ego-ideal.

6. FACER OF ANXIETY

Instead of introducing the word *conflict* at any one point in this little narrative, I have tried to suggest a series of events in which the concept of conflict would become more and more appropriate as we go along. Just as I called the first use of the Narcissus theme the period of the "ego-builder," so I am going to emphasize here the "facer of anxiety" and "resolver of conflict." Now, of course, conflict had always been a prime problem with Freud, and we may ask ourselves in what sense can conflict be introduced as a new theme. It cannot be introduced as a new theme, but it contained a new focal point which by some, and apparently by Freud himself, was thought of as the last of his major fresh psychoanalytic discoveries, as contrasted with the more philosophical interpretations of his last years.

The nature of conflict can be conceived in two ways. One can conceive of conflict imposed upon oneself, where one cannot have two appetizing things at the same time; they are in some such way ordered in time and space and one must choose between them. But conflict arises at times from *inner* preoccupation; there may be two impulses at the same time or two symbols of impulses, between which there has to be a choice. In terms of modern learning theory, one could say that there are conflict situations that represent essentially Pavlovian types of conditioning; one symbol stands for a significant aspect of the environment that would by itself arouse an instinctual response, so that the response is precipitated by the symbol. Such responses can be contrasted with what used to be called *voluntary responses*—now often called *operant responses*—in which there is no simple Pavlovian situation, but a more roundabout voluntary process; instead of being acted on like Pavlov's dogs, as a passive recipient of stimulation, the individual manipulates the environment until he gets what he wants.

Now Freud, in very different language, is making exactly this distinction between classical conditioning and operant conditioning. Freud is agreeing that there are certain primitive types of anxiety that arise from biologically adequate stimulation—for example, situations that are an overload upon the system. (Too much stimulation may break through the stimulus barrier and produce panic or disorientation.) There are, in other words, cases like the Pavlov dog situation in which the person is more or less at the mercy of the environment. But there are also cases in which the individual, often quite unaware of what he is doing, handles life, exercises initiative, in such a way as to gratify needs or ward off threats. The concept of "signal anxiety" is a good way of describing the process by which the ego controls the world in such fashion that an appropriate cue or sign is thrown up which may protect one from having to deal with a catastrophic situation. One may, in other words, inwardly organize life in such a way as to perceive the anxiety signal that one has oneself thrown up for a defensive purpose, and in this way not have to encounter the full course of the adverse situation or threat.

This oversimple statement is designed primarily to show that Freud in his later middle years was still working through new concepts. To say that "anxiety is an ego function" is to go far beyond the definition of an instinctual process as such. The energies have been partly converted into ego form. That is, the I, the first person singular, is still using the energies that are there biologically, is using them against or in control of, or as reconciler of, energies that are functioning at a more primitive level. Freud went on explaining the relation of ego and id. In the *New Introductory Lectures* (1933), which come pretty near the end of his life, we find an expression of the degree to which psychoanalysis had transcended the instinct emphasis of the earlier years and had come to regard the ego, the first person singular, derived from id energies, as having a central or controlling place in life.

7. PHILOSOPHER OF LOVE AND DEATH

The last years of Freud's life were quite literally years in which the relations of love and death were again confronted from a changed perspective. The theme of death, which had been repeatedly voiced in many earlier papers, for example, in *Beyond the Pleasure Principle* and *Reflections on War and Death,* becomes more and more absorbing. It does not require any great guesswork to suggest that the cancer of the tongue, the series of surgical operations, the substitute tissue material that he himself called "the monster," which he had to wear in his mouth, his confrontation of more and more suffering, influenced the writing and influenced the perspective. But Freud would never have wanted to be thought of as a philosopher of love alone, without any recognition of the fact that love and death are co-equal and partners in the scheme of human life. Nor would Freud ever have been satisfied with a hedonistic definition of goals, nor with any notion that the erotization of life functions is a complete biological interpretation of human psychology. There are books in the last years, *Civilization and Its Discontents* and *The Future of an Illusion,* written in the period between the two world wars, which have led some to regard Freud as the town pessimist. As he faces his own last years, and the struggle of the malignant growth in his mouth, and the spread of the Nazi system in the German-speaking world, Freud may seem more and more uncertain, but not, I think, in any way giving up the essential definition of life from the early period, in which the creative process is given co-equal strength with the destructive process. The same is true, of course, of the great philosophical systems of India.

Now for a few words about the historical interrelations of William James, Max Wertheimer, and Sigmund Freud. As we look at these three men, we are impressed, I think, with *pluralism,* as James would call it; scattered richness and multiplicity of incompatible ideas. Freud did not use his last years to create a tighter system. He used them to keep throwing out ideas—some of them, like *Moses and Monotheism,* rather remote from the central creative task—but always with a new turn of thought, always offered in more and more diffidence (as Thomas Mann says, the diffidence of the elderly), with a very strong conviction that what he has done will be advanced by others.

Secondly, despite pluralism, in all three we find *wholeness,* a struggle to find some unitary cosmic and psychological meaning in the system. Certainly all three men were Greeks in the sense in which I have tried to develop the nature of the Greek struggle toward reality. All were worried about disorder everywhere, with loose pieces lying, overlapping, hiding each other; all were concerned with the rebuilding of what might have been an archetypal original order, the making of something that had sense in a reality-testing meaning of the term.

All were tragedians. This becomes particularly clear when Max Wertheimer, with his magnificent attempt at Gestalt, at a unity of all, came back to the discord of life and had to admit that local petty national *Gestalten* often took precedence over anything that could be found at the level of a cosmic scheme as a whole. Certainly with James, the issue of the tragic comes out particularly in the discussion of the "sick soul" and the recognition that with disorder there is tragedy and with tragedy there is disorder; that these are just as deep in reality as are the gratifications that the evolutionist would hope to emphasize.

And all of these three figures are unsatisfied with their efforts. All look beyond. All regard the fragments that lie before them as incapable of meaning anything unless *new empirical fragments* and *new syntheses* are successfully pursued.

One of the many summaries that one might use in describing Freud's attempt to meet the question: How much, after all, has the theory of the unconscious done for us? Look at these vast new meanings in life, which we did not expect but which keep poking their heads up, so that we begin to see and begin to redefine what the growth, what the changes, what the transitions of the future may be! Freud asks us to suppose that we stand there in the office in Vienna. "You want to go to the West. You want to go to Paris. I open the door towards the West. That is as far as we have gone towards understanding the unconscious."

I think that all three of these men, if they had the opportunity to confront the issue in these terms, would say simply: "How little we know."

Index

QUASARS

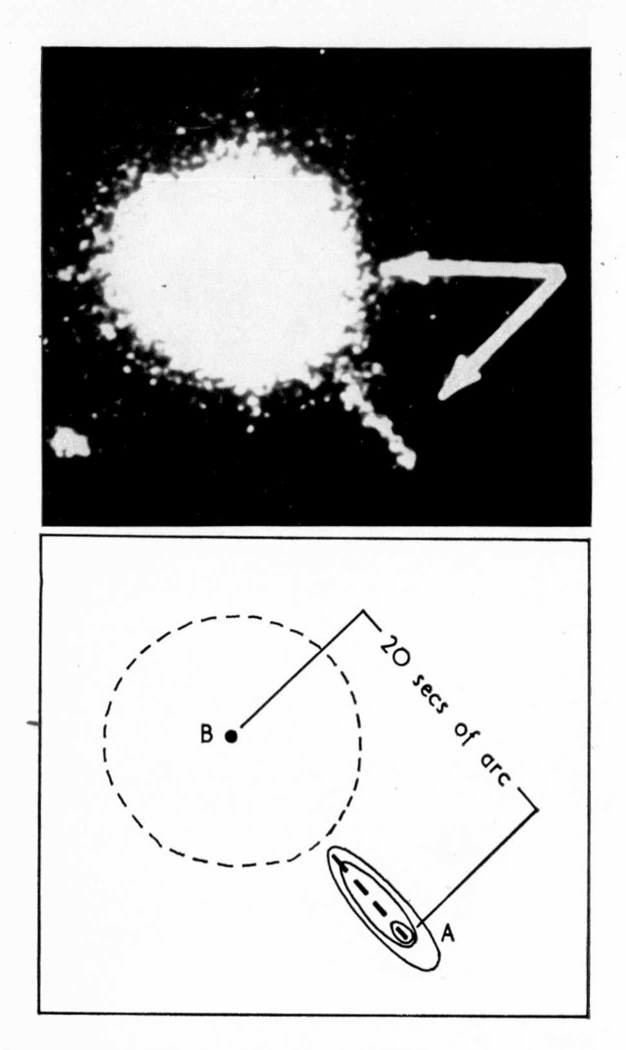

A photograph of the brightest quasar 3C 273. The inclined arrow points to the 'jet', which is called component A, while the horizontal arrow points to the starlike component B. This intensely bright object is probably smaller than 0·01 secs of arc. On this photograph its image is more than 10 seconds across, because of scintillation and halation during the prolonged exposure needed to record the very faint jet. The diagram is to the same scale as the photograph, and shows the positions of the two regions which emit radio energy. The optical and radio properties of this intriguing object are discussed in Chapters II and III.

QUASARS

THEIR IMPORTANCE IN ASTRONOMY AND PHYSICS

by

F. D. KAHN, M.A., D.Phil.

Professor of Astronomy
in the University of Manchester

and

H. P. PALMER, B.A., D.Phil.

Reader in Radio Astronomy
in the University of Manchester

HARVARD UNIVERSITY PRESS
CAMBRIDGE, MASSACHUSETTS
1968

Published by the University of Manchester at
The University Press
316–324 Oxford Road, Manchester, 13

First published, 1967
2nd edition, with corrections, 1968

Printed in Great Britain by Butler & Tanner Ltd., Frome and London

CONTENTS

ILLUSTRATIONS

In addition to the diagrams and stellar photographs, there are a number of illustrations of the optical and radio telescopes used in the observations. These are as follows:

ACKNOWLEDGEMENTS

The authors are grateful to the following institutions for permission to reproduce illustrations. Mt Wilson and Palomar Observatories, Pasadena, California, U.S.A.; The Commonwealth Scientific and Industrial Research Organization, Sydney, New South Wales, Australia; California Institute of Technology, Pasadena, U.S.A.; National Radio Astronomy Observatory, Green Bank, West Virginia, U.S.A.; Central Office of Information, London, England; Nuffield Radio Astronomy Laboratories, Jodrell Bank, Cheshire, England; The National Geographic Society.

CHAPTER I

RADIO GALAXIES IN THE UNIVERSE

We are almost completely ignorant about the early history of the Universe. During this century our knowledge has increased a little, and many great advances have become possible recently as modern developments in science and technology have been used for astronomical research. Some of the most exciting and intriguing of these discoveries are associated with the strange objects now called quasars. This new word is a convenient mnemonic for their full name: quasi-stellar optical objects identified with discrete radio sources. As the name implies, quasars are of interest both to optical and to radio astronomers, and they pose many problems for astrophysicists.

The pioneer radio astronomer Jansky recognized that most of the extra-terrestrial radio radiation reaching the Earth's surface originated amongst the hundred thousand million stars of the Milky Way. This huge disc-shaped galaxy has a diameter of approximately 100,000 light years. Its radio energy is not generated by the stars, but by the acceleration and deceleration of fast-moving electrons in interstellar space. This may occur as a result of their mutual collisions, or under the influence of interstellar magnetic fields. The early radio surveys showed that, in addition to the broad band of radio emission from the Milky Way, some radio waves came from small localized regions which have since come to be known as 'discrete radio sources'. These sources have no connection with any of the bright stars (apart from the Sun), and at first they could not be identified with anything else seen by optical astronomers.

It is now known that detectable radio emission comes from several different types of object. A few are relatively small regions within our Galaxy. Many others have been identified with remote and sometimes unusual external galaxies which are emitting radio energy much more copiously than the Milky Way. Some of these are at extremely large distances, as great as five to ten thousand million light years. In the last two years many of the more intense sources which did not seem to be associated either with galactic objects or with external galaxies have been identified with quasars.

Photographs of the Milky Way galaxy cannot show its form, because from our position within its disc we see mostly the interstellar dust and gas clouds and cannot discern its structure. To appreciate this it is more useful to look at photographs of those nearby external galaxies which are likely to be similar. Figures I/1*a* and I/1*b* show two such galaxies. They are known as M 33 and M 51, the numbers they were given in the list of Messier, the eighteenth-century astronomer who first catalogued them. These galaxies are also listed in the New General Catalogue of nebulae, and are often referred to by their numbers in that catalogue, which are NGC 598 and NGC 5194. Both show the spiral structure characteristic of many giant galaxies, it being more pronounced in M 51 than in M 33. In both cases the galaxies lie with their spirals face on to the telescope. It is likely that the Milky Way galaxy seen at the same distance, and also face on, would be more like M 51 than M 33.

Just above M 51 and apparently at the end of one of its spiral arms another galaxy can be seen. This one, NGC 5195, is classified as an irregular type, for it shows some structure, but not a recognizable spiral form. One of the arms of M 51 lies across the front of it, so that interstellar dust partially obscures the irregular galaxy behind.

Galaxies are not at all evenly distributed in space. All, or almost all of them seem, indeed, to be concentrated into groups or clusters. Groups may have up to about twenty members while giant clusters may contain more than a thousand galaxies. M 33 is a member of the local group to which our Galaxy belongs; fourteen other members are known for certain, with a few more suspected. They are all gathered into a region about three million light years across. Some members of another group which is about six million light years away can be seen in Fig. I/2. These galaxies in the constellation of Ursa major occur within a patch of sky which is approximately 2° square. The spiral near the centre of the photograph is M 81, NGC 3031. It is a weak emitter of radio waves, similar to our own Galaxy and other giant spirals. The irregular galaxy above it in the photograph, M 82, NGC 3034, appears to be distorted, and is a rather more intense source of radio emission.

Optical astronomers have to deal with objects having a very wide range of brightnesses, so they use a logarithmic scale of visual or photographic 'magnitudes' (symbols, m_v or m_p). Each change by one magnitude in the brightness of a star or galaxy corresponds to an increase or decrease in the energy received by a factor of 2·5. Fainter objects are described by larger numbers on this magnitude scale, and the faintest object which can be seen with the naked eye has a visual magnitude of +6.

The galaxies M 81 and M 82 in Fig. I/2 are approximately fifteen times fainter than this, having magnitudes of 8·9 and 9·4. The other two members of the group which can be seen in that figure are about six times fainter again, and hence of the eleventh magnitude. The faintest galaxies visible with the largest telescope have magnitudes greater than +20. That is, they are more than ten thousand times fainter, and so, probably, of the order of one hundred times more distant than the examples mentioned here.

The bright galaxies mentioned so far are easily distinguished from stars, for they have images which are extended rather than point-like. The images of bright stars may also appear to be extended, but they usually have a characteristic diffraction pattern which appears as a cross, and can be used to distinguish them from galaxies. Several examples of this effect can be seen in Fig. I/1*a*. It is more difficult to distinguish between faint galaxies and faint stars but very necessary, for in a cluster the fainter galaxies, which are more difficult to find, are also more numerous. For instance, more than fifty members of the Virgo cluster have been found in the area of sky shown in Fig. I/3.

Part of a cluster of galaxies in the constellation of Virgo can be seen in Fig. I/3, which shows a region three degrees square. The brighter cluster members are marked with a short arrow. In some cases spiral structures can be seen. Many of the others are circular or oval in shape, and have no obvious structure. They are classified as elliptical galaxies. These are usually smaller than spirals, and also probably much older. They may be the central nuclei of old spirals, whose arms have decayed and dispersed.

The galaxy in the Virgo cluster marked with a long arrow in Fig. I/3 is associated with one of the more intense discrete radio sources which has been given the name Virgo A. On this photograph it looks similar to many other members of the cluster, and there seems to be no obvious reason why this particular galaxy should give radio emission. However, this photograph was exposed fully in order to show as many of the fainter members of the cluster as possible and the centre of the image of this bright galaxy is overexposed. On photographs with shorter exposures and greater magnification, such as Fig. I/4, structures become visible in the central region. A jet-like feature about 30,000 light years long appears to be exploding out of the nucleus. The optical spectrum of this jet is most unusual, for no lines at all can be seen, the whole object is unusually blue, and its light is partially polarized. No similar feature has been found in any other elliptical galaxy, though some have been detected recently in quasars, as described in Chapter III. There seems to be an increasing amount of evidence that galaxies become radio emitters after some explosive event in their central regions and these 'jets' may be visible results of such explosions.

Determinations of the distances of external galaxies are among the most difficult measurements in astronomy, for they are far beyond the range of ordinary triangulation techniques. Even when the diameter of the Earth's orbit is used as a yardstick the angles involved in astronomical surveying become too small to measure if the objects are more than a few hundred light years away. Various supplementary techniques have been used to extend this range, first by observations of pulsating stars, and then, at greater distances, by measurements of the intrinsically brightest members of clusters of stars. The margins of error increase as each successive step is made in this chain of measurements and reasoning, linking the size of the solar system to clusters of galaxies. The best estimate at present of the distance of the Virgo cluster is 36 ± 7 million light years. On the scale of the Universe this cluster is relatively nearby, but the errors show that even its distance is uncertain by as much as 20 per cent.

The optical spectra of many of the galaxies in these clusters have been studied, and some of the spectral lines have been recognized. All of these were found to lie rather to the red, or long wavelength, side of their normal position. That is, their wavelength λ had apparently increased by a small amount $\Delta\lambda$ when compared with the values measured in laboratories on Earth. As we shall see this redshift is a very common phenomenon in extra-galactic astronomy. Its value is usually denoted by the fraction $\frac{\Delta\lambda}{\lambda} = z$. For the radio galaxy in the Virgo cluster $z = 0{\cdot}0041$. The famous astronomer Hubble found that, in general, the fainter and presumably more distant galaxies have greater redshifts. Detailed studies of these measurements suggest strongly that, as discussed in Chapter VII, redshift is exactly proportional to distance, even for galaxies far beyond the Virgo cluster.

Measurements of optical redshift can therefore be used to estimate the distance of galaxies, and this is the only method available for the most remote ones.

A second example of an external galaxy associated with a radio source was found in the constellation of Cygnus. Optically this galaxy is about one hundred times fainter than the source in Virgo, and if any similar jet-like features were to exist there, they could not be seen on photographs, even those taken with the largest telescopes. The redshift of this source is $z = 0{\cdot}056$, which is more than ten times greater than that for the Virgo galaxy. So, using the redshift law just described we can calculate the distance of this source, called Cygnus A, as follows

$$\text{Distance of Cygnus A} = \frac{\text{Redshift of Cygnus} = 5{\cdot}6\%}{\text{Redshift of Virgo} = 0{\cdot}4\%}$$

$$\times \text{ distance of Virgo} = 504 \pm 100 \times 10^6 \text{ light years.}$$

Now the energy reaching our telescopes falls off as the square of the distance from the source, yet we receive from Cygnus A about ten times more radio energy than from Virgo A. So we can also calculate that the total radio emission from Cygnus A is $\frac{(5{\cdot}6)^2}{(0{\cdot}4)^2} \times 10 \doteqdot 2000$ times the emission from Virgo A.

By means of special radio observations with interferometers, measurements have been made of the approximate size and shape of the regions emitting the radio energy of the Virgo and Cygnus sources. These were found to be considerably larger than the galaxies which can be seen on optical photographs. The Cygnus source has the more complicated structure, for the radio emission comes from two very large and approximately circular regions, which are each about 75,000 light years across. These lie symmetrically, one on either side of the galaxy. There is no detailed understanding of the processes which generate the radio energy from these sources, and for some time the Cygnus source was thought to emit an unusually large amount, and to be exceptional in other ways. For example, its surface brightness is extremely

I/1a. The external galaxy M 33, (NGC 598) which is a member of the local group.
(*Mt Wilson and Palomar Observatories photograph.*)

I/1b. The giant spiral M 51 (NGC 5194). Above this a second galaxy can be seen, which is named NGC 5195. (*Mt Wilson and Palomar Observatories photograph.*)

I/2. A group of galaxies in the constellation of Ursa Major, which is about six million light years away. The two brightest galaxies are M 81 (NGC 3031), and M 82 (NGC 3034). (*Mt Wilson and Palomar Observatories photograph.*)

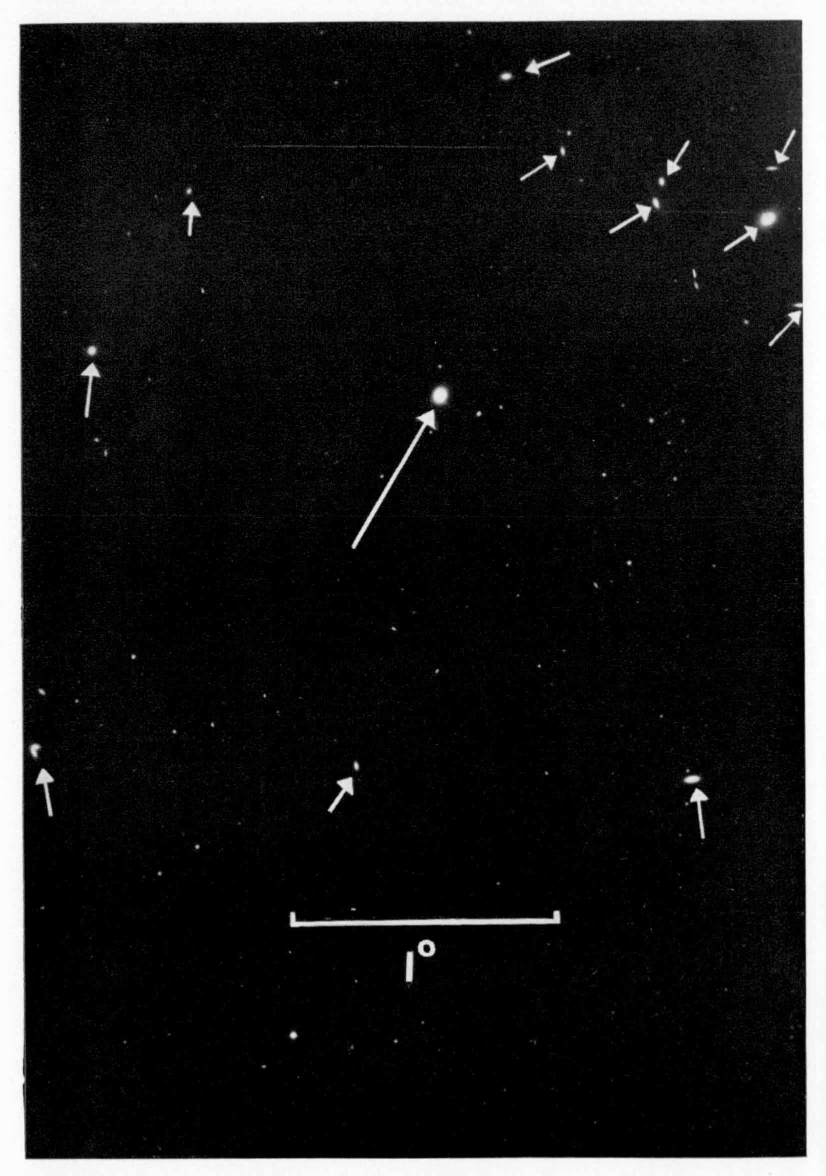

I/3. The region of sky which contains the Virgo cluster of galaxies. Some cluster members are marked with short arrows, and the radio galaxy NGC 4486 with a long arrow. (*Reproduced by permission of the National Geographic Society.*)

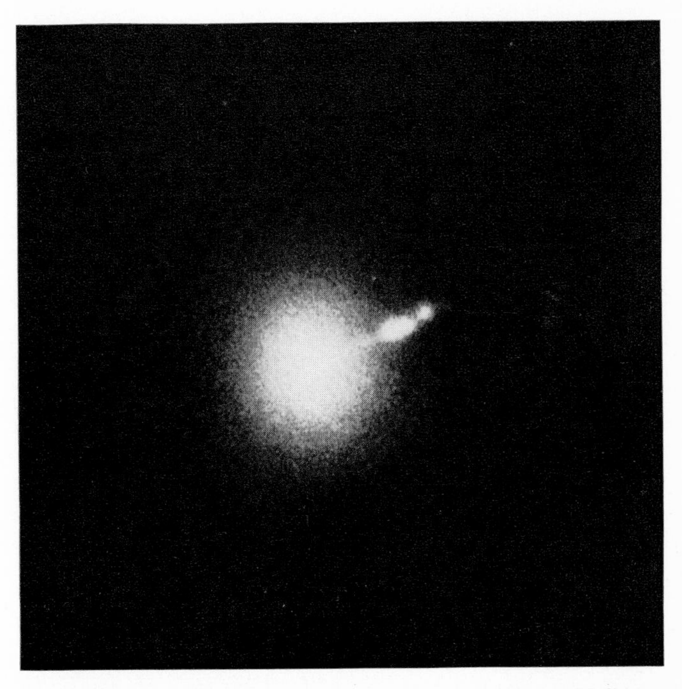

I/4. A short-exposure photograph of the radio galaxy NGC 4486 in the Virgo cluster, showing the 'jet' in its central region. (*Mt Wilson and Palomar Observatories photograph.*)

I/5. The 48-inch Schmidt telescope at Mount Palomar, California, shown with the slit of the dome open. (*Mt Wilson and Palomar Observatories photograph.*)

I/6. The 200-inch Hale telescope at Mount Palomar, California, showing an observer in the cage at the prime focus. (*Mt Wilson and Palomar Observatories photograph.*)

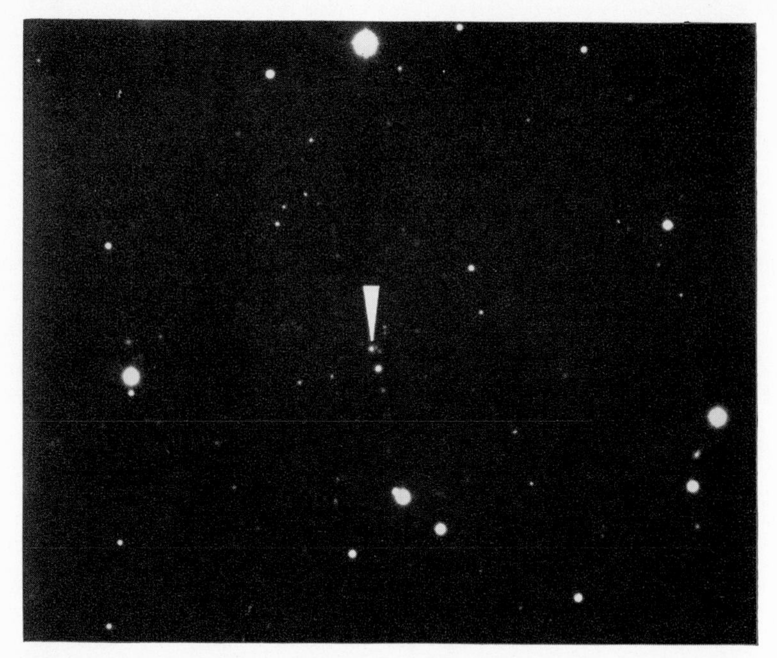

I/7. A remote cluster of galaxies in the position of the radio source 3C 295, photographed by Minkowski with the 200-inch Hale telescope at Mount Palomar. The arrow indicates the brightest member of the cluster, which is identified with the radio source. (*Mt Wilson and Palomar Observatories photograph.*)

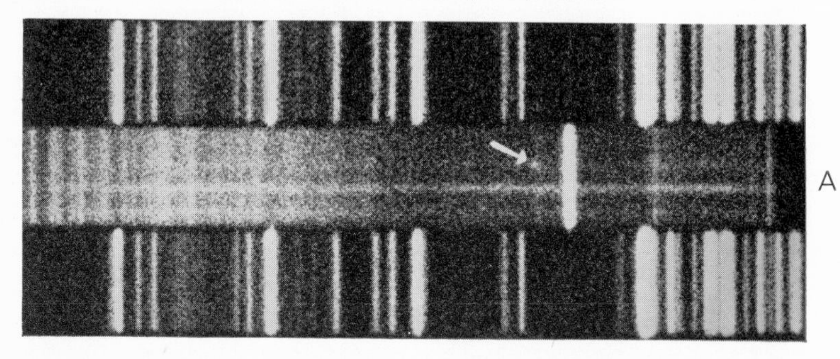

I/8. The optical spectra of some of the galaxies shown in Fig. I/7. An emission line in the spectrum of the radio galaxy is marked with an arrow. It is identified as a double oxygen line emitted at wavelengths of 3726 and 3729 Å. It is observed at a wavelength of 5447 Å, that is redshifted in the ratio 1·47 : 1. The vertical line near it is due to emission at 5577 A.U. from oxygen in the Earth's upper atmosphere. (*Mt Wilson and Palomar Observatories photograph.*)

high. This means that it has a very large rate of radio emission per unit solid angle.[1] There are several ways of describing this, and one of the most convenient is to calculate its radio brightness temperature

$$T_b = \frac{\text{a constant}}{\text{wavelength}^2} \times \frac{\text{energy received}}{\text{solid angle}}$$

Such a calculation would give approximately the correct answer for a red-hot lump of iron or even for a cold planet. But for a radio source the value is rather fictitious, for it refers to regions which are almost perfect vacuum. If a thermometer were placed there it would indicate a temperature dependent on the amount of starlight present, and not on the electrons whose radio emission determines the value of T_b. Nonetheless the brightness temperature has the great advantage of not depending on the distance of the source. It can therefore be used to look for similarities between identified sources, whose distances are known or can at least be estimated, and unidentified sources, although their distances are quite unknown.

A comparison of this sort was one of the arguments which led to the identification of the extremely remote radio galaxy in the constellation of Boötes. This source is number 295 in the Third Cambridge catalogue of discrete radio sources, so it is briefly described as 3C 295. Interferometer measurements showed that this source covers a very small region, a solid angle of less than half a millionth of a square degree. This is about one hundred times smaller than the area covered by the two parts of the Cygnus source, and the radio energy received is also about a hundred times less.

[1] 'Solid angle' measures the fraction of the sky occupied by a celestial object. It can be expressed in square degrees. The whole sky occupies about 40,000 degree^2, the Sun and Moon each about 0·2 degree^2, and the two parts of the Cygnus source each about forty millionths degree^2. This may be compared with the smallest detail which can be seen with the unaided human eye and would fill a solid angle of approximately 300 millionths degree^2.

Thus its brightness temperature is about the same, and it was amongst the two or three highest values known at that time.

This source lies well away from the Milky Way, where there is no significant obscuration of external galaxies by the dust clouds of our own Galaxy. The celestial position of the radio source was measured very accurately, with probable errors which were smaller than 20 arc seconds. It was therefore very likely that if light was emitted by any object associated with this source it might be photographed somewhere within a rectangle on the sky 20 seconds × 20 seconds, and virtually certain that it lay within the larger rectangle 40 seconds × 40 seconds.

The next step was to study optical photographs of that region of the sky, and for this purpose the Sky Atlas was consulted. This is not a book, but a collection of more than a thousand large photographs, each more than a foot square. There are two sets of photographs of the whole sky visible from Mount Palomar, one taken in blue light, and the other in red light, in observing conditions which were as near ideal as possible. This project was undertaken jointly by the Mount Wilson and Palomar observatories, and the National Geographic Society of America, in 1949, and it took eight years to complete. The photograph of Fig. I/3 is about one-fifth of one Sky Atlas field. A 48-inch reflecting telescope was used, which is shown in Fig. I/5. It is of a special design invented (in the thirties) by an Estonian optician called Schmidt. It allows one to photograph a large area of sky at once without the errors and distortions which would be produced if a normal astronomical telescope were used for the same purpose. Complete sets of prints of these photographs comprise the Sky Atlas, and copies are now stored at many observatories, and in university libraries. Since 1960 this set of photographs has been taken again with the same instrument, so that by comparing the two pairs of photographs of any region one can now search for stars or other objects which have moved or changed in the intervening ten years.

Minkowski, one of the Palomar observers, was very interested in the optical problems associated with radio sources. When he heard that the error rectangle associated with the source in Boötes was so small he inspected that part of the sky on the Sky Atlas. He found it empty. If there was any optical object there at all associated with the radio source it was too faint to be photographed with the 48-inch Schmidt telescope. He therefore decided to use the 200-inch telescope to photograph the region again. This great instrument is shown in Fig. I/6. It is so large that the observing astronomer can work in a cage at the prime focus without significantly reducing the amount of light reaching the main mirror, which can be seen below him. Observing time with this instrument is shared between about a dozen astronomers, and there is never enough to satisfy everyone. Nonetheless Minkowski decided to use some of his time for this problem, for he thought that a galaxy of the Cygnus type might be emitting the radio energy of this source in Boötes, and that with the greater light-gathering power of the larger telescope, he might be able to photograph it. This expectation proved to be correct, and he obtained the photograph reproduced in Fig. I/7, which shows an extremely faint cluster of galaxies in that region. One of the brighter members of the cluster is marked with an arrow. The errors in the measurements of the position of the radio source are smaller than the length of the arrow.

The optical spectrum of this object was then examined. A much longer exposure was needed, because the light from the galaxy is dispersed along a line, and not focused into the smallest possible area as in direct photographs. The best spectrum obtained required an exposure of four and a half hours, during which time the telescope had to follow the motion of the sky continuously, and as accurately as possible. The resulting spectrum is the horizontal band at the centre of Fig. I/8. The vertical lines are due to the faint light from the night sky, and to scattered street lighting. The bands of lines at the top and bottom of the figure are calibration spectra, added after the astronomical exposure so that accurate measurements of wavelength can be made.

Three galaxies gave spectra visible on this photograph. The brightest one, just lower than the image arrowed on the direct photograph of Fig. I/7, produced the almost continuous horizontal line marked below the centre of the figure. This spectrum has a redshift of 0·244, but is in other respects that of a normal galaxy. The spectrum of the radio galaxy is marked A in Fig. I/8. The horizontal mark due to its continuum spectrum can only just be discerned. Much of its light is concentrated into one line, which is marked with an arrow on Fig. I/8. Minkowski considered that this line was probably the same as one also observed in Cygnus A which was due to ionized oxygen atoms. In the laboratory this line can be seen to be double, with components at wavelengths of 3726 and 3729 Ångström units (1 Å $= 10^{-8}$ cm). The measured wavelength in the spectrum of the Boötes source was 5447 Å. So the redshift seemed to be

$$z = \frac{5447 - 3726}{3726} = 0{\cdot}4614$$

This value was larger than any found previously, so it was important to check it as far as possible. Two other fainter lines were found in the spectrum which gave the same value for the redshift if they were identified with lines which had also been found in Cygnus A. A second photograph of the spectrum was obtained, on which most of these features could be observed again. As final confirmation Oke examined the overall colour of the galaxy, and showed that it was appreciably redder than nearer ones.

The large value of the redshift showed that the Boötes source is almost ten times as far away as Cygnus A, and all the evidence suggested that it was another exceptionally powerful radio galaxy. This identification, and the suspected similarity to the Cygnus source were made even more probable when further interferometer measurements showed that the radio source in Boötes also had two emitting regions, whose actual size and separation were comparable to but rather smaller than the values for the two parts of Cygnus A.

In all, nearly 200 radio sources have been identified with galaxies in the last ten years. A few of them are 'normal' spirals like the Milky Way, M 33 and M 51. These galaxies are relatively weak radio emitters, with outputs of radio energy of the order of 10^{37} to 10^{39} ergs/sec. Most of the radio galaxies are more like the Virgo source, and have an output of the order 10^{40} to 10^{42} ergs/sec. The sources in Cygnus and Boötes are amongst the most powerful known, with outputs of 10^{44} to 10^{45} ergs/sec. Only seven radio galaxies are known to be as energetic as this.

For some years it seemed likely that most of the discrete radio sources lying in unobscured regions of the sky would in the end be identified with galaxies. This hope has been realized in part, for the more intense sources. In the revised 3C catalogue there are 228 sources lying 15° or more from the Milky Way, that is, in regions where obscuration can usually be neglected. By the beginning of 1966 identifications with galaxies of various types had been published for more than one hundred of these sources, while a further seventy or so were unidentified. In fifty-one cases, which included several of the twenty most intense radio sources in the sky, the correct identification seemed to be with unusually blue star-like objects. These, the quasars, pose puzzling problems. They form the subject of this book.

CHAPTER II

THE DISCOVERY OF QUASARS

Minkowski's successful identification of the remote and very faint galaxy 3C 295 was achieved with the world's largest telescope, the 200-inch reflector on Palomar Mountain in Southern California. He used it to take special photographs of the area of sky surrounding the radio position. Many other comparable 3C sources had been identified with galaxies which were not so remote, but in 1960 there remained several reasonably intense radio sources for which no identification had been suggested. Some of these had marked similarities to 3C 295. They lay in unobscured regions of the sky, in directions far from the Milky Way. Two or more independent and accurate measurements of their radio position were available. In some cases measurements at Jodrell Bank had shown that their radio sizes were as small as, or smaller than, that of 3C 295. Matthews and Sandage decided that three of these sources, 3C 48, 196 and 286, were sufficiently likely to be remote galaxies that a little of the observing time of the 200-inch telescope should be used to photograph them. When all three pictures were studied, however, no sign of any galaxies at all could be found within the search areas, but there appeared to be a rather faint star within 10 arc seconds of each of the radio positions. One of these photographs, of 3C 286, is shown in Fig. II/1. In another case there was a faint wisp of nebulosity extending from 5 to 12 seconds from the star. No star (except the Sun) had previously been shown to give radio emission up to that time, but the coincidences of position were so good, and the cases so similar in very many ways, that the observers were convinced that new identifications had been achieved. The next problem was to persuade the world's astronomers that these really were stel-

II/1. A photograph of the quasar identified with 3C 286. (*Mt Wilson and Palomar Observatories photograph, kindly supplied by Dr Sandage.*)

II/2. The 210-foot diameter radio telescope at Parkes, Australia. (*C.S.I.R.O. photograph, kindly supplied by Professor Bolton.*)

lar identifications, so in search of further evidence they proceeded to examine the colours and spectra of the stars. They found that each star was generating an exceptionally large amount of blue, violet and ultra-violet radiation. Their optical spectra were quite unlike those of normal stars, which always show the characteristic lines associated with hydrogen atoms. In the spectra of most stars many other absorption and emission lines are usually present as well, indicating the presence of numerous other kinds of atoms in their outer layers. These newly discovered stars had continuous emission spectra, which showed no absorption lines and only relatively few emission lines, in one case none. These very unusual and puzzling spectra therefore posed many theoretical problems, but before they were explored at all deeply, the problems were completely changed by the successful identification of the radio source 3C 273. This was achieved in 1962 by Hazard, Mackay and Shimmins working with the 210-ft radio telescope at Parkes in Australia. This instrument was brought into use in 1961. It is shown in Fig. II/2. In 1962 the Moon, as seen from Parkes, appeared to pass three times across the source 3C 273. Such occultations are rare, for the Moon crosses a region of sky $\frac{1}{2}$ degree by 360 degrees, or only a solid angle of 180 degrees^2, in the course of one month. It does not follow an identical path again for nineteen years, so if an occultation is missed there may be a long wait for the next opportunity.

Lunar occultations of planets and normal stars have long been studied by optical astronomers as interesting events from which a variety of astrophysical and even geographical information can be deduced. One result is that the position of the edge of the Moon at any instant is now known extremely accurately, and when all the corrections have been applied, it can be calculated with errors smaller than one hundredth of a second of arc. Baade and Minkowski had pointed out earlier that in favourable cases most of this precision could also be attained in radio observations, if one could measure sufficiently accurately the times at which the Moon covered and uncovered a radio source. If the source is extremely small one might expect it to disappear suddenly, and to reappear equally suddenly. If the source passed behind the Moon near its equator it would remain obscured for more than an hour, while if the source passed near either pole the interval would be shorter. So from the time of disappearance one could calculate one coordinate of the source, and from the interval between disappearance and reappearance, the other coordinate could be found.[1] In the real situation the disappearances and reappearances are not

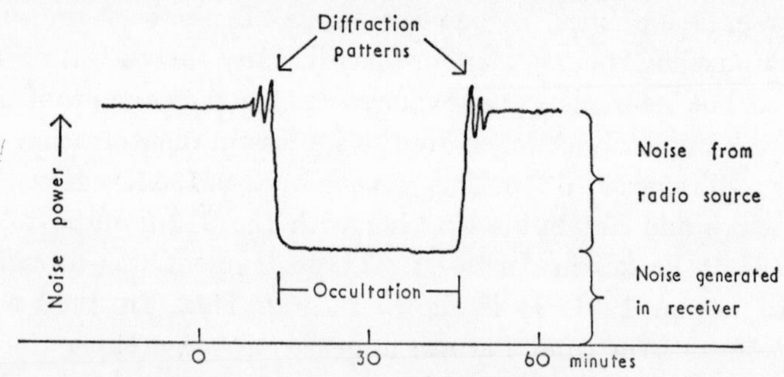

II/3. The record which would be obtained from a radio telescope during the occultation of an intense source by the Moon.

quite sudden, even when the radio source has a very small angular size. Some of the radio energy propagates round the edge of the Moon to a slight extent, so the edges of the geometrical shadow become somewhat blurred. The whole event is a radio astronomical example of the optical diffraction experiments studied in school and college physics courses.

Figure II/3 shows the record which would be obtained if a radio telescope and receiver were used to observe an intense source during an occultation. For sources of sufficiently small diameter diffraction patterns occur when the source disappears and reappears, and these may enable one to estimate

[1] There is an ambiguity in the second coordinate, which can be resolved provided one knows from other measurements whether the source passes behind the north or the south hemisphere of the Moon.

the size of the source, and perhaps to deduce something about its detailed structure.

The occultations of 3C 273 studied at Parkes were a fortunate succession of three which occurred within six months of each other in the autumn of 1962. They were observed at three radio wavelengths, and five of the possible six disappearances and reappearances were recorded. A tracing of one part of these records is shown in Fig. II/4. The full refinements of diffraction theory were used in the interpretation of

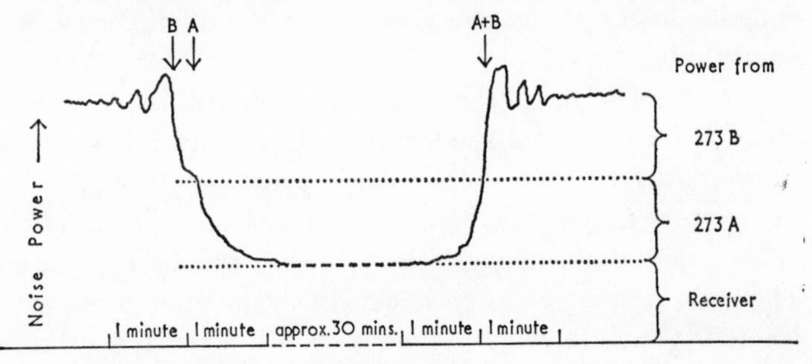

II/4. Tracings of parts of the radio records obtained at a frequency of 410 Mc/s at Parkes, as the Moon occulted the quasar 3C 273 on August 5th, 1962. As the Moon covered the source, its two components disappeared at the times marked with arrows, which are 27 seconds different. No similar step occurred during the reappearance, so the two components must have been uncovered at the same time. (*By kind permission of Dr Hazard.*)

all these data. It was found that the radio source consisted of two components, 19·5 seconds of arc apart, one being rather smaller than the other, and having an unusually flat radio spectrum. The position of each of these radio components was measured with mean errors which were less than one arc second. An inspection of the Sky Atlas showed that the smaller of these components coincided exactly with a rather bright and very blue star, while the more extended component could be identified with a fainter wisp or jet of bluish nebulosity. With positional agreement of such unparalleled excellence there was no doubt that an identification had been achieved, and it seemed to be the fourth stellar one.

The 'star' itself is shown in the frontispiece. Its image is so overexposed that it is about ten arc seconds across. The smaller radio component, 3C 273B, lies at the centre of this image whilst the larger radio component, 3C 273A, is associated with the outer parts of the optical jet, which extends 19·3 seconds of arc from the star.

As the star was relatively bright, Schmidt was able to make a detailed survey of its spectrum. He found six spectral lines which were approximately 50 Å wide, and three broader emission regions, superimposed on a bright and very blue continuum.

The wavelengths of the centres of each of these lines were measured with errors smaller than 10 Å, and tables of the wavelengths of optical lines were consulted to find what atoms were responsible for them. As with the spectra of the other radio stars, none of these lines could be recognized. Then one evening Schmidt decided that he must investigate whether the lines could be understood if a redshift or blue-shift correction were applied. To his considerable surprise he found that if he shortened the wavelength of each line in the ratio 1 : 1·158 (a redshift correction) four could be identified with the lines of hydrogen atoms, and the other two were associated with ionized oxygen and magnesium atoms. The lines then fitted extremely well, with a mean error of only 6 Å. No other explanation of the spectrum was in sight, or has been published since, so it seems that, for this star, a redshift correction $z = 0{\cdot}158$ must be accepted. When the spectrum of 3C 48 was re-examined it was found that with a redshift correction $z = 0{\cdot}361$ two of its lines could be recognized as hydrogen emissions. In addition the same ionized magnesium line was present and possibly one due to ionized oxygen as well. Four other lines were recognized as due to ionized neon. Again, the large redshift seemed well established, no other satisfactory explanation could be found, and as closely related interpretations fitted for each star, they clearly supported each other.

These unexpected results changed completely the astrophysical problems of interpreting the spectra of these 'stars' but did not bring them any nearer a solution. If the objects were stars within the Galaxy, they might be so extremely massive that their gravitational fields were intense enough to cause the redshifts. Alternatively, the redshifts might be due to a high velocity arising from the general expansion of the Universe, in the same way as in the spectra of remote galaxies such as 3C 295. In that case the distances could be calculated in the usual way, but gave values of more than 1000 million light years. These seemed incredibly great, for they implied that these quasars were emitting energy at an enormous rate, more than a hundred times greater than the brightest galaxy known previously. In the three years since these measurements were announced many more quasars have been identified, and still larger values of redshift have been measured. Some of these optical and radio measurements are described in the next two chapters.

CHAPTER III

OPTICAL PROPERTIES OF QUASARS

The measurements of large redshifts for the star-like objects identified with 3C 48 and 3C 273B were very exciting, and stimulated great efforts and interest in many observatories. At once searches were made for further examples of this new and intriguing class of celestial object. Special attention was given to those unidentified radio sources for which accurate measurements of position were available. Many blue star-like objects were found which were as close as a few seconds of arc to the radio positions. Some of these stars were also found to emit exceptionally large amounts of ultra-violet radiation, and in these cases new identifications were reported. At the time of writing more than sixty quasars have been discovered. Most were found by this technique, but several of the fainter ones were found only after even more accurate radio positions had been determined during observations of lunar occultations. All these quasars are fainter than 3C 273B, but several of them are similar in showing jet-like features, or in having faint patches of nebulosity near them.

In the last three years, the accuracy with which the positions of radio sources are known has been improved considerably, until now the mean errors for most of the sources in the 3C catalogue are smaller than 12 seconds of arc in each coordinate. This has enabled astronomers to achieve much greater success in finding optical identifications for the sources. Recently Wyndham, of the California Institute of Technology Radio Observatory, published a comprehensive list of the identifications associated with the three hundred most intense extra-galactic radio sources. Because of the optical obscuration, many of those sources which lie near the

Galactic plane can only be identified if they are associated with relatively bright objects. For the sources which lie further than 14 degrees from the Milky Way, however, more than two-thirds have now been identified. Wyndham gives brief details of each case, and usually a photograph reproduced from the Sky Atlas, of the area in which each source lies. Two examples of these photographs are shown in Fig. III/1. The size of a minute of arc on this scale is shown below the photographs, and also a small black square which represents the size of an error area 12 seconds of arc across. Figure III/1*a* shows the region around the source 3C 49. Its error area is centred on the intersection of the two lines near the middle of the photograph. This radio source is moderately intense, and its size is probably smaller than 3 seconds of arc, so there seemed a good chance that it might be a quasar. Yet there is no object visible on this photograph within thirty seconds of the radio position, and in Wyndham's list it is described as a blank field. The situation with the other source 3C 309.1 is not so difficult, for there is a very blue star of the 17th magnitude exactly at the radio position. The redshift of this source is not known, but as it is the tenth brightest quasar discovered so far, and is only four magnitudes fainter than 3C 273B, it is unlikely to be among the most remote.

The optical objects identified with the 300 extra-galactic radio sources in Wyndham's list may be divided into three groups. The most numerous are the 146 radio galaxies, many of them interacting pairs of ellipticals. Secondly, sixteen of the radio galaxies are classified as N-type, whose characteristic feature is that the central nuclei are much brighter than usual, and have a star-like appearance. The third group comprises the quasars, of which fifty-eight are given in Wyndham's list. This means that more than two-thirds of the extra-galactic radio sources have been identified, and the remaining third are divided between fifty-six cases where either several objects can be seen within the error area, or there is obvious absorption by dust associated with the Milky Way, and forty empty fields like 3C 49. In these there is no object at all bright enough to be photographed by the 48-inch Schmidt telescope, so whether there is a radio galaxy, quasar or some other type of object, it is fainter than 20th magnitude.

Studies of the optical spectra take much longer, but results have already been published for half these quasars. So far thirty values of redshifts have been published, and these are all larger than the value of 0·158 measured for 3C 273B, a few of them being more than ten times as great. At present all such spectral measurements must be made from the surface of the Earth through our shimmering and absorbing atmosphere, for it is not yet possible to make observations of this sort from artificial satellites. These measurements were limited therefore to the range of wavelengths extending from about 3000 to 7000 Å for which the atmosphere is almost perfectly transparent. The spectral lines which fall in this region can be studied with standard astronomical instruments, but for objects with greater and greater redshifts first red, then yellow and then green lines are shifted out of this 'window' into the infra-red part of the spectrum. They are then partially absorbed by the atmosphere, and become much more difficult to observe. Similarly ultra-violet lines not normally observable because of absorption by ozone and other gases in the Earth's upper atmosphere may be moved, by a sufficiently large redshift, into the visible regions of the spectrum. So the identification of spectral lines in quasars was a progressive process. First, a few characteristic lines were found in relatively bright nearby quasars. Then some of the same lines were recognized in more remote quasars with greater redshifts, and in those same quasars some new lines could be seen, not visible before, which had been shifted into the 'window' from the ultra-violet. Then, for the most remote quasars, these ultra-violet lines were recognized, and in some cases, one or two

III/1. Two photographs of areas of the sky containing discrete radio sources. The rectangle below the photographs shows the size on this scale of an error area 12 seconds of arc across. The area of interest lies at the intersection of the two lines on each photograph.

(*a*) 3C 49. No identification is suggested for this source, for the field appears to be empty.

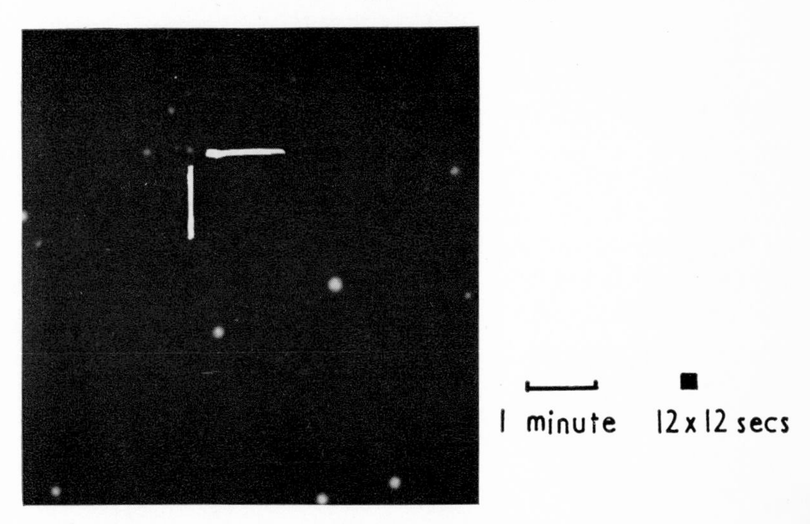

(*b*) 3C 309.1. A quasar of 17th magnitude lies near the centre of this area. (*Mt Wilson and Palomar Observatories photograph, kindly supplied by Dr Wyndham.*)

more were found in the blue, shifted from the far ultra-violet.

As in all spectroscopic work the apparent accuracy of red-shift measurements is remarkably good, with errors smaller than one part in a thousand even for the largest redshifts. But the values are, of course, completely dependent on the correctness of each successive step in the sequence of arguments by which the spectral lines were identified. These are illustrated in Fig. III/2 for three quasars. The symbols in the bottom row represent five of the lines, plotted at the wavelengths at which they are emitted in the laboratory. It will be seen that the Hβ line of hydrogen is near the middle of the 'optical window' and that the magnesium line MgII lies near its blue edge. The two carbon lines CIII and CIV, and also Lyα, another hydrogen line, all lie in the ultra-violet. Above the symbols horizontal rows of short vertical bars indicate the positions to which these lines have been redshifted, for 3C 273B and two other quasars. These last have bigger redshifts, and the top row is for the quasar 1116 + 12, which has the biggest redshift reported so far. (This radio source is given in an Australian catalogue, and the numbers give its approximate celestial position.) The heavy bars indicate lines which have been observed, and the dotted bars the positions of lines which have not yet been detected for these particular quasars.

As the number of known quasars grew steadily, from the original four to more than sixty, the number for which red-shifts have been measured has also increased from two to thirty. Eight other quasars have spectra in which one line can be seen, but at least two lines are needed before a reliable redshift can be deduced. There are also three quasars in whose spectra no lines at all have been found so far.

While some astronomers have tried to identify more quasars, others have examined the brightest ones in more detail, and still others have studied their history by searching observatory collections of old astronomical photographic

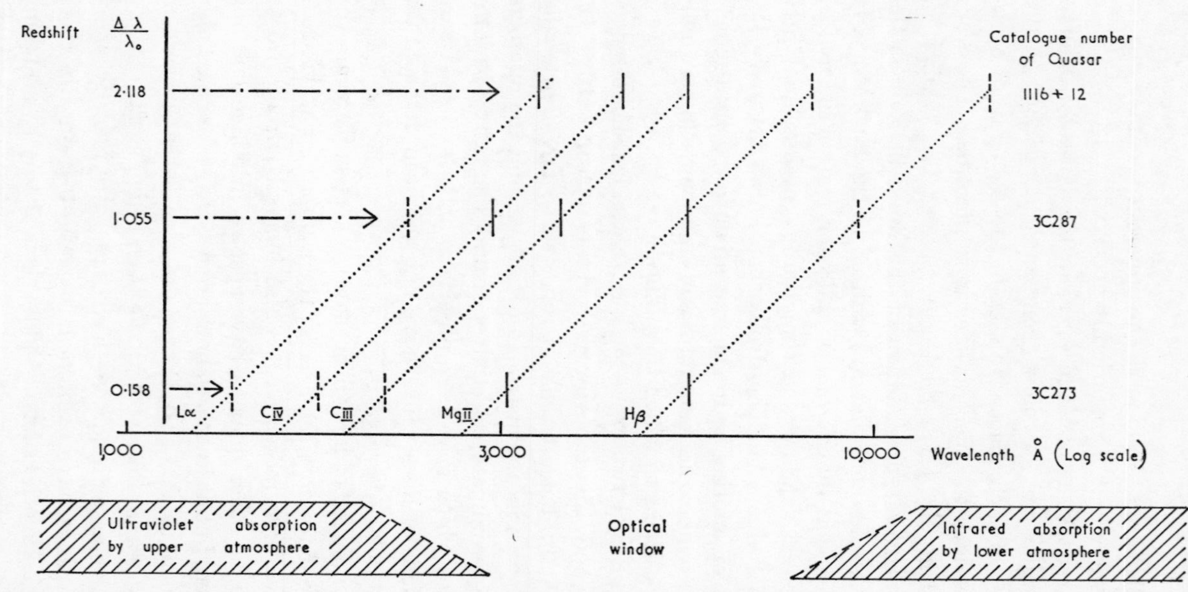

III/2. Some of the optical spectral lines which have been detected for three quasars are shown by solid vertical bars. The dotted bars are lines presumed to be present, but not observed because of absorption in the Earth's atmosphere.

plates. In some collections these plate files go back almost 100 years. The Harvard file of plates was found to contain some 5000 photographs on which the quasar 3C 273B appeared. The earliest of these was exposed during the year 1887 and many were taken with small telescopes of 1½ and 3 inches diameter. The rather fainter 'star' identified with 3C 48 was found to have been recorded on seventy-five plates dating back to 1899.

From the analysis of these old and valuable observations two most important and surprising results emerged. First, there has been no detectable proper motion of the star 3C 273B in almost a century, for it has moved less than 1/400

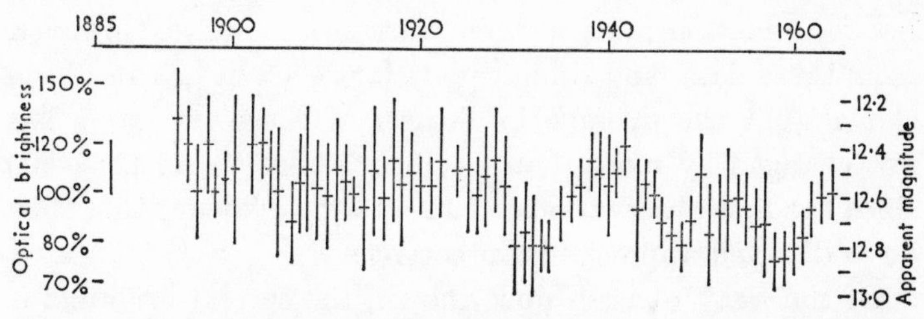

III/3. Annual mean values (where known) of the optical brightness of the quasar 3C 273B plotted against date. The sizes of the vertical bars indicate the estimated errors of the annual values. (*Adapted, by permission, from data published by Professor Harlan J. Smith.*)

second of arc per year relative to the general background of stars. For comparison a steady proper motion as large as 10 seconds of arc per year has been found for a star which is only six light years away. The absence of any detectable motion for 3C 273B suggests that its distance is almost certainly greater than 6000, and probably greater than 60,000, light years. Secondly, the brightness of these stars was found to have varied. In the case of 3C 273B there is a fairly regular periodicity, as may be seen in Fig. III/3, in which the crosses show the annual mean values of the brightness of the star. The more measurements are combined in an average, the more accurate it is, and the vertical lines indicate the accuracy of each point. It can be seen that the errors are smaller in the more recent data, partly because more measurements are available, and also as a result of improvements in telescopes, photographic equipment and technique.

Detailed individual comparisons have also been made between 3C 273B and eight nearby stars which could be used as standards. Such an examination shows whether the size of the error lines in Fig. III/3 is due entirely to inaccuracies of measurement, or whether they have been enlarged significantly by brightness changes of the quasar during each brief period of observation. It was found that during some periods of a few months the quasar had changed its brightness by almost as much as in its thirteen year cycle. However, from these data, and similar plots for 3C 48, it has also been shown that the average brightness of these two stars has not changed by more than 0·2 magnitudes (≑ 20 per cent) since the first observations, so there is no evidence that they have decayed appreciably in a century.

Of the sixty quasars now known, the second brightest is two magnitudes (six times) fainter than 3C 273B, and some of those identified more recently are more than five magnitudes (a hundred times) fainter still. There is very much less information about these stars, or about their history. Already, however, several more of them have been found to have variable brightness. Some of these changes were found by comparing images on the photographs taken ten years apart for the two editions of the Sky Atlas. Others have shown significant variations on the few occasions they have been specially observed in the last two years.

One of these—3C 345, the third brightest quasar—is particularly interesting. Not only was its brightness found to vary by 0·4 magnitudes during twenty days of special observations in 1965, but one of the lines in its spectrum was observed to split and one component to move about 50 Å during the same period. As these changes have so far only been observed once, it is not yet known whether they are regular or erratic. If these spectral shifts are due to relative motions within the quasar, which would be the normal interpretation, they represent speeds of order 3500 km/sec.

For most of the quasars the only features which have been seen are the blue star-like images by which they were identified. These have usually been found on the photograph of the Sky Atlas, but a few have also been observed with larger telescopes. In two of these cases, 3C 48 and 3C 196, very faint patches of glowing nebulosity have been seen a few seconds of arc away from the quasar. Sandage also reported recently that, using the 200 inch telescope and an especially sensitive photographic plate, he had been able to detect very faint filaments at the edge of the image of 3C 48. He thought it looked like an extreme case of an N-type galaxy, which had a particularly bright star-like nucleus, surrounded by a vestigial glowing envelope or halo. Another non-stellar feature has been reported for the quasar 3C 279. This is almost four magnitudes fainter than 3C 273B, but has a jet-like structure emerging from it which extends up to 36 seconds of arc from the star. This is an angular distance which is almost twice as great as that for the jet in 3C 273. Yet the redshift measured for 3C 279 is 0·535, which is more than three times larger than the redshift for 3C 273. So if one assumes, as usual, that redshifts are proportional to distances, this second jet is at least one million light years long, and, if we see it in projection, may be much longer.

During some of the early searches for quasars several blue star-like objects were found, which emitted unusually large amounts of ultra-violet radiation, yet did not coincide with any catalogued radio sources. This led Sandage and others to wonder how many of the blue objects previously classified as stars in the halo of our Galaxy may, in fact, be extragalactic. More than 8000 stars of this sort have been catalogued, and in the last twelve months some have been reexamined. There are basically three types of measurements which can help to elucidate this problem. If a star is found to have a measurable proper motion it must be within the Galaxy, but the converse is not true. A star may be so far away in the galactic halo that its angular motion is immeasurably small, and anyway a small fraction of nearer galactic objects may be moving directly towards or away from us, and so have no transverse motion. But if it should be confirmed, as the evidence now suggests, that an unusually high proportion of the stars emitting excess ultraviolet radiation have transverse motions too small to be measured, then it is probable that many of these objects are extragalactic. Secondly, it may be possible to detect radio emission from these quasars even though they are too faint to appear in the catalogues of radio sources which have been published so far. This point is discussed in the next chapter. Sandage has suggested the name 'quasi-stellar galaxy', or QSG, for these objects which look like quasars but have not given detectable radio emission. Finally if upon examination the spectrum is found to be a recognizable stellar type, then the object is almost certainly a galactic star. Most of the halo stars seem to be of this sort, particularly the explosive or erratic types known as 'white dwarfs' and 'old novae'. On the other hand if spectral measurements show that the object has a large redshift, then it is almost certainly extragalactic. This has been established in four cases, and values of z ranging from 0·02 to 1·91 have been reported.

Table I contains some details of the optical properties of a few of the quasi-stellar objects for which redshifts have been published. The catalogue number of each object is given, and its observed optical magnitude. Then follow the redshift, and a note of the number of spectral lines used for its determination. The first three objects in the table are the brightest and the first two have the lowest values of redshift, of those known at present. The next three were selected because they have particularly interesting optical or radio properties. The remaining objects are three of the radio-quiet quasi-stellar

TABLE I

Optical properties of some quasi-stellar objects

Catalogue number	*Optical brightness (Magnitude m_v)*	*Redshift* $\frac{\Delta\lambda}{\lambda} = z$	*No. of lines in spectrum*	*Notes*
Quasars				
3C 273B	12·8	0·158	6	Brightness varies with period of approx. 13 years and quasar also shows 'flashes' lasting a few days. Proper motion less than 1/400 second of arc per year.
A	19	—	—	Jet extends to 19·5 seconds of arc from B.
3C 249.1	14·8	0·311	4	Second brightest quasar.
3C 345	15·0	0·595	3	Light output variable. In 1965 one spectral line was observed to move 50Å in 20 days.
3C 48	16·6	0·367	8	Light output variable. Nebulosity 5 seconds of arc from quasar.
3C 279	17·8	0·536	4	Light output variable. Jet 36 seconds of arc long.
1116+12	19·3	2·118	3	The largest value of redshift reported by August 1966.
Quasi-stellar Galaxies				
PHL 256	15·9	0·131	9	No reports of variable light output or of proper motions.
PHL 938	16·9	1·93	3	
BSO 1	17·0	1·24	2	

galaxies described by Sandage, for which redshift measurements have been published. Notes on optical peculiarities are given in the last column. Most of these were found during observations with telescopes larger than the 48-inch Schmidt. It seems likely that if similar observations of other quasars were available this list of peculiarities would be considerably longer.

In conclusion, a graph of observed optical brightness against redshift is shown in Fig. III/4 for the quasars whose redshifts have been published. If all these quasars were identical with 3C 273B then, if distance is proportional to redshift, all the points would fall on the dotted line at least until

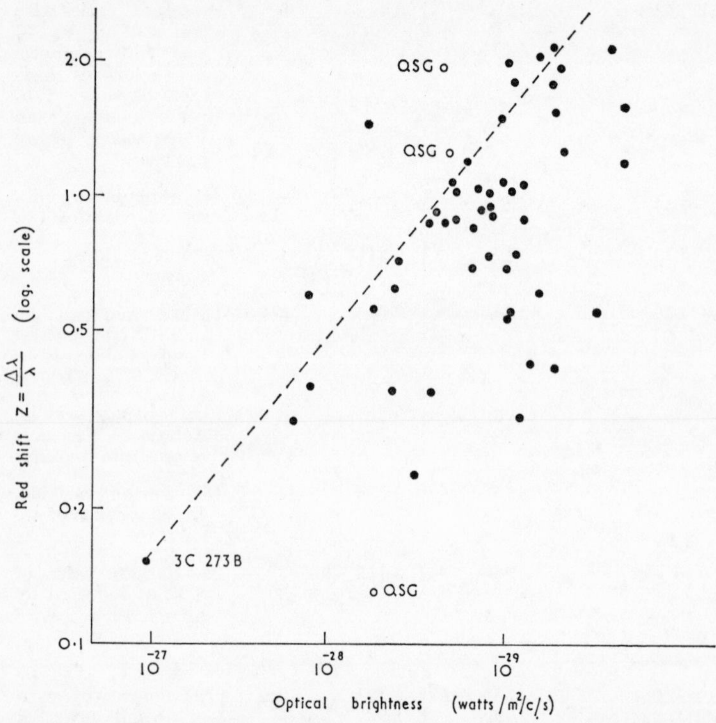

III/4. The points represent the observed optical brightness of quasars and QSG's plotted against redshift, on logarithmic scales. The points would fall on the dotted line if all were of similar brightness to 3C 273B, and the inverse square law were obeyed exactly. If the quasars are at very great distances, cosmological effects would make this line more nearly horizontal for the greatest redshifts.

the distance became so great that the inverse square law was no longer obeyed exactly. Then a curved line would be more likely. The observed points show a large spread about these lines, which presumably indicates that their optical output differs from one to another by more than a factor of ten.

CHAPTER IV

THE RADIO PROPERTIES OF RADIO GALAXIES AND QUASARS

Quasars as a class are defined by their optical rather than their radio properties. Photographs or spectrograms obtained during one or a few nights may be sufficient to add one more to the catalogue of quasi-stellar objects. Although radio astronomers can often observe all day as well as at night, they are more limited than their optical colleagues in the measurements they can make and they gain information more slowly.

The fundamental radio measurements of discrete sources are of their celestial positions and of the radio energy received from each at one or more wavelengths. Difficulties arise in making accurate measurements of position, because the radiation used has wavelengths which are approximately a million times longer than those of light. To casual visitors radio telescopes seem large, especially when compared with optical ones. But in relation to the wavelength of the radiation being studied, they are very small instruments. Measurements of source positions and sizes made with single telescopes are correspondingly less precise. The accuracy with which angles can be measured, and the smallest details which can be distinguished within a particular discrete source depend on a property of telescopes known as resolving power. This is defined as the smallest angular distance between two adjacent areas of the sky which can just be recognized to be distinct. This angle is approximately λ/d radians, or $\lambda/d \times 57 \times 60$ minutes of arc, where d is the diameter of the telescope, and λ is the wavelength of the radiation. For example, the Jodrell Bank Radio Telescope Mark I has a diameter of 250 ft, i.e. 76 metres, so that when it is used at a wavelength of 21 cm, λ/d is 1/275 radians, or 12 minutes of arc. This means that at any instant the telescope receives all the radiation coming from an area of sky 12 minutes of arc across. The contributions from different directions within that cone cannot be separated. In radio terminology the cone is called the 'main beam' of the telescope which defines a 'beam area' on the celestial sphere. This is the order of accuracy with which the position or angular size of a radio source can be measured with that telescope when it is used by itself at a wavelength of 21 cm.

More accurate measurements of source positions can be

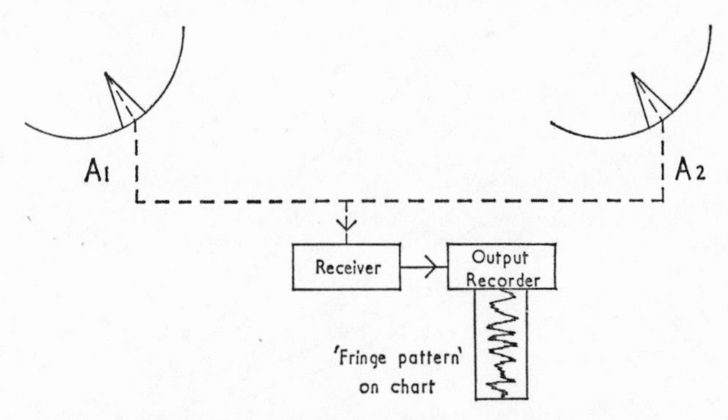

IV/1. A block diagram of the simplest type of radio interferometer.

made with radio interferometers. These consist of two or more widely separated telescopes used together. A diagram of a simple interferometer is given as Fig. IV/1. It shows the two radio telescopes A_1 and A_2, connected together by a cable, whose mid-point goes to a well-stabilized receiver. If radio waves from an intense source arrive within the main beam of each aerial, and induce voltages in the cables which reinforce each other at the receivers, then there is a large deflection of the output pen. This falls to zero when the voltages induced in the cables cancel out. Whether the voltages reinforce or cancel depends on the exact time of arrival of a wavefront, and hence on the exact direction of the source relative to a line joining the two telescopes. We say that the combined beam of the telescopes has been divided into a number of fan-shaped lobes as shown in Fig. IV/2. As the radio source moves through these lobes, a characteristic pattern, called a fringe pattern, is drawn by the pen recording the receiver output.

With some modification of the circuits of the receiver one

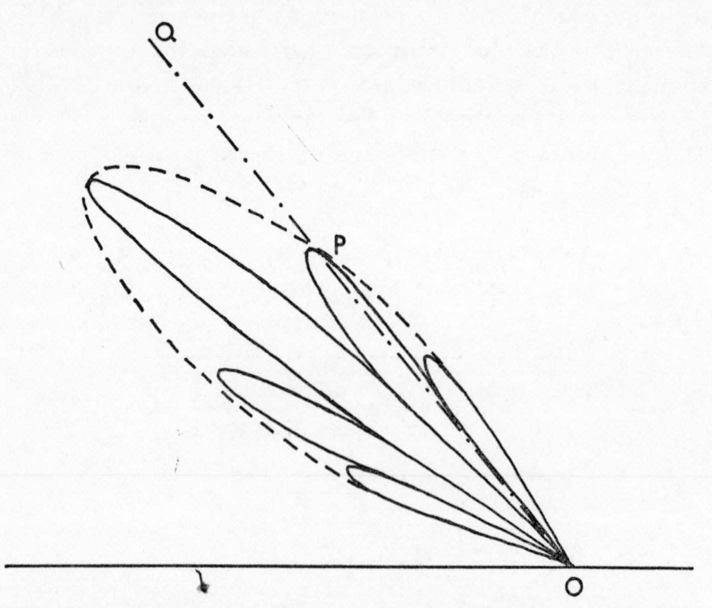

IV/2. The response of an interferometer may be represented by this pattern of lobes within a main beam, provided the telescopes are pointing in the same direction. The distance OP from the origin to the end of a lobe shows the relative sensitivity of the system in the direction OQ.

can arrange that a symmetrical fringe pattern is recorded, which looks like a sine wave, as in the example of Fig. IV/3A. The pattern there is almost perfectly smooth, as would be observed for an intense discrete source. The great majority of sources are rather faint, so it is necessary to increase the gain of the receiver until their pattern becomes visible. A limit to this process is reached, however, when the pen begins to make erratic deflections due to the amplification of minute random variations of voltage in the input circuits of the receiver, and not as a result of radiation from radio sources. We then say that 'noise' dominates the record. An example of a noisy record is shown in Fig. IV/3B, and of a fringe

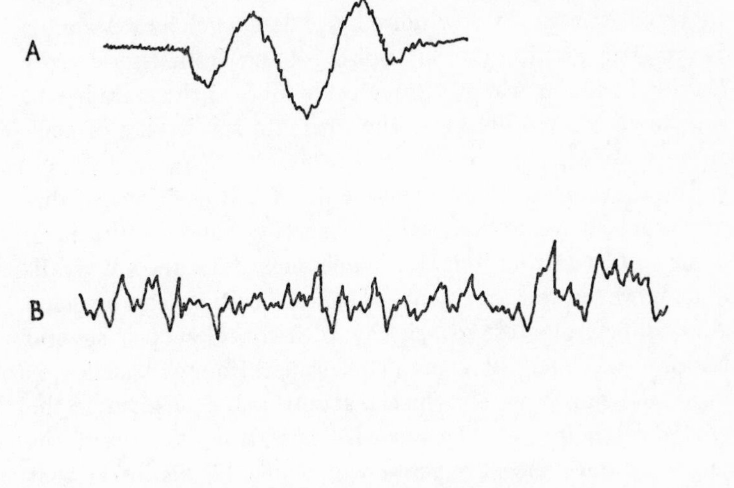

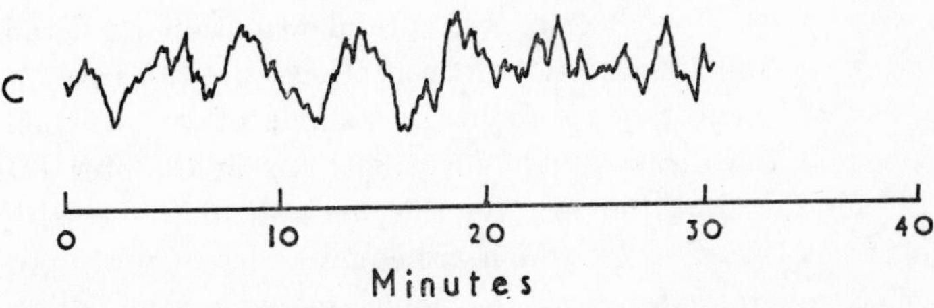

IV/3A. A symmetrical fringe pattern such as would be obtained if an intense radio source passed through the five lobes of Fig. IV/2.
IV/3B. A 'noisy' record, in which no fringe pattern can be discerned.
IV/3C. A 'noisy' interferometer record, showing a fringe pattern whose amplitude is approximately twice that of the noise.

pattern whose amplitude is only about twice noise in Fig. IV/3C. There is a calculable chance that deflections comparable with the noise may be due to random changes rather than to radiation from a radio source. The danger of being misled in this way is greater if one is studying even fainter sources, and for such work it would obviously be highly desirable to use a larger radio telescope, or improve the performance of the receiver. If neither is possible, one must arrange to take averages over longer periods of observation, possibly using a computer to do the arithmetic. The noise arising in the input stages of the receiver can be reduced by the use of special low-noise amplifiers, such as masers, or parametric amplifiers. But noise coming from the sky, or leaking from the ground through side-lobes of the main beam, sets fundamental limits to the ultimate sensitivity of such radio systems.

The most accurate measurements of the positions of discrete sources are determined by observing lunar occultations, as described in Chapter III. When such data are not available, however, measurements of source positions can be made with interferometers consisting of two telescopes several hundred wavelengths apart. Their separation, or baseline, is measured very precisely. Special attention is then given to the cross-over points on the record. These times represent the most accurate measurements which can be made on that source. With large telescopes, careful attention to detail, and many repetitions of the observations, positions can be measured accurately to about 12 seconds of arc, as mentioned in the discussion of identifications in Chapter III. Interferometers to be used for this work should have fairly short lengths of cable, which are equal and preferably protected from rapid temperature changes in underground ducts.

The second fundamental type of radio measurement is of the radio flux density, that is the energy received from a discrete source. The energy passed to the receiver is proportional to the collecting area of the telescope and to the width of the band of frequencies studied. In order to compare different measurements it is usual to calculate the energy received per square metre of collecting area in a unit frequency band one cycle per second wide. A convenient unit of radio energy or flux density is the flux unit, which is defined as 10^{-26} watts/m^2/c.p.s. Errors arising from unwanted random noise, and from the noisy nature of the 'signal' from discrete sources also affect measurements of flux density. Such measurements can be made either with a single telescope, or with an interferometer, and each method has its own advantages, and difficulties. Clearly the most reliable values are obtained when the two methods agree. The basic difficulty is to separate the radiation from a particular discrete source, so that the measurements are not confused by radiation from nearby sources or from the background. It is also necessary to measure the background level, that is the radiation arising from diffuse clouds in our own Galaxy. This is particularly important at wavelengths greater than 1 m, where this galactic radiation is strongest. It has proved extremely difficult to make reliable comparisons between different telescopes, or interferometers, and even between observations with the same telescope working at different wavelengths. When such measurements have been satisfactorily carried out and compared with each other as well as possible, the best overall accuracy achieved so far in values of flux density is about 10 per cent. The results show that for most discrete sources less energy is received per unit bandwidth at the higher frequencies, but that there are significant differences between sources in the way in which their power falls off, that is in their radio spectra. For most sources the flux received is almost inversely proportional to wavelength, or falls off slightly slower than that. For the quasars, on the whole, it does not fall off so rapidly, and in a few cases may even increase again at radio frequencies of the order of 8000 Mc/s and above. These higher values of flux may even extend into the infra-red parts of the spectrum.

Figure IV/4 shows some examples of the radio spectra of discrete sources. That of the radio galaxy Virgo A (NGC 4486) is apparently straight, except for a possible falling off at the lowest frequencies. The spectrum of the galaxy 3C 295 is slightly curved, but approximately parallel to that of Virgo A. The great majority of radio sources appear to have spectra of these types. The spectrum of the quasar 3C 286 is more nearly flat, while that of the quasar CTA 102 has a definite maximum at about 1000 Mc/s. The spectrum of 3C 279 shows

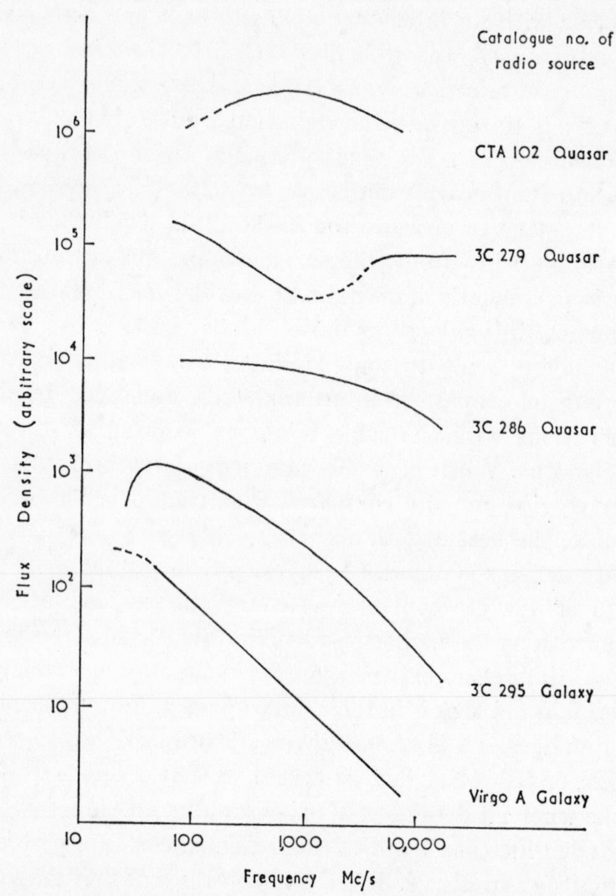

IV/4. The radio spectra of some radio galaxies and quasars. (Logarithmic scales.) The vertical scale of flux density is arbitrary, and the graphs have been displaced vertically, so that they do not overlap.

a pronounced increase at short wavelengths. The radio spectrum of the quasar 3C 273 did not seem particularly interesting until the occultation data enabled the spectrum of the two components to be plotted separately as shown in Fig. IV/5.

Interferometers such as those shown in Fig. IV/1 can also be used to measure the angular size and to some extent the shape of discrete sources, for their resolving power in directions parallel to the baseline is λ/D, where D is the separation of the telescopes. In order to make a survey of the

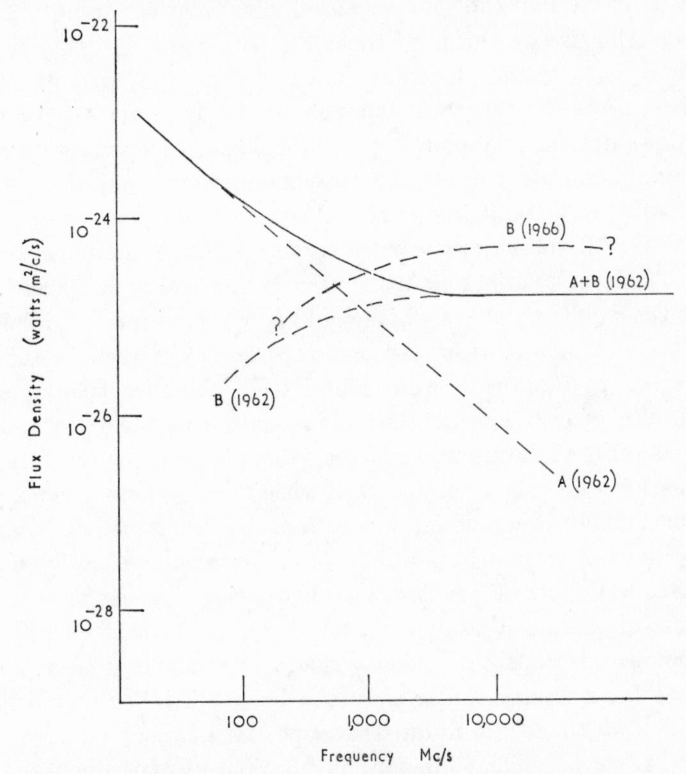

IV/5. The radio spectrum of the quasar 3C 273, showing the different contributions of the components A and B.

approximate angular scale of a group of sources one can observe them with interferometers of steadily increasing baselines. The separation between the lobes of the interferometer pattern therefore becomes smaller, and when it is comparable with the size of the source the amplitude of the fringe pattern is reduced. We then say that the source is partially resolved and we can calculate the approximate size of the source. A survey of the angular sizes of 174 discrete sources with a cable link interferometer was carried out at a wavelength of 30 cm, at the Owens Valley Radio Observatory in California, using the telescopes shown in Fig. IV/6. It was found that nearly half the sources were larger than one minute of arc. Almost two-thirds of these had two radio emitting regions, such as the examples shown in Fig. IV/7. In both of these cases the two radio components lie on either side of a faint elliptical galaxy, and were substantially larger than the galaxy. In these sources the components were found to have unequal radio emitting power, but many other sources identified with galaxies appear to have two similar components.

The largest aerial separation used in this survey was 2200λ, so the smallest sources which could be resolved were of order 1 minute of arc. However half the sources studied in this survey in California were found to be smaller than one minute of arc. The detailed investigation of the sizes and structures of these small sources, which include many of the quasars, can only be undertaken with interferometers having very much larger aerial separations. Interferometers have been in operation at Jodrell Bank for many years which use a radio link rather than a cable to bring together the outputs of the receivers at each telescope. The distance to the remote telescope can then be made very much greater, so that far smaller angular sizes can be studied. For much of this work the 250-ft Radio Telescope Mark I was used at one end of the baseline, while for the more recent experiments at wavelengths of 11 cm and below, the Mark II was used. These telescopes are shown in Fig. IV/8. Figure IV/9 shows photographs of two of the telescopes which have been used at remote sites.

A simplified block diagram of this radio link interferometer is shown in Fig. IV/10. It will be seen that this is rather more complicated than the instrument shown in Fig. IV/1, and that a radio link system is used which has two

IV/6. The two radio telescopes forming the interferometer of the Owens Valley Observatory, operated by the California Institute of Technology. (*Photograph kindly supplied by Dr Moffet.*)

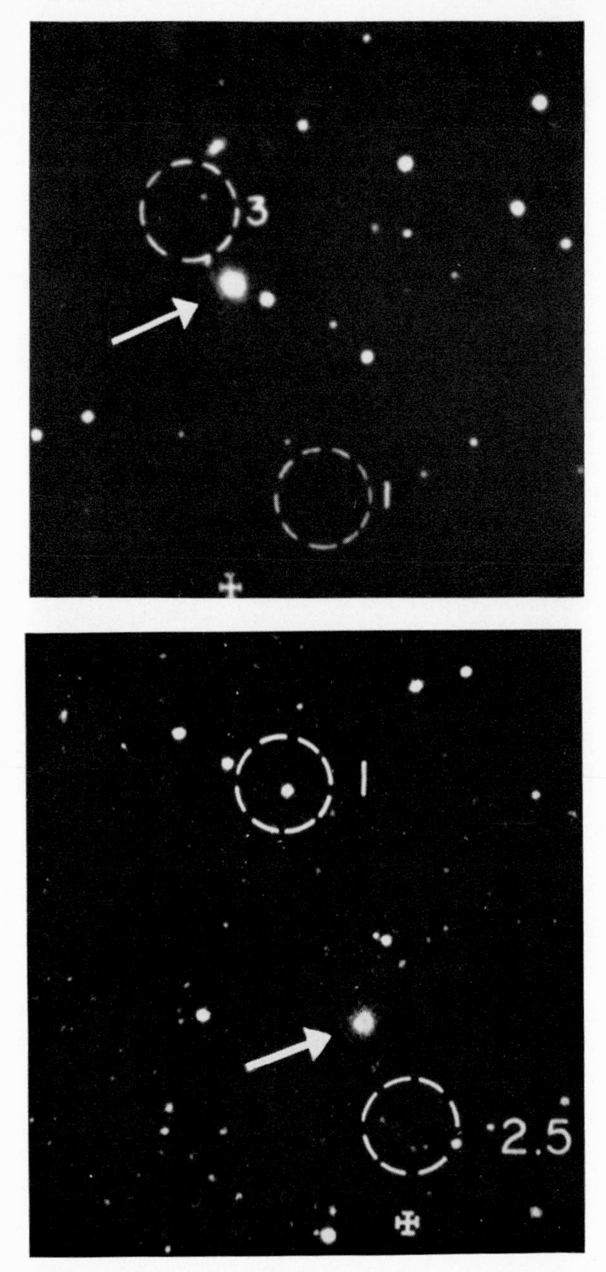

IV/7. The arrows on these photographs indicate elliptical galaxies identified with the double radio sources 3C 33 and 3C 98. The small cross indicates the accuracy of the radio position measurements used, and the figures the relative radio intensity of the two components at 960 Mc/s. (*Mt Wilson and Palomar Observatories photographs, kindly supplied by Dr Matthews.*)

IV/8. The two major telescopes at Jodrell Bank. The 250-foot diameter Mark I is on the left. The elliptical Mark II (125 ft by 83 ft) is just behind the buildings in the foreground on the right. In this photograph they are seen parked in their 'safe' positions during a gale.
(*Photograph kindly supplied by Colin Ronan.*)

IV/9. Two of the radio telescopes used at distant sites during the Jodrell Bank long baseline interferometer programme.

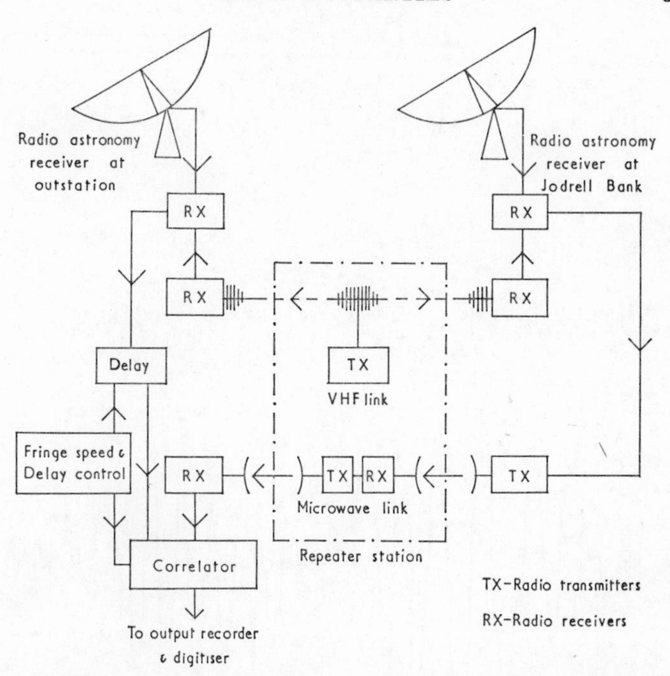

IV/10. A simplified block diagram of a radio interferometer, using microwave and VHF link systems, with one repeater station.

parts: one, a microwave system of television standard, is used to convey a broad band radio astronomy signal from the remote aerial to the main interferometer; a second, normally a narrow band VHF system, is used to compare the frequencies of all the oscillators in the system, and in a recent development, to compensate for any variations by continuous and automatic adjustments of one of them. Equipment of this type operating at a wavelength of 2 metres in the period 1958–61, was set up at three of the sites. It was used for investigations of the angular scale of more than 200 discrete sources most of which were smaller than one minute of arc. Figure IV/11 shows an example of the fringe patterns which were recorded during this investigation. The results showed a range of angular dimensions going down to less than one second of arc in a few instances. Similar work has been

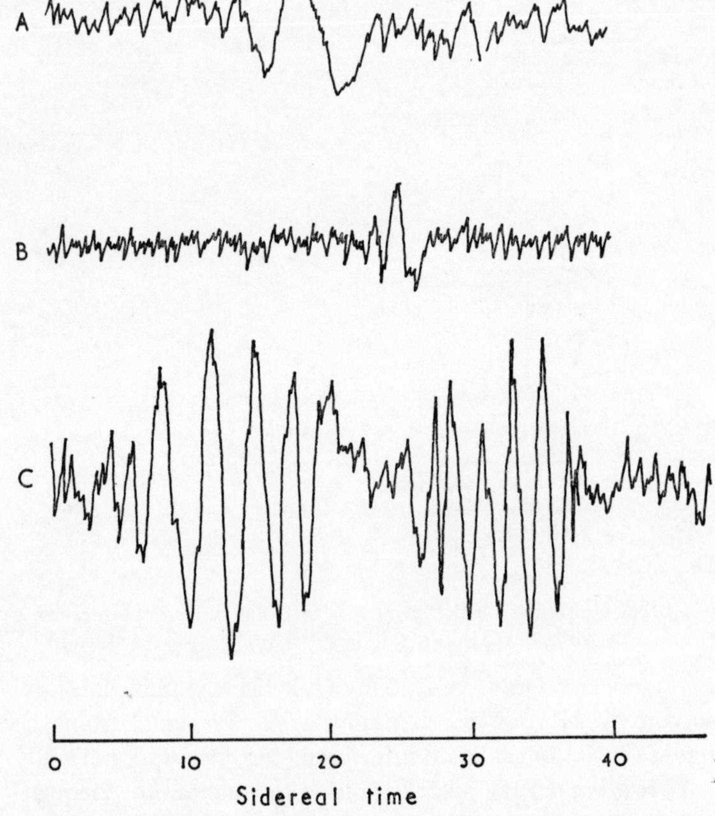

IV/11. Examples of fringe patterns observed with radio link interferometers.

A. 3C 147 observed at 159 Mc/s with D = 10,640λ on 20.12.55.
B. 3C 218 observed at 159 Mc/s with D = 32,000λ on 29.5.60.
C. 3C 273 observed at 408 Mc/s with D = 180,000λ on 28.8.64.

reported from the Radio Observatory at Green Bank in West Virginia, USA., using the interferometer which is shown in Fig. IV/12. In this case the wavelength of observation was 11 cm. With the telescopes at either end of the long track shown on the photograph the length of the baseline was 22,000λ.

IV/12. These telescopes at Green Bank, W. Va., form a cable link interferometer with a baseline of 22,000 λ at $\lambda = 11$ cm. (*National Radio Astronomy Observatory photograph, kindly supplied by Dr Heeschen.*)

IV/13. One of the 85-foot telescopes operated by the Royal Radar Establishment, Malvern, as used during the cooperative interferometric observations with Jodrell Bank in 1965. (*Central Office of Information photograph.*)

Results of high accuracy cannot be obtained from surveys of the angular scale of a fairly large number of radio sources based on observations at only a few interferometer baselines. Because of the complex and double structures of many of the sources such measurements are only approximate. Recent work at Cambridge has shown that, for sources smaller than one second of arc, approximate size estimates can also be based on observations of the radio scintillation effects produced by irregularities in the interplanetary medium.

More detailed information can be obtained by observing sources with a tracking interferometer as they move across

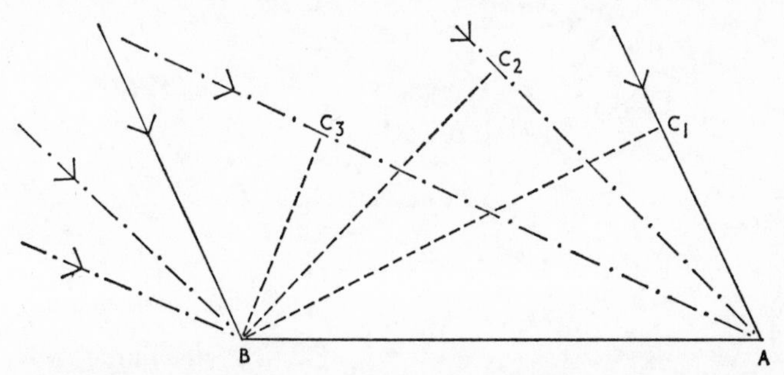

IV/14. The change in effective baseline from B C_1 to B C_2 to B C_3 as a discrete source is observed at different times of day. The direction of the baseline relative to any structure in the source may also change.

the sky. Then the effective aerial separation, that is the distance BC_1 between rays from the radio source to the two telescopes changes to BC_2 then to BC_3 in about six hours. If such observations can be repeated with several values of aerial separation, then a reasonably complete and accurate picture of the source shape can be derived down to the resolving power of the longest baseline used. Clearly this method takes a very great deal of time, both in the operation of the remote aerials and in the observation of each source from rising to setting on several occasions. It has so far been possible to make observations of this sort for only about twenty sources altogether, and for only five of the smallest of them.

The most recent experiment of this sort was undertaken jointly by Jodrell Bank and the Royal Radar Establishment at Malvern. One of the Malvern instruments is shown in Fig. IV/13 The radio telescopes operated by these institutions are 127 km. apart. A three 'hop' microwave and VHF link, shown in Fig. IV/15, was established during the summer of

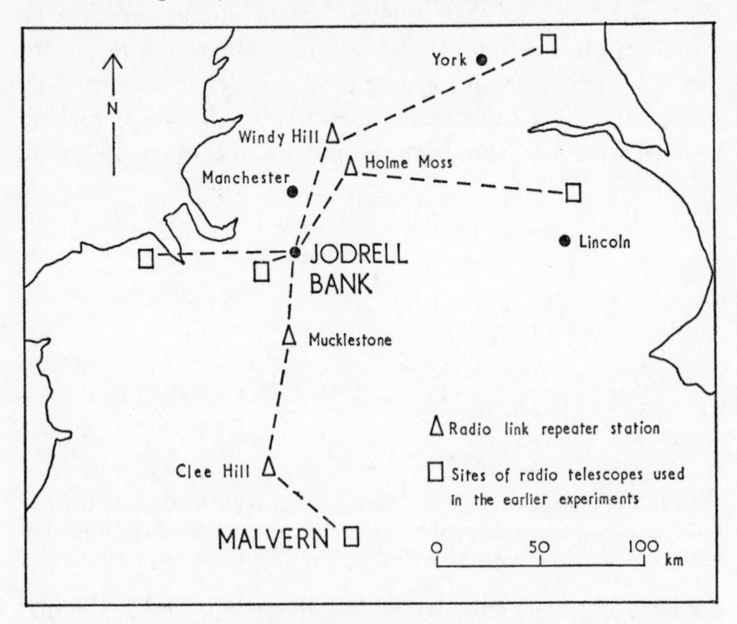

IV/15. A map showing the radio link paths used during the Jodrell Bank–Malvern observations and some earlier experiments.

1965. These telescopes could then be used together at a wavelength of 21 cm., when their separation is greater than half a million wavelengths. About two months of observations were undertaken, and in this time continuous following observations were made of about six sources. These showed that one source CTA 102 was smaller than 0·1 second of arc in all directions. It was also found that the other five sources had structures which were smaller than 0·1 seconds of arc, in some directions, but somewhat larger in others. The shape of these structures is not known.

Three other types of special radio observations connected with quasars should be mentioned. Variations of the radio flux received from some quasars have been detected in the last two years. As indicated in Fig. IV/5 for 3C 273B these are most marked at the shortest wavelengths. There is good but not perfect correlation between those quasars which show radio variations, and those which are variable in their light output. However, as this is a very new field of study, the statistics are poor, and it may merely be that the observations made so far are incomplete or not sufficiently accurate. Secondly, in the study of radio spectra it is found, in general, that they are very much simpler than, for instance, the optical spectra of stars. However a few absorption and emission lines have been detected in radio spectra at wavelengths of 21 cm and 18 cm due to non-ionized hydrogen and the hydroxyl radical OH. In the last year it has been found that an absorption line due to hydrogen can be detected in the emission from the source Virgo A, (3C 274) and also that from 3C 273, which is only about 10° away. In both cases the line is redshifted by $z = 0{\cdot}0041$, the amount of the redshift of the Virgo cluster. One interpretation is that neutral hydrogen in the outer parts of the Virgo cluster is responsible for this absorption in both cases. If this is correct, the quasar must be beyond the Virgo cluster. Even this is not quite certain however for it has also been suggested that this absorption may be due to a cloud of hydrogen which is nearer to our Galaxy, and happens by chance to be moving away at the same speed as the cluster. This second explanation seems rather improbable.

Finally, a recent report from Italy describes a search for radio emission at 408 Mc/s for some of the radio-quiet quasi-stellar galaxies reported by Sandage. During observations of their celestial positions, no radio emission was detected which could be attributed to them individually. However, when the mean of all the observations was inspected, it seemed likely that, on average, a radio flux of 0·1 f.u. was coming from each.

TABLE II

Radio data on some Quasars and radio galaxies

Catalogue number	Redshift $\frac{\Delta\lambda}{\lambda} = z$	*Radio flux density* w.m.$^{-2}$(c/s)$^{-1}$ $\times 10^{-26}$ *at*					Notes (*angular sizes in seconds of arc*)
		38	178	408	1420	3000 Mc/s	
Quasars							
3C 273(A + B)	0·158	—	72	48	40	31·2	Flux increasing by 10–15% per year at 1420 Mc/s and above. B probably smaller than 0·05 sec.
3C 345	0·595	27	11	9·2	6·6	4·5	Smaller than 0·05 sec, flux decreasing by 10–20% per year at 8000 Mc/s.
3C 279	0·536	—	20	12·5	6·4	4·6	Smaller than 0·05 sec, flux decreasing by 10–20% per year at 8000 Mc/s.
3C 9	2·012	—	15	6	3·1	—	Appears to be bigger than 10 secs at 159 Mc/s.
3C 47	0·425	125	20	13	4·2	—	Two components 62 secs apart.
1116 + 12	2·112	—	—	5·5	1·9	1·6	Probably larger than 10 secs at 159 Mc/s.
CTA 102	1·037	5·1	—	7	6·6	4·7	Russians report flux variability at 1000 Mc/s, with period of 100 days. Spectrum curved. Smaller than 0·05 sec.
Radio Galaxies							
3C 33	0·057	150	49	32	13·4	6·3	Two components 210 secs apart. Flux ratio 2·5 : 1 at 970 Mc/s.
3C 84	0·018	470	62	33	13·0	8·9	Halo 280 secs across, with core smaller than 0·1 sec.
3C 98	0·030	150	41	20	105	6·2	Two components 205 secs apart. Flux ratio 3·0 : 1 at 970 Mc/s.
3C 274	0·0040	3310	970	460	300	99	Halo 390 secs. Core 36 secs. Pip smaller than 0·1 sec. with 2% of flux at 1420 Mc/s.
3C 405	0·056	12,500	8700	4700	1400	610	Two components 80 secs apart each 42 secs by approx. 15 secs.

(The flux values are from many observers, and may not all be on identical scales.)

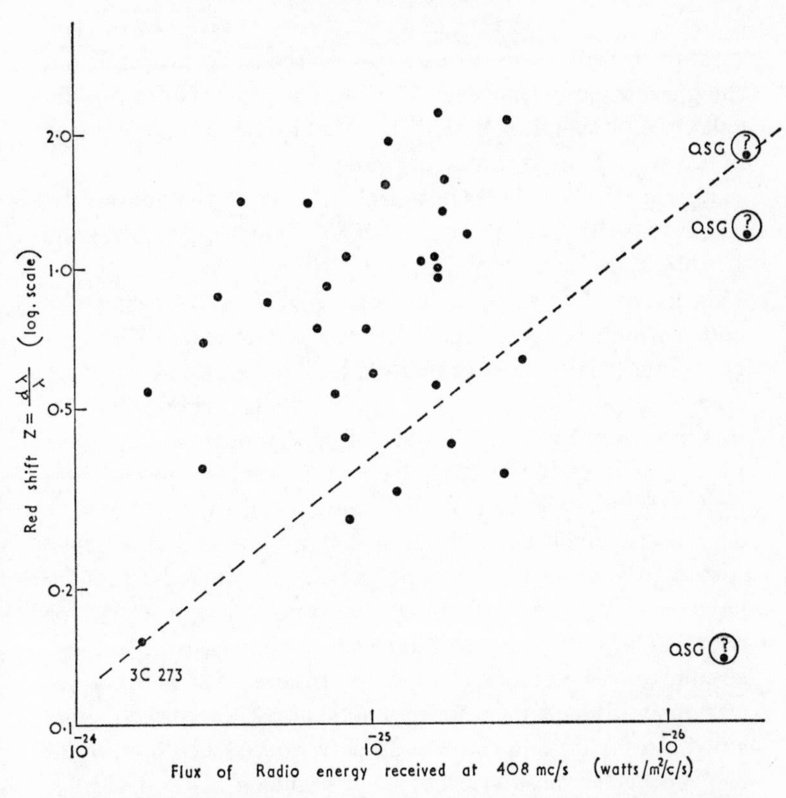

IV/16. The points represent the observed values of radio flux density at 408 Mc/s for quasars, and possible values for some Q.S.G's plotted against redshift, on logarithmic scales. The points would fall on the dotted line if all radiated as much radio energy as 3C 273, and the inverse square law were obeyed exactly If the quasars are at very great distances, cosmological effects make this line more nearly horizontal for the greatest redshifts.

The radio properties of the galaxies and quasars discussed in this chapter are summarized in Table II and Fig. IV/16. The table contains data for most of the quasars in Table I, and for five radio galaxies. For each of these objects the values of radio flux at several frequencies are given, with notes on any special features in its radio spectrum or any observations of changes in its radio output. The available information about radio angular sizes and structures, is given in the last column. It will be seen that most of the radio properties of the quasars can be matched by a similar property for a radio galaxy, and even if a clear distinction exists it is not evident in the radio data available at present.

Figure IV/15 includes data from almost all the quasars for which redshifts have been published. Values of radio flux at 408 Mc/s are plotted against redshift, on logarithmic scales. This figure is a radio version of Fig. III/4. As before the points would be expected to lie on the dotted line if the inverse square law were obeyed and if all quasars had the same energy output as 3C 273(A + B). The scatter shows that, on this interpretation, their values of energy output may differ by as much as 10 : 1. If the report of weak radio emission from QSG's is confirmed, then the spread in radio output may be as much as 1000 : 1, which would be much larger spread than in their optical properties. Hoyle and Burbidge have recently used a similar diagram to argue that, for quasars, redshifts have nothing to do with distances. In these circumstances cosmological interpretations of radio data are obviously difficult until individual sources are better understood. In favourable cases radio astronomers can now equal or even better most types of measurements made optically, both in positional accuracy and resolving power. But because of the very low energy density of the radiation they study, each measurement takes a longer time, and many require special equipment. For most of the quasars, many of the possible measurements have not yet been made. Those that are available suggest that the radio emission from galaxies is associated with very violent events. The radio data suggest that the quasars are even more extreme objects.

CHAPTER V

DYNAMICS

We shall now describe results taken from several branches of physics, which may help us understand the nature of quasars. Even though we are often tempted to postulate new laws of nature to explain some particularly strange effects, we should first try to find an explanation in terms of physics as it is known now. Scientists studying extragalactic phenomena seem especially prone to invent new theories, but they ought to resist the temptation. We shall do our best not to speculate in this way.

In the present chapter we deal with various important dynamical effects. In the following six chapters we shall consider useful aspects of relativity, cosmology, stellar structure, and so on.

We begin with the mechanics of charged particles. It is certain that fast moving charged particles are abundantly present in quasars. It is also probable that quasars are permeated by magnetic fields. A great deal is known about the interaction of, say, an electron with a magnetic field. If a particle carrying charge e moves with speed v through a magnetic field H then it experiences a force $(1/c)evH \sin \theta$ at right angles to both the velocity and the field. In the formula c stands for the speed of light, and θ is the angle between the direction of motion and the lines of force (see Fig. V/1).

The direction of the force is defined by the right-hand rule: if a screwdriver were turned from the direction of the velocity to that of the field then a right-handed screw would be driven along the direction of the force.

The resulting motion of the electron is very simple, particularly when θ equals 90°. The electron will then be continually accelerated towards the same point on a particular

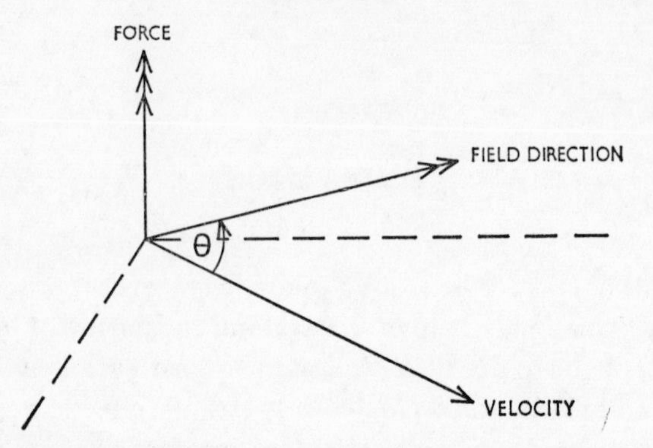

V/1. To show the relation between the directions of the velocity, the magnetic field and the resultant force on a charged particle.

line of force. Its path is therefore entirely similar to that of a stone held on a string. Like the stone, the electron will move around a circle whose centre is at the point towards which the force acts (Fig. V/2).

If the electron is not moving at right angles to the lines of force, then we have to decompose the velocity into two parts. The parallel part $v_{\parallel}$ is along the magnetic field lines, and

V/2. Motion of an electron.

(*a*) with velocity at right angles to lines of force,
(*b*) with velocity not at right angles to lines of force.

produces no force. The perpendicular part $v_{\perp}$ produces a force $ev_{\perp}H/c$. The superposition of the two components results in motion round a circle whose centre slides forward along a line of force with velocity $v_{\parallel}$. In other words the electron moves along a helical path.

So far we have described what happens when the lines of force are straight. If the lines of force are curved then the electron's path is deformed. The track still looks like a helix but now it bends so as to follow approximately a particular line of force. We say that the electron remains 'tied' to a line of force. There will also be a drift component in the motion of the electron, which tends to displace the electron gradually from one line of force to another. But we shall ignore the drift, because it is slow and unimportant in most cases of physical interest.

Another important effect is associated with motion in a non-uniform magnetic field. Suppose that an electron is spiralling around a given line of force, and that as it moves forward it penetrates into a region where the magnetic field

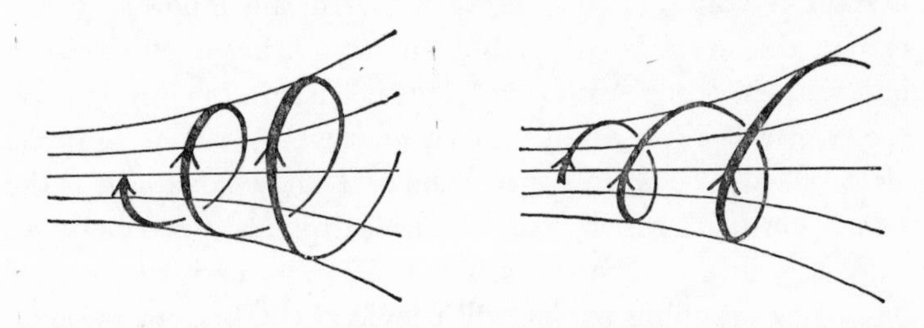

V/3. Electron paths in a non-uniform magnetic field. The field strength decreases from the left to the right.
(*a*) Path to mirror point.
(*b*) Path from mirror point.

strength is larger. One can readily show that there must then be an increase in ω, the angular velocity (or the rate of turning) of the electron about its guiding line of force. If ω increases, the radius r of the helix decreases so as to keep constant the angular momentum, which is proportional to $r^2\omega$. But this in turn implies that there will be an increase in $v_\perp (= r\omega)$. Finally we know that no work can be done by a static magnetic field on a moving charge. Radiative losses apart, the total kinetic energy of the electron therefore cannot change, and this implies that an increase in $v_\perp$ must be balanced by a decrease in $v_\parallel$. We have now shown, by this lengthy argument, that the forward velocity of the electron must decrease as it moves into a region where the magnetic field is stronger. Eventually the field strength may become so large that the forward velocity becomes zero. The electron is reflected at this point and thereafter travels back along another helical path around its guiding line of force. The point where the electron is reflected is called its mirror point.

Now in almost all configurations of magnetic fields the typical line of force runs from a region of high field strength to a region of low field strength, and then on again to another region of high field strength. As a rule an electron on a given line of force is therefore trapped between two mirror points. This property can be used to imprison charged particles in certain regions of a magnetic field. In the laboratory one can in this way confine a hot gas consisting exclusively of ions and electrons (a plasma). This is basic in experiments on the controlled release of nuclear energy by fusion. Trapped electrons also occur in nature: the best-known example is the van Allen belt, which consists of electrons trapped between mirror points in the outer parts of the Earth's magnetic field. The trapping works well provided the lines of force do not have sharp bends, and as long as the charged particles do not suffer appreciable deflections in mutual collisions, or with other particles.

In contrast to a static field, a magnetic field that changes with time can communicate energy to the particles, and we shall describe several possible processes later. For the sake of brevity we have, up till now, considered the electrodynamic properties of electrons only, but of course other charged particles behave in very similar ways.

The forces experienced by a moving electron have a very familiar analogue. They are exactly the same as the force which acts when an electric current is passed down a wire placed in a magnetic field. In other words the force which ties an electron to a line of force is the same as the force which drives an electric motor. To continue the analogy we shall now describe some other dynamical effects which may occur in quasars and which also have a familiar counterpart. A dynamo works on the principle that a potential difference is set up between the ends of a wire moving across the lines of force of a magnetic field. Common experience shows that it is quite easy to turn the dynamo if its terminals are connected through a high resistance. The potential difference induced then produces only a small current, and we have merely to overcome the force arising from the interaction of this small current and the magnetic field. But it becomes much harder to turn the dynamo when the circuit is closed by a small resistance. A given rate of turning now induces a much larger current and is opposed by much larger forces.

The corresponding astrophysical effect occurs when gaseous material moves in a magnetic field. Gases in stars, in space and in quasars are usually ionized, that is they normally contain some free electric charges. This makes them excellent conductors of electricity. Potential differences will be set up in such a gas when it flows across the lines of force of a magnetic field. But the electrical resistance of the gas is low, and so large currents will flow in response to the potential differences. We have here a good analogy to the case of a dynamo terminated by a low resistance, and we conclude that it will be difficult to maintain the relative motion of the gas and the lines of force. In fact the gas will behave as though it were 'frozen' to the lines of force. This may not seem very surprising, following our earlier description of the spiralling of moving charges in a magnetic field. But there is a difference. The gases we are now describing do contain free charges, but now the motion of the charges need not be unimpeded. The results we established earlier hold only if the electrons do not make collisions. On the other hand the free electrons in the type of gas we are now considering may make few or many collisions, but the gas is still frozen to the lines of force. The study of the motion of such gases is called 'magneto-hydrodynamics' (or MHD, for short), and has become an important part of astrophysics.

Two general results from MHD are particularly striking. A conducting gas in a strong magnetic field cannot flow across the lines of force and cannot distort them. It can therefore only flow along the lines of force, and this condition is very restrictive. The opposite happens if the energy of the conducting gas much exceeds the energy stored in the magnetic field. Then the lines of force must follow the motion of the gas, and thus the field can change considerably. In particular the field energy usually increases in such cases, at the expense of the kinetic energy of the gas. It is widely believed that interactions of this kind lead to the building up of cosmical magnetic fields such as those of the Earth, the Sun or the stars. In the case of the Earth, though, the moving fluid is a conducting liquid in its core. It is also possible that large scale motions within quasars lead to the growth of magnetic fields there. Fig V/4 illustrates a particular case.

Our pictures show a simple example of eddying motion in a fluid (or a plasma) and of its tendency to amplify existing magnetic fields. Such eddies typically occur when the fluid is turbulent. This is a very common state of motion, which can easily be observed in smoke or on water. A good example can often be seen in the smoke rising from a cigarette. At first the smoke rises smoothly, in a narrow thread-like stream. The flow of the smoke here is 'laminar'. But this flow is unstable and it breaks up some distance above its source. It then becomes 'turbulent'. After watching it for long enough

---

V/4. To show how motion of a conducting fluid can change the lines of force. Here a magnetic field has straight lines of force to begin with. When an eddy begins to turn, the lines of force are distorted. In the second picture the fluid at the centre of the eddy has turned through 180°, in the third picture through 360°. The outer edge of the eddy remains at rest. The lines of force are brought closer together by the motion. This means that the strength of the field increases. In the third picture the field strength has increased approximately threefold. The energy of the field varies as the square of the field strength: between the first and the third stage the magnetic energy stored within the eddy has therefore increased ninefold. The additional energy is derived from the kinetic energy of the fluid.

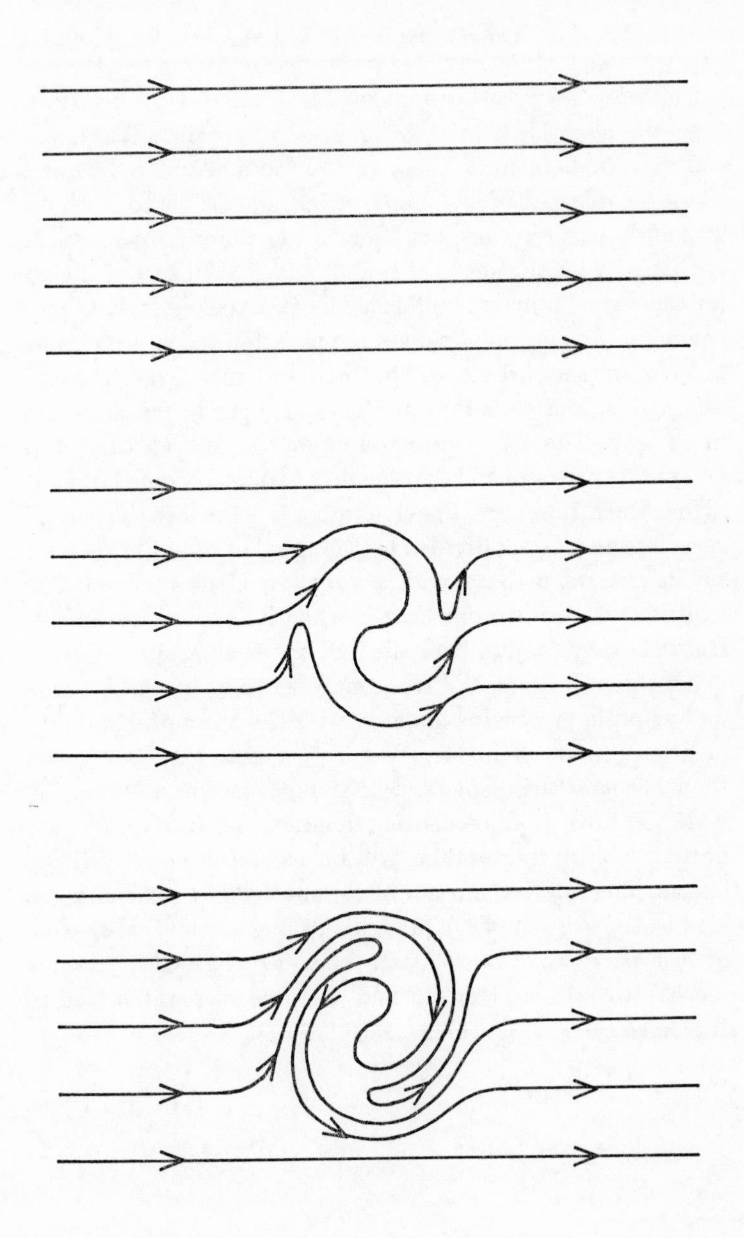

one notices how the turbulent motion is made up of many superimposed eddies. This is quite characteristic.

There are many other familiar instances of turbulent motion, for example white water in a mountain stream, the water at the bottom of a weir or the wake behind a steamer. These are all cases of low speed, or incompressible turbulence. The motion is irregular, but the velocity differences are small compared with the speed of sound, and the density of the air (or the water) remains uniform. The air expelled from the jet engines of an aeroplane moves much faster and it is also turbulent. But the turbulence now involves much larger velocity differences, and therefore produces changes in pressure and in density. These generate sound waves, and so the jet is noisy. The pressure and density fluctuations become larger at higher Mach numbers. (Mach number is defined as the typical speed of the motion, divided by the speed of sound.) Cigarette smoke rises at a speed with a very low Mach number: this explains why we cannot hear it when it becomes turbulent. But it is very easy to hear the exhaust from a jet.

All these dynamical effects may occur in quasars. For a quasar probably begins to shine after the onset of instability in a large mass of matter. We expect that the matter will then become turbulent, and that high speeds will develop which in turn produce density fluctuations. In a quasar the growth of such fluctuations will be assisted by gravitational effects. The relative motion of the matter in the quasar can lead to the growth of magnetic fields and to the acceleration of fast particles. Later in this book we shall discuss some mechanisms of acceleration and the processes which lead to the emission of radiation.

CHAPTER VI

RELATIVITY

Quasars present the physicist and the astrophysicist with the strangest phenomena yet discovered in the Universe. They are exceedingly distant and extremely powerful sources of radiant energy. The quasar 3C 273 emits energy at a rate several hundred times that of all the stars in the Milky Way put together. Yet the energy source appears to fit into a space which is, by astronomical standards, extremely compact. The energy producing regions of a quasar may be little bigger than the solar system, and this represents a concentration of energy and mass much larger than any known previously. Gravitational fields may then be more intense than in normal physical situations, and they must play a more important role. To understand how they act one has to apply relativity theory, and we shall now describe how this may be done.

Relativity theory comes in two varieties. The first kind is special relativity, discovered by Einstein in 1905, and much used since then. It has survived every experimental test and must be regarded as one of the most secure foundations of modern physics. Whatever we say about a quasar, it must not violate special relativity. Briefly, the theory gives an explanation of some unexpected results found by Michelson and Morley. Their experiments showed that, no matter how an observer may move, his measurement of the speed of light always yields the same result, 186,000 miles/second (or 300,000 km/second). We call this value c. This invariance cannot be understood according to the common-sense point of view of pre-relativity physics. If observers A and B both look at the same source of light, A standing still in his laboratory and B moving at some speed u away from the source, then in pre-relativity days one would have expected B to measure a speed smaller than that measured by A. In fact the difference would just be equal to u. A pre-relativity physicist would have been content to add or subtract speeds just like two everyday commodities. If A measured a speed v and B a speed v', then the relation between v and v' would be expected to be

$$v' = v - u.$$

But according to Einstein the correct formula is different and reads

$$v' = \frac{v - u}{1 - vu/c^2}; \quad . \quad . \quad . \quad (1)$$

this is the result for subtraction of velocities. For the addition of velocities we must change the minus signs into plus signs. It is easy to verify, in the formula, that if $v = c$ then also $v' = c$, so that both observers now measure the same speed for light, whatever the speed of the second observer relative to the first.

Another consequence, very important for us, is that even if we accelerate a mass continually, we can never make it reach the speed of light. It follows that c is larger than the largest possible speed of a material particle. Formula (1) for the subtraction of velocities shows that, no matter how fast a particle may be moving past an observer, it would have to increase its velocity by c, relative to its own frame of reference, in order to be moving at the speed of light relative to that observer. But no force, however large, will produce more than a small change of speed in a small interval of time. At the end of that interval the speed of our particle will still be less than c. The same result applies to the next time step, and the one after that, and so on. An outside observer might see the particle picking up speed all the time, but the particle would never attain the speed of light. Thus no particle travels through space faster than light. Speaking (only slightly) loosely we can go on to say more: signals are carried through space either by material particles or by radiation. Radiation travels at speed c, material particles at less than c. It follows that no signal travels faster than light. If then an event happens at a point O, say I push a button to set off a fuse, the bomb cannot explode at P before time l/c later, l being the distance from O to P.

This has a direct consequence for our quasar, in particular for 3C 273. The original observation showed that it consisted of two parts. One part, 273 B, coincided with the central, quasi-stellar object, while the other, 273 A, is a long tongue of material, stretching out to a distance of 150,000 light years. We can look at it two ways, but get the same result. If the tongue was ejected from 273 B then at least 150,000 years must have passed for it to reach its present length. But suppose the tongue contains matter which has always been in its present position, and that this material has been made luminous by a powerful pulse of energy from 273 B. Once again it would have taken at least 150,000 years for the pulse to reach the far end of the tongue. One can, admittedly, make up some apparently more sophisticated models to reduce the age of the quasar. As they only lead to still greater troubles, there seems little point in discussing them here. Our first conclusion is this: the picture we see of a typical quasar is that of an object at least 150,000 years of age.

But now we can use a similar argument and conclude that in some very important respects a quasar looks like a highly compact object. Many observations show that the light from a quasar is not steady. Regular variations have been noticed in the brightness of a number of quasars, usually having periods of the order of a year. But abrupt changes have also occurred, some within times as short as a week. The most striking of these is the newly found change in the wavelength of one of the magnesium lines observed in 3C 345. This apparently altered by some 50 Å within a week.

One possible inference is that the emission of the magnesium line is triggered by some form of illumination coming from a central object. On September 24th a pulse of light, or a cloud of fast moving electrons, must have encountered one group of atoms. By October 1st it picked out quite another group moving with quite a different speed—hence the wavelength change. This makes one think that the illumination in a given part of a quasar can be turned on and off within a week. For this to be possible one would expect that the source of the light is less than a light week across, or less than 2×10^{16} cm in diameter. Such a distance is very small by astronomical standards, for it is only about twenty times as large as the diameter of the solar system. We shall discuss this problem again, from a rather different point of view, in Chapter XII.

There are many other important aspects of special relativity. For example the theory shows that the energy and the mass of an object are strictly related, so that one unit of mass corresponds to c^2 units of energy. To put it graphically, if one could tap all the energy in one gram of matter, say a small lump of sugar, one would extract some 30 million kw-hours of energy—probably enough to supply all the electricity consumed in one month by all the households in a town like Edinburgh. (Incidentally, this makes the lump of sugar worth about £200,000 at the present day price of electricity.)

At present we know of no process that actually occurs and can release all this energy from a lump of matter; the nearest approach to it is the release of nuclear energy in the stars. Here the conversion of hydrogen into helium liberates about $0{\cdot}006\ c^2$ units of energy per unit of mass, or some 180,000 kw hours per gram. At this rate we should need about 6 ounces, rather than one lump, of sugar to keep the city warm for a month.

Special relativity also leads to a useful formula for the Doppler shift of light. Suppose that an object, seen at rest, gives out light of wavelength λ_0. If that object is seen moving away at speed u, it will appear to give out light at wavelength λ, where

$$\lambda = \lambda_0 \sqrt{\frac{1 + u/c}{1 - u/c}} \quad . \quad . \quad . \quad (2)$$

One can easily verify that this formula checks with formula (1), for the addition of velocities. Imagine the following experiment. Light of wavelength λ_0 is emitted by A, and

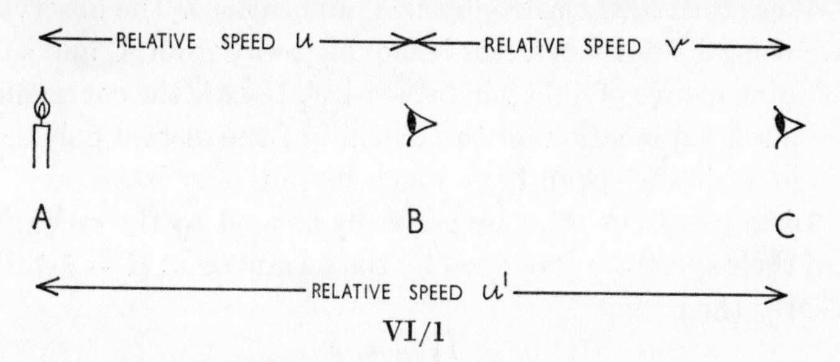

VI/1

observed by B and C. B is moving at speed u away from A; C is moving at speed v relative to B and at speed u' relative to A. Then formula (1) states that

$$u' = \frac{u + v}{1 + uv/c^2}$$

Further B thinks that the light has wavelength

$$\lambda = \lambda_0 \sqrt{\frac{1 + u/c}{1 - u/c}} \quad . \quad . \quad . \quad (3)$$

and C thinks the light has wavelength

$$\lambda' = \lambda_0 \sqrt{\frac{1 + u'/c}{1 - u'/c}}$$

$$= \lambda_0 \sqrt{\frac{c + \dfrac{u + v}{1 + uv/c^2}}{c - \dfrac{u + v}{1 + uv/c^2}}}$$

$$= \lambda_0 \sqrt{\frac{1 + u/c}{1 - u/c}} \times \sqrt{\frac{1 + v/c}{1 - v/c}}$$

$$= \lambda \sqrt{\frac{1 + v/c}{1 - v/c}} \quad . \quad . \quad . \quad . \quad (4)$$

With the formulae we have given, C can therefore calculate the Doppler shift correctly in two ways. Either he works out his velocity relative to A and uses formula (3). Or he asks B what wavelength he observes, and then applies a Doppler formula to allow for his own motion relative to B. Only relativistic formulae lead to this logical result.

We return to the astrophysical implications. The observed wavelength λ is longer, if B is moving away from A, and so a receding source of light will be 'redder'. Here is the commonly accepted explanation for the redshift of the distant galaxies, about which we shall have much more to say later.

Distances to quasars are generally gauged by the redshifts z of their spectra. z is defined by the formula $z = (\lambda - \lambda_0)/\lambda_0$; clearly then

$$z = \sqrt{\frac{1 + u/c}{1 - u/c}} - 1$$

A quasar with z equal to 2 has $u/c = 0{\cdot}8$. We judge that it was moving, relative to us, at 80 per cent of the speed of light at the time when it emitted the radiation by which we now see it.

General relativity was introduced by Einstein in 1916. It is a much deeper and more difficult theory. It includes all special relativity, and it also explains how bodies move under the gravitational influence of other massive bodies. Now an explanation had already been given by Newton some centuries before. But whereas Newton's theory invokes forces acting between the bodies, Einstein's theory has a much subtler form. It invokes the distortion of space near massive bodies, and postulates differences in the rates of running of identical clocks, one placed close to and the other far away from such a body. In most of the cases studied as yet by physicists the predictions made according to Einstein's theory differ only minutely from those made following Newton's theory. The consequence is that general relativity has hardly been tested yet; only one of its predictions has been experimentally verified, and this relates to the rate of time-keeping by different clocks. General relativity therefore has a status which is very different from that of special relativity. Its acceptance by physicists rests almost entirely on their feeling that it is inherently right, but this may be a form of prejudice, rather than a reasoned judgement. With this proviso we can now discuss some important consequences.

The first of these concerns the radiation emitted from a gravitating mass M having a radius R. Let the frequency of the light on emission be f_*; when observed at a large distance let its frequency be f_∞. It seems to the distant observer that clocks go slow on the mass M. In other words he knows that in his laboratory the radiation should have frequency f_*, but he sees it arriving from M with a redder colour, and a frequency f_∞ lower than f_*. The general theory of relativity predicts a relation

$$f_\infty = f_*\left(1 - \frac{2GM}{Rc^2}\right)^{1/2}$$

where G is the universal gravitational constant. For light from the Sun, $2GM/Rc^2 = 4{\cdot}3 \times 10^{-6}$, and so we see sunlight red-shifted by about 2 parts in a million. This is so small an amount that the effect has not yet been verified astronomically.

A successful experimental verification has, however, been made with γ-rays by means of the Mössbauer effect. The Mössbauer technique leads to the production of spectral lines having extremely well-defined frequencies. Very small discrepancies in frequency can therefore be detected. In the relevant experiment the line-shift measured was about one part in 10^{15}. This was produced, in a terrestrial laboratory, by the difference in gravitational potential resulting from a vertical distance of some 40 ft between the source of the radiation and the detector.

Since the experiment was restricted to a very small frequency shift all one can in fact deduce is that f_∞ is related to f^* by a formula which takes the form

$$f_\infty = f_*\left(1 - \frac{GM}{Rc^2}\right) \quad . \quad . \quad . \quad (5)$$

for small values of GM/Rc^2. A large variety of different formulae are indistinguishable from (5) for such values.

But the formula chosen by Einstein fits in best with general relativity. It also has a startling consequence. When a mass M shrinks to a radius R so small that $2GM/Rc^2 = 1$, then the frequency f_∞ becomes zero, whatever the value of f_*. Thus no radiation can escape from an object which is more highly condensed than this. In fact when this degree of compactness is reached, the object cuts itself off from the rest of the Universe. In the technical phrase it has disappeared inside its Schwarzschild sphere.

This tells us one more useful fact. We might consider that the power of our quasar could be derived by tapping the gravitational energy of some large mass or system of masses. This energy could be released if the various parts of the mass were to come closer together under their mutual self-attraction. Such a form of power generation is of course very well known. It is just by an application of this principle that power is made available to drive a hydro-electric power station. The power there is derived from the work done on water falling under gravity and being made to turn the turbines. Quite analogously work can be done by a collapsing body of great mass. But there is a limit. The energy cannot escape if ever R becomes smaller than $R_* = 2GM/c^2$. At this stage each unit mass could have released an amount of energy of the order of $\frac{1}{2}GM/R_* = c^2/4$; this is a quarter of our previous 'best' estimate. We shall show in Chapter XII that the quasar 3C 273 has probably emitted 10^{60} erg, or more, in its lifetime. To provide this 10^{60} erg we must therefore draw on at least the energy available in some 10^{40} gm of matter, or a mass about 5 million larger than that of the Sun. But we still have to consider how such large masses behave when they exist in a highly condensed state.

CHAPTER VII

COSMOLOGY

Cosmology is concerned with the large-scale properties and history of the Universe. The observational information required comes from the study of the positions of other galaxies in space. It enables us to construct some simple models of the Universe. This is important for our work. A model enables us to convert the redshifts of quasars into distances in the Universe. As we shall see, the cosmological observations at present available refer mainly to relatively nearby objects; in this connection 'relatively nearby' means that the objects concerned may be as much as 100 million light years away, but this is only about one per cent of the distance to the most remote objects we know. In consequence we have no definite indication of the actual structure of the Universe at large distances. Fortunately several quasars seem to be very far away indeed, and perhaps by observing them we shall be able to clear up this uncertainty.

The results drawn from the study of the galaxies are easily summarized. Their spectra are, in general, red-shifted. The redshift is interpreted as being due to the Doppler effect, and is therefore taken to imply that the galaxies concerned are receding from us. We recall from Chapter VI that the redshift z is conventionally defined by the formula

$$1 + z = \frac{\lambda}{\lambda_0}$$

where λ_0 is the laboratory wavelength, λ the observed wavelength of the spectral line in question and

$$1 + z = \sqrt{\frac{1 + v/c}{1 - v/c}},$$

where v is the velocity of the galaxy concerned. For redshifts rather smaller than unity it is approximately true that

$$z = v/c \quad . \quad . \quad . \quad . \quad (1)$$

The interesting cosmological observation is that a simple relation exists between the distance R to a galaxy and its velocity v, determined from the measured redshift with the help of equation (1). The relation is best expressed by the formula

$$v = HR \quad . \quad . \quad . \quad . \quad (2)$$

Equation (2) looks straightforward. In fact, though, it is very hard to find accurately the distance to any one galaxy, and measurements of such distances involve a sequence of complicated arguments. In consequence the best estimates for H have been much revised since the early work by Hubble. According to the latest data it seems best to say that $1/H = 10{,}000$ million years, to within an accuracy of about 50 per cent.

A simple formula must have a simple meaning. In the case of the velocity–distance relation (2) the easiest interpretation is as follows. To travel a distance R at speed v takes a time $t = R/v$; by formula (2) the time t is the same for all galaxies. We therefore could make up a model of the Universe in which all the galaxies started out from the same position at a time $1/H$ ago. They began their motions with a range of different velocities, and their distances from us now are simply proportional to their original velocities. On this basis an object with a redshift $z = 0{\cdot}16$, say (like 3C 273), has a speed $v \approx c/6 = 50{,}000$ km/sec, and is now some 500 Mpc ($= 1500$ million light years) distant. This shows at once how one arrives at great distances for the quasars if one interprets the line-shifts in their spectra as being due to cosmological effects.

In discussing formula (2) we have already made an implicit assumption for which we have no real justification. This is that the speed of recession of any individual galaxy has remained unchanged since the beginning of the Universe—or, alternatively, that at any one epoch $1/H$, as measured then, equals the age of the Universe. But there may be forces acting on each galaxy due to the gravitational attraction of all the other galaxies, and possibly due to some other large-scale fields of force. When such interactions are taken into account it becomes possible to construct a variety of different models for the Universe. In all these the distances of the galaxies from each other increase with time, but the rate of increase need not be the same at all epochs. It is therefore probably fairer to interpret formula (2) as implying that the age of the Universe is of order $1/H$, rather than that it equals $1/H$ exactly.

There is another important question which is not settled by formula (2). The relation $v = HR$ has been verified observationally only for galaxies with relatively low speeds of recession. The more distant galaxies, which recede faster, are very faint, and it becomes progressively harder to determine their redshifts. There is thus a considerable uncertainty about the correct form of the velocity-distance relation (or the redshift–distance relation) for the more distant parts of the Universe. This in turn makes it difficult to interpret the redshifts of the more distant quasars exactly.

It may be more profitable to look at this problem the other way round. With continued intensive study it should eventually become possible for astrophysicists to understand the nature of quasars as well as they now understand galaxies. This means that they would then be able to set up a distance scale for quasars in terms of their luminosities and other properties in just the same way as a distance scale has been set up in the past for the galaxies. There would be a great advantage, though, in using quasars, because some of them are so very distant, with redshifts as large as $z = 2$, much larger than the shift for any known galaxy. When enough data have been collected it should be possible to decide whether the Universe has been expanding uniformly in the past and whether it is finite or infinite. One will also be able to judge how physical conditions in the past differed from those we know now. This can be done because, in receiving light from a very distant object, we see the object as it was at the time when the light was emitted. It takes a light signal a very long time to reach us from a quasar with a redshift of, say, $z = 2$. In fact one can show quite generally that, if the ratio of observed to emitted wavelengths is $\lambda : \lambda_0 = z + 1 : 1$, then this is also the ratio of the radius of the Universe at present to the radius at the time of emission. If we see a quasar with $z + 1 = 3$ then we are looking at an object which belongs to a Universe with a radius one third as large as the radius of the Universe at present. Clearly we may hope to gather some fundamental information about the origin and early history of the Universe in this way.

But these are all hopes for the future. At present the distant quasars have been used for only one important cosmological observation, though they may soon be used for a second. The observation which has been made concerns the abundance of atomic hydrogen in intergalactic space. Atomic hydrogen has a strong absorption line at $\lambda_0 = 1216$ Å. In observing the quasar 3C 9, for which $z + 1 = 3$, we see this wavelength displaced to $\lambda = 3648$ Å (approximately). Any intergalactic hydrogen in the space between us and 3C 9 will have a redshift somewhere between $z = 2$ and $z = 0$, so that the hydrogen should appear to us in absorption, in a range of wavelengths between $\lambda = 3648$ Å and $\lambda = 1216$ Å. In fact no such absorption is observed. This sets a very low upper limit to the mean density of atomic hydrogen in intergalactic space.

But we cannot immediately conclude that there is very little hydrogen in intergalactic space, for the hydrogen present may be ionized rather than atomic. If so there will be one free electron available for each hydrogen atom. If there are free electrons in space then this affects the propagation of radio waves, so that waves of low frequency will travel at a speed slightly different from waves of higher frequency. Over very long distances the differences in travel time become appreciable. There is hope that one may be able, eventually, to observe sudden outbursts on distant quasars at a range of frequencies, and do so with such accuracy that one can note the differences in transit time for the various frequencies. The observation would lead to an estimate for the density of ionized hydrogen. If one knows the abundance of both non-ionized hydrogen and ionized hydrogen then one can be fairly certain that one has a good estimate for the density of intergalactic matter. This is an important datum for any dynamical model of the Universe.

CHAPTER VIII

STARS

Stars have been known much longer than quasars. They, too, generate much radiant energy, though many orders of magnitude less than the quasars. For example, the luminous output of the Sun is 4×10^{33} erg/sec. The intrinsically brightest star known has a luminosity of about 4×10^{39} erg/sec, one million times larger than that of the Sun. The quasar 3C 273 is thought to have a power output of 2×10^{47} erg/sec. This is 50 million times larger again.

Thus the luminosities of the various stars spread through a wide range of values. Since there are also stars intrinsically much less bright than the Sun the range is, in fact, even greater than this factor of one million. One therefore wonders whether the mechanism that powers a typical star can be extended sufficiently to work for a quasar. To answer this question we should first understand some basic properties of the structure of a star. The best example on which to test our theories is, of course, the Sun. Here the data are as follows:

$$\begin{aligned} M_\odot &= \text{mass of Sun} &&= 2 \times 10^{33} \text{ gm} \\ R_\odot &= \text{radius of Sun} &&= 7 \times 10^{10} \text{ cm} \\ L_\odot &= \text{luminosity of Sun} &&= 4 \times 10^{33} \text{ erg/sec.} \end{aligned}$$

The most common element in the Sun is hydrogen. It is present almost fully ionized, that is with the electrons detached from the protons. This makes the mean weight of the free particles in the Sun equal to $m \doteqdot 10^{-24}$ gm.

We shall now state some quite elementary and self-evident propositions. They are:

(1) Gravitation plays an important role in the mechanics of the Sun.

(2) The Sun's material is entirely gaseous, because of its high temperature.

(3) On the whole the matter in the Sun is not in a state of violent motion.

(4) The internal gas pressure of the Sun prevents the material of the Sun from collapsing onto itself under gravitation.

(5) The Sun is much hotter in its deep interior than at its surface.

(6) Energy flows from the hotter to the cooler parts of the Sun, and therefore from the inside to the outside. Eventually it escapes from the surface as radiation.

(7) The energy is generated in the deep interior by nuclear reactions, probably the conversion of hydrogen to helium.

(8) The Sun has existed in, roughly, its present state for some 5000 million years. Its structure is therefore very stable.

We can now use the statements (1), (2), (3) and (4) and make estimates of typical pressures, temperatures and densities deep down in the Sun, or in any star. A mass M distributed through a sphere of radius R has a density of order M/R^3. The typical acceleration of gravity within the sphere is of order GM/R^2; thus the pressure gradient required to support the gas against its self-gravitation is of order $\frac{M}{R^3} \times \frac{GM}{R^2} = \frac{GM^2}{R^5}$. This also equals p/R, which is the typical pressure divided by the radius of the star. It follows that the typical pressure in the star is $p = GM^2/R^4$.

We can next use Charles' law to relate pressure, density and temperature. The law states that

$$p = \frac{k}{m}\rho T,$$

where k is Boltzmann's constant, and m the mean weight of the free particles (defined earlier in this chapter). We shall show later that Charles' law cannot always be used. But if it can, we find that

$$\frac{kT}{m} = \frac{p}{\rho} = \frac{GM}{R},$$

approximately. In the case of the Sun this leads to the estimate that the average temperature T equals 13 million deg. K, actually quite close to the values found by more exact calculation. At such a temperature nuclear reactions can occur with a rate adequate to supply the luminosity of the Sun. Our general scheme therefore seems to be reasonable.

Now we shall verify whether we can, in fact, use Charles' law in the way we have done. It is possible, at a high enough temperature, for the pressure of the radiation trapped in a gas to become more important than the gas pressure itself. The law relating temperature T and radiation pressure p_R is that

$$p_R = \tfrac{1}{3}aT^4,$$

with $a = 7{\cdot}5 \times 10^{-15}$ erg/cm^3. deg^4. Our calculation has already suggested a value for the typical temperature of the matter deep inside the Sun. On substituting this value we find that the radiation pressure becomes

$$p_R = \tfrac{1}{3}a\left(\frac{m}{k}\right)^4\left(\frac{GM}{R}\right)^4$$

The ratio of p_R to the typical gas pressure p_G is given by

$$1 - \beta : \beta = p_R : p_G$$

In the Sun $1 - \beta$ is small, and we find that

$$1 - \beta = \tfrac{1}{3}a\left(\frac{m}{k}\right)^4 G^3M^2 \quad . \quad . \quad . \quad (1)$$

If we substitute numerical values for the Sun we find that $1 - \beta = 0{\cdot}005$, approximately. Thus radiation pressure contributes about half a per cent to the total pressure in the Sun. In more massive stars, $1 - \beta$ becomes larger, as our formula (1) shows. Thus while we can clearly forget about radiation pressure when discussing the Sun, we cannot do so when discussing more massive stars. We shall come back to this point later. At present we shall only recall an estimate from Chapter VI. This was that a quasar needs a mass of at least some millions of solar masses in order to provide the energy which it seems to consume in its lifetime. Following our argument, we can be quite certain that radiation pressure will be dominant in any object which is in static equilibrium, and which is so much more massive than the Sun. It appears very likely that there are violent motions in quasars, and that they are not quiescent objects like the Sun. We shall now show that objects in which radiation pressure dominates are much less stable.

An excellent test for the stability of any mechanical system in equilibrium is to give it a small push, and watch its subsequent motion. If the system is stable it will, after experiencing this push, try to return to its previous position of equilibrium. A simple example of stability is a child's marble, lying at the bottom of a glass bowl. However, if the system is unstable, it will go further and further from the equilibrium position after being disturbed. An example of this is the case of a pencil, carefully balanced to stand on its point. More familiarly, and almost as correctly, we might equally well take a house of cards as an example.

To test for the stability of the Sun we then imagine an experiment in which every particle on the Sun is moved, say, one per cent nearer to the centre of the Sun. Of course such an experiment can never be carried out, but we can calculate that the following changes should take place:

Typical distances	change by	-1%
volume	changes by	-3%
density	changes by	$+3\%$

The principle behind this calculation is quite simple. Volume varies as the cube of the typical distance. If the typical distance is reduced by 1 per cent, this means that it is multiplied by a factor $1 - 0{\cdot}01 = 0{\cdot}99$. The volume is therefore multiplied by $(0{\cdot}99)^3 = 0{\cdot}970299$, or, near enough, by a factor $0{\cdot}97 = 1 - 0{\cdot}03$. A reduction by 1 per cent in the typical distance implies a 3 per cent reduction in volume. Then we work out the change in the typical density, which varies inversely as the volume. If the volume is multiplied by 0·97, the density is multiplied by $1/0{\cdot}97 = 1{\cdot}0309\ldots$, or 1·03. The density thus increases by 3 per cent. We shall use the same principle again later for working out related changes in the state of a star.

If the disturbance is applied quickly enough the gas will heat up on being compressed but the heat will not have time to flow any appreciable distance. This is called an 'adiabatic' compression. During such changes pressure p and density ρ usually obey the relation $p = \kappa\rho^{5/3}$, so that we find that if the density changes by +3 per cent then the pressure changes by +5 per cent.

Finally the pressure gradient varies like the typical pressure divided by the typical distance. Hence the pressure gradient changes by +6 per cent.

Thus the pressure builds up within the Sun and tends to prevent compression. Obviously this helps to restore the Sun to its equilibrium size after being disturbed. But we have not yet considered all the consequences. The gravitational force exerted by any particle on any other particle in the Sun varies inversely as the square of their distance apart. Thus upon shrinking the Sun by 1 per cent, we increase the mutual attraction of all its particles by 2 per cent, or the acceleration of gravity changes by +2 per cent. We also know that the density has increased by 3 per cent and so the inward force per unit volume, due to gravity, has changed by +5 per cent.

Finally equilibrium is maintained by the balance between the pressure gradient, pushing outwards, and the inward pull of gravity. The former increases everywhere by 6 per cent in our experiment, the latter only by 5 per cent. Thus a net outward force results, and the Sun, after being compressed, will spring back to its former size. We confirm that the Sun is stable, as assumed in point (8) of our list of plausible propositions.

Now we can follow through the same argument in the case of an object supported solely by radiation pressure. Once again we apply our 1 per cent contraction, once again the density rises everywhere by 3 per cent, but in the case of matter supported entirely by radiation pressure the adiabatic law becomes $p = \kappa\rho^{4/3}$. This means that now the pressure changes by +4 per cent and the pressure gradient by +5 per cent only. The percentage change in the pressure gradient is just the same as that in the inward force, per unit volume, due to gravity. Both forces change by the same amount; if they were in balance before the shrinkage they will still be in balance after the shrinkage. There is no resultant force tending to restore the old equilibrium, and the object can equally well remain in its new, disturbed state. We have here a case of neutral equilibrium. Our conclusion is that a star supported solely by radiation pressure is not at all firmly held together. If it is very largely supported by radiation pressure, with only a small contribution from gas pressure, then it will be stable, but only just.

There is another aspect of the stability problem. Suppose we wish to discover a process which shrinks a star by 1 per cent and does not allow it to spring back. We consider first a star supported by gas pressure, and argue as follows. When the star is compressed by 1 per cent, the gas density rises by 3 per cent and the gas pressure by 5 per cent. Now Charles' law $p = \frac{k}{m}\rho T$ implies that the temperature has increased by 2 per cent. There is a corresponding increase in the thermal energy content of the star. If we allow the star to dispose, by radiation, of half this increase in thermal energy, then the resultant increase in pressure will be only 4 per cent and the corresponding increase in the pressure gradient 5 per cent. Thus if just half the increase in thermal energy were allowed to escape, the star would attain a new equilibrium position. Put another way, this means that a star can condense gradually, if, at each stage, it radiates away half the increase in thermal energy resulting from the contraction. In condensing, the star loses energy into space. If therefore we take the original dispersed condition of the stellar material as the zero energy state, then we may say that, after condensing into a star, the matter is in a state of negative energy. The diagram below shows schematically how this negative energy depends on M/R, M being the mass of a star. We shall call M/R the degree of condensation.

In the figure, curve (1) refers to a body having about the mass of the Sun, in which gas pressure predominates. As the body condenses, M/R grows and $\mathscr{E}$ decreases steeply.

Curve (2) refers to a body of larger mass, in which radiation

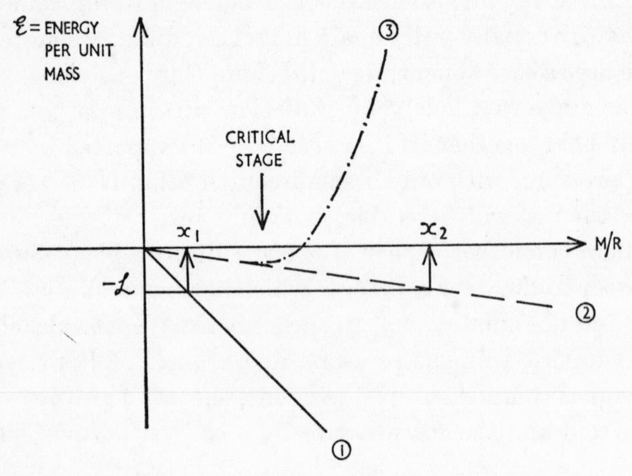

VIII/1. To show how the energy $\mathscr{E}$ depends on the degree of condensation.

pressure dominates and gas pressure contributes only to a small extent. $\mathscr{E}$ still decreases as M/R grows, but not so steeply. Such a body still emits radiant energy into space as it condenses. But to liberate a given amount of energy now calls for a much greater degree of condensation. The diagram indicates how much condensation is necessary to liberate energy $\mathscr{L}$. We have drawn a horizontal line opposite the value $\mathscr{E} = -\mathscr{L}$. The line cuts curve (1) when $M/R = x_1$ and curve (2) when $M/R = x_2$. The values of x_1 and x_2 give the degree of condensation needed in the two cases. It is clear that x_2 much exceeds x_1.

Curve (3) indicates how the predictions for case (2) are changed if one takes account of the general theory of relativity. For small values of M/R, that is for small degrees of condensation, there is little difference. But soon one has to allow for the changes in mechanics which the general theory requires. They are that

(i) time measurements made deep down in the body do not agree with time measurements made near the surface;

(ii) the geometry of the space occupied by the mass becomes non-Euclidean; in particular a sphere of radius R does not have a surface area $4\pi R^2$;

(iii) in any element of the body the mass density is increased by $4p/c^2$, p being the local pressure, c the speed of light. Of this increase $3p/c^2$ comes from the additional internal energy, and p/c^2 from the relativistic pressure term.

This last change has the most drastic consequence. The material of the star behaves as if its density were

$$\sigma = \rho + \frac{4p}{c^2} \quad . \quad . \quad . \quad . \quad (2)$$

We take the relation between p and ρ to be adiabatic, with an index γ just larger than 4/3, so that

$$p = \kappa\rho^{\gamma} \quad . \quad . \quad . \quad . \quad (3)$$

We recall that a relation like (3), with $\gamma = 5/3$, describes adiabatic changes in a medium where only gas pressure matters. The value $\gamma = 4/3$ describes a medium where only radiation pressure matters. A value of γ just larger than 4/3, say $\gamma = 4/3 + \epsilon$, refers to a case in which radiation pressure dominates and gas pressure contributes a little.

But now we must realize that in working out the mechanics of our model we should replace ρ by σ. From relations (2) and (3) we conclude that, approximately,

$$\sigma = \rho + \frac{4\kappa}{c^2}\rho^{4/3}$$

or

$$\rho = \sigma - \frac{4\kappa}{c^2}\sigma^{4/3} \quad . \quad . \quad . \quad (4)$$

A useful relation between p and σ may then be found from (3) and (4). It states that

$$p = \kappa\left(\sigma - \frac{4\kappa}{c^2}\sigma^{4/3}\right)^{\gamma}$$

$$\doteqdot \kappa\sigma^{\gamma}\left(1 - \frac{16}{3}\frac{\kappa}{c^2}\sigma^{1/3}\right), \quad . \quad . \quad (5)$$

approximately again. We shall give a better description of the mechanics of a massive body if we pretend that σ is the density, and that (5) gives the correct adiabatic relation. The new relation evidently differs somewhat in form from the relation we have used until now. But one can still define an effective adiabatic index Γ, and a simple calculation, not to be given here, shows that

$$\Gamma = \gamma - \frac{16}{9}\frac{\kappa}{c^2}\sigma^{1/3} = \frac{4}{3} + \epsilon - \frac{16}{9}\frac{\kappa}{c^2}\rho^{1/3}, \quad . \quad (6)$$

to a reasonable approximation. Γ is not now a constant, but depends on $\kappa\rho^{1/3}$, which we can express in terms of the condensation M/R, as follows. The typical pressure and the typical density deep inside the massive body are

$$\left.\begin{aligned} p(\doteqdot \kappa\rho^{4/3}) &= \frac{GM^2}{R^4} \\ \text{and} \qquad \rho &= \frac{M}{R^3} \end{aligned}\right\} \quad . \quad . \quad . \quad (7)$$

From these two equations it follows at once that a typical value for $\kappa\rho^{1/3}$ is GM/R, and that equation (6) can be written

$$\Gamma = \frac{4}{3} + \epsilon - \frac{16}{9c^2}\frac{GM}{R} \quad . \quad . \quad . \quad (8)$$

This result can be interpreted quite simply. The effective adiabatic index Γ depends on the condensation M/R of the massive body. When M/R is small, and the body has condensed only a little, Γ is nearly equal to $4/3 + \epsilon$, and therefore larger than the critical value $4/3$. But Γ decreases with increasing condensation and becomes equal to 4/3, according to our estimate, when

$$\epsilon = \frac{16}{9c^2}\frac{GM}{R} \quad . \quad . \quad . \quad . \quad (9)$$

The body is then in neutral equilibrium. If it radiates any more energy into space it will contract still further and Γ will be less than 4/3. There must follow a catastrophic collapse.

Our argument has been rather rough, even if it is moderately simple. We have come to a result of the right form, and the factor 16/9 is nearly right. In Chandrasekhar's classical discussion of this effect the correct factor is found to be between 1 and 2. Any discrepancy makes little difference to us here

Important conclusions will follow from (9) if we can express ϵ in terms of the mass of the body. We therefore note that for a relatively large mass M, $\gamma = 4/3$, $\epsilon = 0$ and $\beta = 0$, and for a relatively small mass M, $\gamma = 5/3$, $\epsilon = 1/3$ and $\beta = 1$t

This suggests that ϵ and β are related by

$$\epsilon = \tfrac{1}{3}\beta \quad . \quad . \quad . \quad . \quad (10)$$

But β is the fraction of the total pressure provided by the gas. We know from some results found earlier in this chapter that, when the radiation pressure p_R dominates,

$$p_R = \tfrac{1}{3}aT^4 = \frac{GM^2}{R^4},$$

while the gas pressure p_G is given by

$$p_G = \frac{k}{m}\rho T.$$

Thus

$$\beta \doteqdot \frac{p_G}{p_R} = \frac{3k\rho}{maT^3} \quad . \quad . \quad . \quad (11)$$

Once again

$$\rho \doteqdot \frac{M}{R^3}$$

and we eventually find, after a short calculation, that

$$\epsilon = \tfrac{1}{3}\beta = \left(\frac{M_0}{M}\right)^{1/2} \quad . \quad . \quad . \quad (12)$$

The mass M_0 in this relation is defined by

$$M_0 = \frac{k^2\sqrt{3}}{9m^2G^{3/2}a^{1/2}} \qquad . \quad . \quad . \ (13)$$

We know the numerical values of k, a, G and m, and on substituting them into the formula, we find that

$$M_0 = 3 \times 10^{33} \text{ gm},$$

which is one and a half times the mass of the Sun. Now on referring back to relation (9) we conclude that a body of mass M reaches the point of instability when

$$\frac{GM}{R} = \frac{9c^2}{16}\left(\frac{M_0}{M}\right)^{1/2} \qquad . \quad . \quad . \ (14)$$

Relation (14) leads to the answers to two crucial questions:

(1) What is the temperature deep inside a massive body which is at the point of instability?

(2) The body radiates energy into space. How much gravitational energy can it make available for radiation before it reaches the instability point?

Question (1) is easily answered. The formula for the radiation pressure is

$$\frac{GM^2}{R^4} = p_R = \tfrac{1}{3}aT^4 \qquad . \quad . \quad . \ (15)$$

With a little algebra one finds from (14) and (15) that

$$T = \frac{3{\cdot}7 \times 10^{46}}{M} = \frac{1{\cdot}9 \times 10^{13}}{(M/M_\odot)} \qquad . \quad . \ (16)$$

This relation means that the temperature reached at the instability point depends on the mass of the body: the larger the mass, the smaller is the temperature. Now obviously the body can get no hotter than temperature T before the collapse. The table below shows some typical values.

These values lead to an interesting inference. There is a limit to the amount of nuclear energy which can be released by a massive body. A temperature of at least 10^7 deg. K is needed before nuclear reactions will go on at an appreciable rate. Our table then shows us that collapse sets in before such

Mass of body (in solar masses)	*Highest temperature (degrees Kelvin)*
10^5	$1{\cdot}9 \times 10^8$
10^6	$1{\cdot}9 \times 10^7$
10^7	$1{\cdot}9 \times 10^6$
10^8	$1{\cdot}9 \times 10^5$
10^9	$1{\cdot}9 \times 10^4$

a temperature is reached in a body with a mass larger than about 2×10^6 $M_\odot$ or 4×10^{39} gm. Each gram of hydrogen gives up at most 6×10^{18} erg, so that no static massive body can release more than about $2{\cdot}4 \times 10^{58}$ erg of nuclear energy.

The conclusion is therefore that during a smooth contraction nuclear energy is available in very massive bodies, but that it cannot be extracted before instability occurs. The release can occur only below a certain mass; but such masses cannot supply all the energy which is needed by a quasar. It therefore becomes very important to answer the second question. We have all the necessary information now.

The energy carried by the gas in the body (as opposed to the energy carried by the radiation trapped in the gas) has a density equal to U, where

$$U = \tfrac{3}{2}p_G = \tfrac{3}{2}\beta p_R \quad . \quad . \quad . \quad (17)$$

Equations (12) and (15) give values for β and for p_R. We use them to find that

$$U = \frac{9}{2}\left(\frac{M_0}{M}\right)^{1/2}\frac{GM^2}{R^4}$$

On multiplying this by the volume of the body we find that the total energy carried by the gas in the body is

$$E_G = 6\pi\left(\frac{M_0}{M}\right)^{1/2}\frac{GM^2}{R} \quad . \quad . \quad . \quad (18)$$

From equation (14) we know the value for GM/R at the instability point. We use it in equation (18) to find that

$$E_G = \frac{27\pi}{8} M_0 c^2 = 2 \cdot 5 \times 10^{55} \text{ erg} \qquad . \quad (19)$$

approximately.

This helps to answer our previous question. For we know, from an earlier discussion, that at every stage in the condensation a certain amount of gravitational energy is given to the gas, and that at the same time an equal amount of energy is radiated into space. At any time, then, the value of E_G equals the total amount which gravitational effects have contributed to the radiation emitted by the body. The conclusion is that, no matter how massive the body may be, it can never release into space more than $2 \cdot 5 \times 10^{55}$ erg before it reaches the instability point.

In this chapter we have treated a quasar as though it were a static body of great mass, gradually contracting under the influence of its self-gravitation. We now find that we cannot insist on this view. No matter whether we propose to draw on the gravitational or the nuclear energy available, our static body must break up before it has produced enough. We shall obviously have to look for a better model, and will do so later.

Earlier in this century the subject of astrophysics was opened up by the genius of Eddington. We have tried to follow his lead and to write this chapter, as best we could, in the way in which he might have done. But one of Eddington's other interests was to try to understand why the constants of nature take the values that they have. One such constant, namely the mass M_0, has been found in this chapter. In relation (13) it is defined in terms of k, G, m and a. But a can itself be expressed in terms of k, c and h (Planck's constant).

If we make the substitutions we find that

$$\frac{M_0}{m} = 0 \cdot 016 \left(\frac{hc}{Gm^2} \right)^{3/2} \qquad . \quad . \quad . \quad (20)$$

hc/Gm^2 is a pure number. It gives a measure of the strength of the gravitational force between two particles of mass m. Relation (20) states that if we know the mean molecular weight of our massive body then we can calculate what number of particles will contribute their gravitational energy before the body must collapse. In our case the number is 3×10^{57}.

CHAPTER IX

ELECTRON PROCESSES

We have already discussed the problem of the energy requirements of a quasar. Our discussion shows that we do not yet know the source of the radiant energy which is seen to leave a quasar. But without knowing where the energy comes from we cannot claim that we understand how a quasar works at all. Even if we can see how the energy is supplied this still does not give us a full understanding. We also have to know how the energy is converted into radiation, and shall now discuss the role played by electrons in the conversion mechanism.

There are essentially two kinds of radiation to consider. The first is continuum radiation, observed at radio and at optical wavelengths. In continuum radiation the energy content is spread out smoothly over large ranges of wavelength. On the other hand in spectral line radiation the intensity is confined to narrow and well-defined ranges in wavelength, and each wavelength observed in the laboratory corresponds to a transition between particular states of a particular atom, molecule or ion. One knows from experiment that a given atom (or ion or molecule) has only a certain number of configurations for its electrons, and that the atom can maintain equilibrium only in those configurations. Most of these states are not stable, and an atom remains in an unstable state for only a very short time (about 10^{-8} second, as a rule) and then reverts to another equilibrium state. There is always a difference in energy between two equilibrium states of an atom; if χ_a, χ_b are the energies of the two states, then the energy difference $\chi_a - \chi_b$ is radiated into space after the transition. There are also other ways in which the state of an atom can be changed. Most important for us is the process of inelastic or superelastic collisions with electrons.[1] In this an electron interacts with an atom, in state a, say, and transfers it to state b. Suppose that the energy difference $\chi_a - \chi_b$ is negative. Then the electron will have to supply energy $\chi_b - \chi_a$ to accomplish the transfer. This can only happen if the electron has at least energy $\chi_b - \chi_a$.

Cases where χ_a exceeds χ_b are different. Here the electron carries off the surplus energy.

Both processes can occur in the gaseous nebulae which envelop the typical quasar. There is, though, one further complication. Many so-called 'forbidden' spectral lines show up in quasars—and in the more ordinary excited nebulae known to the astrophysicist. Forbidden lines arise from states which are only just unstable; according to the technical term the upper state is 'metastable'. The life-time of such a state can be very much longer, perhaps as large as one or even a hundred seconds, and this has the following consequences.

Suppose that we were to consider a volume of gas containing a certain species of atom, and a very few electrons which can excite it to emit radiation. Then a particular atom will, at any one time, be most probably in its state of lowest energy. If it interacts with an electron and is raised to a state of higher energy then it will spend a little time there, make the transition to a lower state, emitting some radiation, and then continue to make such transitions, with emission of radiation, until it again reaches a stable state.

If the density of electrons is increased then there is an increase in the rate at which atoms are excited, and the various spectral lines emitted by the gas will become stronger. But one cannot go on indefinitely stepping up the emissivity at this rate. For if the excited states of the atoms are metastable, and have appreciable lifetimes, then there is a definite chance that an atom in an excited state will make a downward transition from that state not by radiation, but by

[1] The electrons lose kinetic energy in inelastic collisions, and gain kinetic energy in superelastic collisions.

being de-excited in a super-elastic collision with an electron. Or, to put it another way, the following processes take place when the electron density is relatively high and the excited states of the atoms are metastable. The atoms are raised from their lowest energy states by taking energy from the electrons in inelastic collisions, but much of this energy is returned to the electrons again in super-elastic collisions. The proportion of energy which escapes in the form of radiation is only small. By applying theoretical arguments of this form it is possible to set limits on the density of those regions in a quasar in which the line emission occurs. It should be noted, though, that calculations like this may be based on assumptions which are difficult to justify. For example there is the well-known discussion by Greenstein and Schmidt, who analysed the spectrum of a quasar in just this way. But they tacitly assumed that

1. the emission is caused by electrons at a temperature of the order of 10^4 deg. K;
2. the total charge on the electrons per unit volume just balances the charge on the positive ions per unit volume, so that there is no net charge;
3. the emission takes place in a medium which is more or less uniform, that is, no allowance is made for possible fluctuations in density.

If one makes these assumptions in interpreting the observations one finds that the electron density in the medium is about 10^4 particles per cm^3. But can the assumptions be reconciled with the recent observation in which it was seen that a component of one of the magnesium lines in a quasar shifted its wavelength by 50 Å within a week? The atoms that emitted the radiation at the beginning of the week must have had a different velocity from those that did so at the end of the week. Let us see what would be implied if the same group of atoms were responsible for the emission all along.

First, a change in wavelength by 50 Å calls for a change in velocity of the order of 3500 km/sec, or $3{\cdot}5 \times 10^8$ cm/sec. This has to occur within a week, or 5×10^5 seconds, and requires an acceleration (or deceleration) of some 700 cm/sec^2, which is very large by astrophysical standards. If the emission of the magnesium line were confined to a small fraction of the volume of the quasar it might be possible to imagine that there are forces large enough to cause the implied change in velocity. One would then wonder why the line emission occurs only in this restricted volume—in fact a basic assumption in the work of Greenstein and Schmidt is that emission occurs throughout a jacket of substantial volume enclosing the quasar. The observation of the change in wavelength clearly implies that important non-uniformities do occur.

If the magnesium emission takes place in only a restricted volume, and if the emission occurs in a given group of atoms, then we may safely expect that a considerable amount of heat will be dissipated among those atoms during the deceleration. This suggests a picture quite different from that constructed by Greenstein and Schmidt. There will be a sequence of events by which different parts of the quasar can be raised, intermittently, to very high temperatures, possibly as high as 100 million deg K. These hot spots must provide the major part of the line radiation. If conditions were otherwise there could be no sudden wavelength changes; a relatively quiescent nebula enveloping the quasar will certainly not produce them. Indeed, if the quiescent part were to contribute most of the line emission then it would make only a very small difference if some minor portion of the nebula were involved in a sudden velocity change.

One might consider another interpretation. It may be true that the magnesium atoms, observed at the beginning of the week, had a different velocity from those seen at the end of the week. But did we observe the same group of atoms on both occasions? Perhaps one should, rather, think in terms of a burst of radiation, or a group of fast-moving electrons, coming from some central point in the quasar. The outburst interacts with different parts of the nebula at different times, as its effect is propagated outwards. Both radiation and relativistic electrons travel at about 300,000 km/sec; in the course of a week they cover distance of $1{\cdot}5 \times 10^{16}$ cm. One might then argue that the quasar is surrounded by a gaseous nebula, different parts of which move at different speeds. During the passage of a group of fast electrons through a particular region that region is made to shine, and we observe its radiation at the Doppler shifted wavelength appropriate to its speed. When the electrons have moved on elsewhere, we observe a different Doppler shift, determined by the velocity of the gas with which they are now interacting.

If this second speculation is right, then we must find a source for the fast electrons. Some possibilities will be discussed in Chapter X. But here we return to a description of other mechanisms which can cause fast electrons to radiate.

Basically, an electron will radiate if it is accelerated. Any change in the motion of an electron causes a time-dependent change in the surrounding electric and magnetic fields. These changes are propagated through space at the speed of light, and can be observed elsewhere as radiation. For example, when an electron passes close to an unbalanced electric charge, the electric field there causes a deflection in the electron's motion, and some radiation is produced as a result. There are, of course, many ionized atoms in and around a quasar, and one may expect some radiation to escape every time that an electron passes such an ion. This process is known as free-free emission, and almost certainly occurs in the atmospheres of stars, and in diffuse nebulae in our Galaxy. But it is rather inefficient and cannot account for any appreciable proportion of the radiation from a quasar.

Synchrotron radiation is another possible process. It is well known from the study of conventional radio sources and supernova remnants. Here the fast electron moves under the

CHAPTER X

PRODUCTION OF FAST PARTICLES

There is excellent evidence that quasars contain large numbers of fast electrons, and that these fast electrons play an important part in producing the radiation by which quasars are observed. In the present context the word 'fast' means that the electrons move at a speed comparable to c, the speed of light. According to the theory of special relativity the energy of an electron moving with a speed v is $mc^2/\sqrt{1-v^2/c^2}$. When $v = 0$, the electron is at rest, and its energy is mc^2. For small values of v the energy is not much above the rest energy, mc^2, and it equals $2mc^2$ when $v/c = \sqrt{3}/2 = 0{\cdot}866$. Very roughly this is about the dividing line between the non-relativistic and the relativistic electrons. The energy becomes much larger for speeds v still closer to c. It is quite possible that quasars (and their radio sources) contain electrons with energies as large as 20,000 mc^2. A convenient unit for expressing these energies is the Mev, or mega-electron volt. It is the amount of energy acquired by an electron on passing through a potential difference of a million volts. The rest energy mc^2 of an electron is about 0·5 Mev; our rather arbitrary division between the non-relativistic and the relativistic electrons occurs at an energy of just one Mev. There is also a useful relation between the concept of temperature and these energies. When the temperature T of an electron gas reaches 10^{10} deg. K the typical electron has an energy of about one Mev.

High energy electrons have long been known to the physicist. They can be produced in the laboratory, they are observed in cosmic ray showers and they are known to exist trapped in the Earth's radiation belts (the van Allen belts). The laboratory electrons have to be accelerated to their high speeds by rather sophisticated, specially designed machines. But the cosmic ray showers and the van Allen electrons may have analogues in a quasar. It is therefore worth our while to consider their physical properties further.

Cosmic rays are charged particles with high energies. They enter the Earth's atmosphere from outer space. Most probably they originate in interstellar space or possibly in very disturbed regions like the remnants of supernovae. There is also a suspicion that some of the most energetic cosmic rays come from intergalactic space. The overwhelming majority of cosmic ray particles are positively charged nuclei: many elements are represented, with hydrogen and helium being by far the most common. Energies of cosmic ray particles range from about 100 Mev upwards. More energetic nuclei are not as common as less energetic ones, but energies as large as 10^{13} Mev have been observed. Electrons are also present in cosmic rays, but they are only about 1 per cent as abundant as the cosmic ray nuclei. This discrepancy is, at first sight, surprising, because any natural process which gives energy to positively charged particles should also accelerate negatively charged particles. But there is an explanation. The different behaviour is not due to the difference in charge, but in rest mass. The electrons, having a much smaller rest mass, will radiate far more easily than protons or other nuclei. In the previous chapter we described some of the ways in which relativistic electrons can be made to radiate. All these would work for positively charged nuclei as well. The difference in the rest mass of the particles, however, means that a nucleus, having rest mass M_0 and a fixed energy E, will, under given conditions, emit at a rate only $(m_0/M_0)^4$ times that of an electron with equal energy E and rest mass m_0. If the nucleus is a proton, then $M_0/m_0 = 1840$ and the factor $(m_0/M_0)^4 = 8{\cdot}5 \times 10^{-14}$. Fast electrons therefore lose their energy much more easily than the fast nuclei do. This limits the number of cosmic ray electrons. But the size of the factor $(m_0/M_0)^4$ also explains why we attribute effects in quasars to high energy electrons and not to high energy nuclei. The nuclei may have high energy, but they do not radiate efficiently, and they could not possibly produce the amount of electromagnetic radiation which is observed.

We can now see why cosmic ray showers are relevant. A shower (in this case) consists of a cloud of electrons and positrons travelling along with a cosmic ray primary. The primary is the nucleus which comes from outer space. On passing close to the atoms in the atmosphere the primary sparks off secondary particles and anti-particles. The particles are the electrons, the anti-particles are the positrons. (The positrons are in most respects very similar to electrons, except that their charge and magnetic moment are opposite. An electron and positron can mutually annihilate when they meet: their energy is then converted to electromagnetic radiation. This is a simple example of the interaction of matter with anti-matter. We shall consider some other such interactions in Chapter XII.)

Abundant cosmic-ray showers in the Earth's atmosphere seem to be produced when the primaries have energies above 10^9 Mev. An appreciable fraction of the energy of the primary goes into the formation of the secondaries. It is possible that a similar process takes place in a quasar. If so then we know one source for the fast electrons, but we still have to discover how the nuclei are accelerated.

The electrons in the van Allen belt have a different origin and different properties. They are observed in a loop-like region which girdles the Earth, and has a diameter of ten or twenty Earth radii. Their properties and distribution in space are closely controlled by the Earth's magnetic field. They also seem to be strongly affected by the explosion of nuclear devices in the upper atmosphere, and by changes in the strength of the solar wind. (This wind consists of hot gas evaporated from the surface of the Sun.)

It is not known just how the van Allen electrons are produced, nor why the solar wind has such a marked influence on them. The most promising speculation is that the solar wind presses on the Earth's magnetic field, and that the pressure is not constant or uniform. The variability in the pressure sets up waves in the magnetic field and the electrons pick up some of the wave energy. The waves are particularly strong after the outburst of a solar flare when the solar wind blows harder and becomes more gusty. The student of quasars can regard this as a useful experimental result. He may not have a theoretical explanation of the effect. But he knows that electrons can gain energy when they are trapped in a magnetic field, which is subjected to changes in the pressure of the medium in which it is embedded.

Another interesting analogy follows from the observation that the van Allen belts were much enriched after the explosion of a hydrogen bomb at high altitude. Somehow the explosion must have energized the electrons in the belts. This was most probably due, at least in part, to the passage of a shock wave across the belts. The explosion would have sent off shock waves in all directions. The wave travelling away upwards moves into progressively more tenuous parts of the atmosphere. This results in a steady increase in the Mach number of the shock wave. As the Mach number increases so does the temperature of the material that has passed through the shock. Paradoxically, as the shock travels further upward from the site of the explosion, it produces progressively higher temperatures. This can result in a very marked increase in the energy of the van Allen electrons.

Even if this is not the full explanation of the enhancement of electron energies, it quite probably has a close connection with some astrophysical effects. Stars of certain kinds occasionally have explosions in their deep interior. Shock waves coming from such an explosion attain very high Mach numbers when they reach the outer layers of the star, where the gas density is low. Here they will produce intense heating, and consequently an abnormal number of energetic electrons. In a quasar the shock waves are probably set up when two condensations within the quasar collide with one another. The cause of the shock waves might now be different, but their general effect would still be the same.

The intensification of shock waves may seem rather strange. But it is quite closely related to the phenomenon of breakers on the sea shore, which almost everyone must have seen at some time. The relationship exists because there is a great similarity between the properties of waves on water and waves in air. Sound waves and surface waves on water have many properties in common. Shock waves are very similar to breakers; a shock wave advancing into a region of decreasing density in an atmosphere is very much like a breaker travelling up a sloping beach. It is a very common observation that the breaker becomes higher and higher as it comes closer to the shore. The reason is that the water is shallower near the shore, but the breaker must still transport a certain amount of momentum. In places where there is less water for the breaker to disturb, the disturbance of the water available must be correspondingly stronger. The shock amplification in the outer layers of a star is due to an exactly similar cause: a certain amount of energy must be transported outwards. In places where there is less gas to carry the wave, the disturbance due to the wave necessarily becomes greater.

Finally, there is the Fermi mechanism for accelerating charged particles. This is a more gradual process. Fermi originally proposed it as a description of the way in which cosmic ray particles are accelerated in interstellar space. The particles were assumed to interact with the interstellar gas clouds. These are known to be in a chaotic state of motion; Fermi also assumed that each cloud carried with it its own magnetic field. The fields prevent any charged particles from penetrating into the clouds. Instead the particles bounce around among the clouds. In doing so they exchange energy with the clouds. One can easily show that the particles will gain, on average, and that the clouds will lose.

Consider a head-on collision between a relativistic particle having energy E and a cloud having mass M and velocity u. To a good enough approximation, we can say that before the collision the particle, shown in Fig. X/1, has momentum E/c leftward; after collision it has momentum E/c rightward.

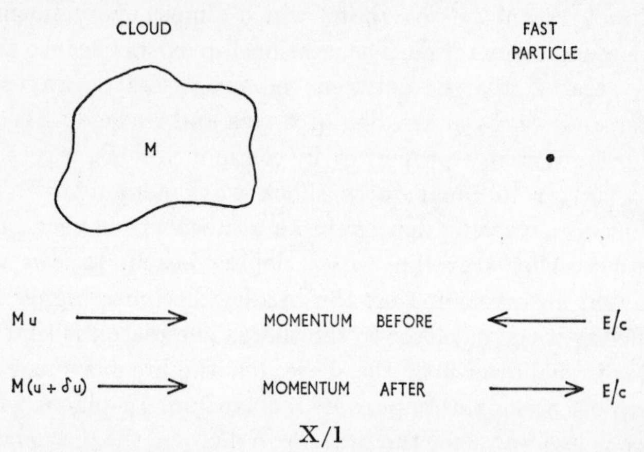

X/1

The velocity u of the cloud changes to $u + \delta u$ during the interaction; the change is necessary because the cloud gives momentum $2E/c$ to the particle. To conserve momentum we require that

$$M\delta u + 2E/c = 0$$

so that

$$\delta u = -2E/cM \quad . \quad . \quad . \quad (1)$$

It follows from (1) that the cloud changes its kinetic energy by

$$\tfrac{1}{2}M(u + \delta u)^2 - \tfrac{1}{2}Mu^2$$
$$= Mu\delta u = -2Eu/c \quad . \quad . \quad . \quad (2)$$

Thus in a head-on collision the cloud loses energy $2Eu/c$ and the particle gains $2Eu/c$.

There are also overtaking collisions. An overtaking collision with a cloud having speed u is equivalent to a head-on collision at speed $-u$. The particle then loses energy $2Eu/c$. There would be no net gain in energy if overtaking collisions were as frequent as head-on collisions. But of course they are not. The frequency of collisions between moving objects is directly proportional to their relative velocity. For head-on collisions with clouds having speed u the relative velocity is $c + u$, for overtaking collisions it is $c - u$. The ratio of probabilities is therefore

$$c + u : c - u, \text{ or } \tfrac{1}{2}(1 + u/c) : \tfrac{1}{2}(1 - u/c).$$

A fraction $\frac{1}{2}(1 - u/c)$ of collisions are of the overtaking kind, and after they are balanced by an equal number of head-on collisions, there still remain a fraction u/c of unbalanced head-on collisions. This leads to a net average gain of energy $2Eu^2/c^2$ per collision.

The net rate of gain of energy by a particle is proportional to the energy it already has. This is rather like the growth of a sum of money invested at a certain rate of interest, say x per cent. At compound interest the investment doubles after about $69/x$ years. In the case of the relativistic particles the energy doubles after $\dfrac{69c^2}{200u^2}(= 0{\cdot}345\, c^2/u^2)$ collisions, the 'rate of interest' being $200\, u^2/c^2$ per cent per collision.

This turned out to be too low a rate of interest, when numerical values were substituted for the conditions in interstellar space. In principle the Fermi process would work; in practice the interstellar clouds do not move fast enough and collisions are too infrequent. But conditions may be more favourable in a quasar.

There is another good comparison between the Fermi mechanism and a savings bank. Some depositors leave their money in a bank for a very long time, and their capital grows very large. But most depositors leave their money only for shorter periods and they do not grow so rich. In the absence of inflation savings banks therefore produce some very rich people and many more moderately well-to-do people. It is just the same with the Fermi process. A particular particle remains in the accelerating region only for a certain length of time—just how long it does so is largely determined by chance. The few particles which remain for a long time acquire very high energies, but many more particles acquire only moderately high energies.

We have described three possible mechanisms of acceleration in this chapter. All of them require the existence of chaotic motions within the quasar. In two of the mechanisms the moving condensations are required to carry magnetic fields as well. In the third mechanism, the one which involves shock waves, a magnetic field may or may not be present. On the whole one can probably not construct a plausible model of a quasar which is entirely free of magnetic fields.

CHAPTER XI

SYNTHESIS OF THE ELEMENTS

One of the mysteries of physics concerns the creation of matter. No one can at present say how the matter now in the Universe came into existence. Yet one conclusion seems certain. Whatever form matter was created in, it was surely not created in the form of 92 different elements, most of them with several isotopes. Thus it is a legitimate exercise in physics to try to construct a scheme to describe how matter, having been created in some simple form, eventually acquired its present composition after undergoing a suitable sequence of nuclear reactions. Several such schemes exist, but to date only one has been really convincing. This is the theory proposed by Burbidge, Burbidge, Fowler and Hoyle (B^2FH for short).

Let us consider another scheme first, due to Lemaître. This postulates that matter came into the Universe in the form of one vast nucleus. The Universe was then very condensed. As it expanded the super-nucleus split into progressively smaller pieces, eventually to form the nuclei as we know them now. But the idea does not work. What one expects to happen is that the large nuclei will continue to split up, by radio-active decay, and will emit energy into the Universe. Eventually they will reach a small enough size to become stable. Whatever happens they cannot easily go on splitting to reach sizes smaller than that of the iron nucleus. There are good physical reasons for our making this assertion.

It is well known that iron is the most stable of all the elements. Nuclei heavier than the iron nucleus can split into smaller nuclei; nuclei lighter than iron fuse together to form heavier nuclei. In other words when light nuclei are involved in reactions, they release energy by forming heavier rather than lighter nuclei. Thus the natural tendency of nuclear reactions is to produce nuclei of about the size of the iron nucleus. Once an iron nucleus has been formed it becomes quite hard to destroy it again.

Obviously this leads to a very fundamental difficulty for the Lemaître scheme. It is a well-established observational fact that the lightest elements, hydrogen and helium, are also by far the most abundant. In fact the known data on cosmic abundances suggest that the various elements were formed by a process of building up from smaller nuclei, rather than by the fission of large nuclei.

Briefly the observations show that hydrogen and helium are very abundant, that elements between helium and iron are moderately abundant, and that elements heavier than iron are rather rare. (This explains, in part, why gold and platinum are expensive, but water is cheap.)

Other scientists, notably Alpher, Bethe and Gamow (or $\alpha\beta\gamma$ for short), have investigated the consequences of forming the Universe with an initial content of hydrogen only. It may have been possible for nuclear reactions to occur then, provided that the initial state was sufficiently hot and dense. It is not entirely certain that this was so. But suppose that the matter in the Universe had originally been very hot and dense. Hydrogen nuclei would then have been able to combine to form helium. Helium nuclei in turn would combine to form heavier nuclei, such as those of carbon, oxygen, and so on, but with one proviso. Reactions to form heavier elements from helium require higher temperatures than those involving the formation of helium from hydrogen. If, then, conditions are right for the formation of other elements from helium, they are even more suitable for the formation of helium from hydrogen. In other words, in a medium where heavier elements can form from helium, there will automatically be nuclear reactions which exhaust the hydrogen content of the medium even faster. But we know that hydrogen is still very abundant in the Universe. We therefore deduce that element formation, other than the formation of some helium, cannot have taken place in the initial phases of the Universe.

The site where the elements heavier than helium were formed must therefore contain hot and dense material, but little hydrogen. This conclusion suggested to B^2FH that element formation goes on inside stars which have completed much of their evolution, and have burnt up all the hydrogen in their deep interior. Theoretical studies have shown that, granted reasonable enough assumptions, all the elements can be thus formed in about the required proportions. Again extensive discussions have been given of the external appearance of stars at various stages of their evolution. Here computation and observation agree that stars at first consume the hydrogen they contain, and later feed on the energy released by nuclear reactions involving helium. The problem remains of discovering how the transmuted material is returned to interstellar space, where it is observed later. It is customary here to suppose that many stars experience supernova explosions in their final stages. These are so violent that much (or all) of the content of the stars is thrown out into space again.

Such events tend to change the composition of the inter*stellar* material, which becomes richer in the elements heavier than helium. On the other hand it is unlikely that the inter*galactic* material will be so enriched. Most probably the matter, ejected when a star explodes in a particular galaxy, remains in that galaxy. Only an exceptionally powerful explosion could throw its debris right out of a galaxy. Our conclusion is that intergalactic material consists of hydrogen and helium; interstellar material usually contains some heavier elements as well.

These arguments can now be applied to the case of the quasars. In the first place we note that observation shows the presence of elements such as carbon, oxygen, nitrogen and magnesium. Many other common elements will doubtless also be seen when more time has been spent on analysing the spectra. This means that quasars contain processed material. We therefore have some further explanations to give if either:

(i) a quasar forms from a condensation of intergalactic matter, or
(ii) a quasar forms from a part of the Universe which is rather late in expanding.

This second possibility needs a brief comment. Almost all cosmologies (see Chapter VII) describe model Universes with a finite radius. As the Universe ages the radius grows larger, or, one might say, the curvature decreases. It is customary to study only models of the Universe which have the same curvature in all their parts at any time. But it has been suggested that there might, in the real Universe, be pockets of high curvature. These pockets would be virtually cut off from the rest of the Universe until their own curvature had become low enough. Then they would become visible—perhaps as quasars.

If we accept either possibility then we also admit that the heavier elements contained in a quasar must have been synthesized in that quasar. Some part of the quasar must therefore have become hot enough for nucleosynthesis to take place: the minimum temperature needed for this process is about 10^9 deg. K. Referring back to the table of temperatures in Chapter VIII we see that such high temperatures can occur only in masses which are not larger than about $10^4 M_{\odot}$. A typical quasar would therefore contain sub-units of this size. Further it follows that the hydrogen in the quasar would, at least in part, be converted into helium, even before nucleosynthesis had taken place, and so the nuclear energy stored in the hydrogen would be released. Finally, the heavier elements should increase in abundance as the quasar evolves. Recent astrophysical work has made it possible to arrange the different types of star in a sequence of increasing age. Perhaps it will eventually become possible to do the same for quasars. If either possibility is correct then a quasar should show a marked change in composition with increasing age.

The third possibility is that a quasar forms as an occasional catastrophe in an ordinary galaxy.

If so, there will be no difficulty in accounting for the presence of the heavier elements, and there would be less noticeable changes in their abundance as the quasar evolves. Further, this idea is supported by other circumstantial evidence, notably the occurrence of violent events in galaxies like M 82, or the existence of the so-called Seyfert galaxies.[1] Violent events result in the expulsion of matter at high speeds from the centres of galaxies; Seyfert galaxies also show evidence of very violent motions in objects which are otherwise fairly ordinary. Both classes of galaxy seem to have much in common with quasars, although the energies involved in their activity are much lower. On the whole our view is therefore that quasars occur in ordinary galaxies as a result of some extraordinary sequence of events. But we are unable to propose a detailed scheme which shows how a quasar comes into existence.

[1] Named after C. K. Seyfert, who first described their properties a quarter of a century ago.

CHAPTER XII

A MODEL OF A QUASAR

We shall now try to summarize and draw some conclusions. The crucial discovery in the study of quasars was made in 1963 by Maarten Schmidt when he identified their spectra. At the time it was known that quasars were radio sources of very small angular size and that they were associated with optical objects. Then Schmidt showed that the spectra of quasars were all systematically red-shifted, each quasar having its own characteristic redshift z.

There are two acceptable explanations for the existence of a redshift: the Doppler shift and the Einstein gravitational redshift. It would require exceedingly strong gravitational fields to produce a large enough value of z for most quasars. Schmidt (together with Greenstein) easily showed that the existence of such strong fields in quasars would prevent the emission of some of their characteristic spectral lines. There has been hardly any further serious discussion on this matter, and we accept his conclusion.

If therefore we interpret the redshift z as a Doppler shift then we also admit that the quasars are rapidly moving away from us. But it is known that the Universe is expanding, and that the distant galaxies are systematically receding from us. It is natural to conclude that the recession of the quasars is a cosmological effect. We can estimate the distances to the various quasars by the known relation between redshift and distance. Many quasars have large redshifts and so the inferred distances are also large. We can then calculate the rate of energy emission (or the luminosity) of a quasar. Being very distant, quasars are found to have large luminosities, typically 1,000 or even 10,000 times those of a galaxy like our own. Finally it is known that part A of 3C 273, the nearest quasar is a tongue of luminous material at least 150,000 light years long. This suggests that the quasar itself is at least 150,000 years old; if its luminosity has remained roughly the same throughout all this time then its total emission of energy is at least 10^{60} erg, or about 10^8 times the total energy radiated by a star like the Sun in its lifetime.

These large luminosities and energies worry some astrophysicists. Their anxiety is deepened by the observation that the radiation from many quasars is not steady, but shows sudden and irregular fluctuations, occasionally on a time scale of a few days only. One expects that such luminous objects cannot be confined in a small space. But if the object is large and uniform then the disturbances we observe should not be sudden because synchronization cannot be achieved, since light from the far parts of the object has to travel rather further to reach us and will therefore be seen rather later than light from the near parts.

These seem to be powerful objections. We shall later propose a model for a quasar which, we hope, will meet them. Nevertheless we shall first discuss one possible alternative view according to which quasars are much closer to the Earth. In this 'local origin' theory the displacement of the spectral lines is still ascribed to the Doppler shift, but the velocities of recession are not associated with the expansion of the Universe. Instead the known quasars are all imagined to have been produced and set in motion in a vast explosion. The event is supposed to have occurred, perhaps, one hundred million years ago. We know the speeds of the quasars; if we accept the theory then we conclude that they are now between ten and a hundred million light years distant from the site of the explosion. No blue-shifted quasars have yet been observed. This means that among the quasars we know none is approaching us, and therefore we are closer to the site of the explosion than any of them. The explosion must therefore have occurred quite close to our Galaxy.

Certain difficulties are removed by this theory: the quasars are now calculated to be much nearer, and their inferred luminosities are much smaller, although still quite large. (For example 3C 273 now has a luminosity about as large as that of our Galaxy.) The quasars have presumably been shining ever since the original explosion, and so their minimum life-times are at least a hundred million years, and if anything are rather larger than before. Finally the rapid fluctuations in luminosity are a little easier to understand, since we can now assume that quasars are more compact.

Even so a quasar still needs a mass of 10^5 or 10^6 $M_\odot$ to be able to liberate all this energy ($M_\odot$ = the mass of the Sun). The total mass of all the quasars is therefore between 10^7 and 10^8 $M_\odot$ .If we assume that the typical quasar has a redshift $z = 1$, then we can calculate that its kinetic energy is about $\frac{1}{4}c^2$ per unit mass, or 2×10^{20} erg per gram. The hypothetical explosion must have released between 4×10^{60} and 4×10^{61} erg, as much as or even more than the total integrated luminosity of 3C 273, according to the more orthodox theory.

As we have seen, the theory requires that the explosion must have occurred quite near us, and at an epoch quite close to our own. We cannot suppose that the Earth is in a privileged position nor that we live at a privileged time. If we adopt the local origin theory we must admit that other parts of the Universe and other epochs also have their quasars. We estimate therefore that there might be up to a million other groups of quasars contemporary with ours (since our local group of quasars only fills about one millionth the volume of the Universe), and that there might have been a hundred previous generations. This estimate for the total energy required is clearly much larger than the estimate given by the orthodox theory.

That is not all. The initial explosion must have been very powerful since it evidently threw out debris with very high speeds. One would expect that the debris would then spread more or less evenly throughout a large volume. Instead of doing so it apparently condensed into some hundred small objects. The forces accelerating the debris during the explosion would have been very great, and would have destroyed any subsidiary condensations then. As the material expands, its self-gravitational forces grow weaker. The later condensation of large fragments thus becomes less and less likely. This is probably the most telling objection to the local hypothesis. We shall say no more about it.

Here we return to the main theme of this book, and follow up the consequences of assuming a cosmological origin for the quasars. There are then two possible energy sources; the first of these is by the release of gravitational energy, which we have already described, and shall reconsider later. The second is by the annihilation of matter with anti-matter. This is an attractive idea, which has sometimes been considered but never fully worked out. We shall briefly discuss it next.

Matter, as far as the astrophysicist is concerned, consists of protons (p), neutrons (n) and electrons (β^-) in various combinations. This needs little explanation. Anti-matter, correspondingly, includes anti-protons ($\bar{p}$), anti-neutrons ($\bar{n}$) and positrons (β^+), and it can be produced in the laboratory. The existence of anti-matter is therefore an established experimental fact. A proton, p, has the same mass and spin as an anti-proton, $\bar{p}$. But the electrical and magnetic properties of $\bar{p}$ are exactly opposed to those of p. Thus p carries a positive charge and $\bar{p}$ a negative charge. Similarly β^- and β^+ have equal masses and equal spins, but opposite electromagnetic properties. n and $\bar{n}$ are not electrically charged, but their magnetic properties are opposite. If we superpose a p with $\bar{p}$ (or n with $\bar{n}$, or β^- with β^+), then the resulting particle has mass and spin, but no charge and no magnetic moment. It behaves just like one (or rather two) photon(s) of radiation. If a particle and its anti-particle come close enough together they can thus spontaneously annihilate and turn into radiation. The photons emitted have high energy and short wavelength, with λ about equal to 0·01 Å, for annihilation of β^- and β^+, and about equal to 0·00001 Å for p with $\bar{p}$, or n with $\bar{n}$. 'Close enough' means roughly that the particle and anti-particle will annihilate if they approach to within a distance λ. From this one concludes that a β^+ can travel a total distance of about one centimetre in air at NTP before annihilation. The time taken to do so is about 10^{-7} second. A $\bar{p}$ or an $\bar{n}$ must come closer to a p or an n before the reaction occurs. Either could in fact travel a total distance of about 10 km and would take a few seconds to react.

Anti-matter does not occur naturally in the Solar System and most probably not even in the Galaxy. But theoretical physicists feel that matter and anti-matter should be balanced in the Universe as a whole. It may therefore be that other parts of the Universe contain anti-matter, just as our part contains matter. There would be boundary surfaces in intergalactic space between the regions where matter and those where anti-matter predominates. One might expect that annihilation reactions would take place there, but the density of the intergalactic gas is very low, and even β^-, β^+ reactions would go on too slowly to be noticeable.

Now, it is commonly believed that the intergalactic gas can form condensations, which evolve into galaxies or even clusters of galaxies. The condensations develop because of the gravitational self-attraction of the gas. Gravitational forces do not distinguish between matter and anti-matter. Condensations can therefore form consisting entirely of matter or of anti-matter, or partly of matter and partly of anti-matter. In the first two cases there would be no spectacular results. But if a mixed condensation forms, then particles and anti-particles will be drawn together into a body of higher density, and annihilation reactions might become important. About 5×10^{17} erg could be released by the annihilation of all the β^- and β^+ contained in one gram of matter and anti-matter, present in equal proportions. A body containing about 10^{43} gm of the mixture would thus be needed to supply adequate energy to 3C 273. A brief calculation, which we shall omit, suggests that the reactions would go on fast enough to account for the luminosity of the quasar when the radius of the body was about 10^{22} cm (or 10,000 light years). At the accepted distance of 3C 273 this corresponds to an angular size a little larger than one second of arc, which is too large to fit in with observation.

But the body may contract until there is rapid enough annihilation of p with $\bar{p}$, or n with $\bar{n}$. The same calculation suggests that only 10^{39} or 10^{40} gm are now needed to provide the energy; in round figures, a million solar masses. The energy is generated fast enough when the body has shrunk to a radius of about ten light years. At the distance of 3C 273 the corresponding angular size is about 0·001 seconds of arc, well below the upper limit set by observation.

The idea is attractive, yet severe problems remain. The worst is that the energy is released as radiation of extremely short wavelength, but quasars emit strongly at optical and radio wavelengths. It is not clear by what mechanism the radiation can be converted. Nevertheless we cannot rule out this hypothesis.

We finally come back to the theory that the energy is released by gravitational effects. We have already described much of the theory. The most important result established was that relatively little energy can be released by a body of large mass, while it is contracting slowly through successive states of equilibrium. As we explained in Chapter VIII, most of the gravitational energy released remains confined within the body as radiant energy.

But these results have been established only for the case of rather idealized conditions. No allowance was made for any mass motions within the body. Yet we know that the body emits radiation into space and must lose energy. Therefore, as long as it can release energy by contracting, it will do so—until it reaches its critical state. In fact, as that state is approached, the rate of contraction must grow faster and faster, for the curve of energy versus condensation becomes steadily less steep there (see Fig. VIII/1).

No calculation has yet been made which allows for this motion, or for some other essential features of the process. We do not know how the energy is carried from the inner parts of the body to the surface; it is quite possible that it is carried outwards by convection currents, for which a realistic description must allow. Clearly we do not know how the critical state is approached; all that we do know is that at a certain degree of condensation the mass becomes unstable in some way.

We are therefore rather short of facts when we try to predict what should happen after instability. The most promising guess is as follows. At the instability point the mass M breaks up into several secondary masses M'. These cannot escape from their mutual gravitational fields and must therefore go into orbit about one another. But the equilibrium of the original mass has been broken, and therefore the radiant energy can escape into space, together with some of the matter which has failed to condense. Perhaps this explains the origin of the great luminous tongue of 3C 273, and of the tongue-like structures round other quasars, notably 3C 48.

The secondary masses M' can shrink to smaller sizes before they, too, become unstable. As their contraction continues they also reach their critical radii, and divide up into tertiary masses M''. The fragmentation can continue with further subdivisions. Our picture then is of a hierarchy of condensations, a mass M containing several masses M' in orbit about each other, each mass M' containing several masses M'' in orbit about each other, and so on.

This model of a quasar obviously agrees with many observational results and with deductions made from them. The condensations in their orbits travel along complex and irregular paths. Any magnetic field initially present in the quasar will be stretched by and gain energy from the motion of the condensations. An unsteady magnetic field develops and this may lead to the acceleration of the electrons present. Again, a bodily collision between two condensations will lead to the creation of shock waves, and they, too, will produce fast electrons.

We can try to estimate typical values for the mass and the size of a quasar. First, we might expect that the radiant energy released at the time of the original instability should have been enough to supply the energy needed by 3C 273A. It has been estimated that part A is, overall, about one per cent as bright as part B. If part B has emitted 10^{60} erg in its lifetime, part A will have emitted 10^{58} erg. Now a mass M reaches its critical radius R_c when

$$\frac{GM}{R_c} \doteqdot \frac{9}{16}\left(\frac{M_0}{M}\right)^{1/2} c^2$$

with $M_0 = 3 \times 10^{33}$ gm. At that stage an amount of gravitational energy GM^2/R_c, approximately, has been turned into radiant energy. The radiant energy available is about $\frac{9}{16}(M_0M)^{1/2}c^2$, which equals $2{\cdot}5 \times 10^{57}$ erg when M equals 10^{40} gm (in round figures). The corresponding value of R_c is about 4×10^{15} cm.

But then we face a difficulty. The fragments formed at the time of the collapse would have acquired orbital speeds typically equal to $\left(\frac{GM}{R_c}\right)^{1/2} = \frac{3}{4}\left(\frac{M_0}{M}\right)^{1/4} c$; with our assumed values this equals 3×10^8 cm/sec, which is of the order of the typical spread of velocities expected in a quasar. The orbital velocities will increase when the masses M' subdivide into masses M'', and so on. Perhaps, though, we have underestimated the energy required by part A. If part A really needs 10^{60} erg, then M must equal $1{\cdot}6 \times 10^{45}$ gm; the predicted orbital velocities are then reduced to 3×10^7 cm/sec, which is more plausible. The total mass of a quasar is now larger than that of a galaxy. If so, the formation of a quasar can hardly be a typical event in the evolution of a galaxy; but circumstantial evidence suggests that it is.

We can make another estimate from the observations on

3C 345, which showed that a velocity change of about 3×10^8 cm/sec can occur within rather less than a week, say in 10^5 seconds. The change was most probably caused by a collision between two condensations: the typical size of the condensations involved is then $3 \times 10^8 \times 10^5 = 3 \times 10^{13}$ cm, or about two Astronomical Units (one Astronomical unit equals the distance from the Earth to the Sun). It is not known how often collisions like this occur. But suppose, for argument's sake, that they happen once in 10^7 seconds, and that the energy they release is an important contribution to the power supply of a quasar like 3C 273B. They must then release energy at a mean rate of some 10^{47} erg/sec, or 10^{54} erg per collision. If this equals the relative kinetic energy of two condensations before collision, then their masses must be about 10^{37} gm each, or about 5,000 $M_\odot$. We refer back to Chapter VIII, and find that quite high temperatures can be attained inside condensations as light as this before they reach instability. Thus we cannot maintain that nuclear reactions will be unimportant: they may in fact supply a large fraction of the energy which the quasar requires. If a body of 5,000 $M_\odot$ is allowed to contract to its critical radius its interior temperature may even become high enough for the synthesis of some of the heavier elements. This somewhat weakens our argument that quasars must form in galaxies, from 'processed' material.

There are other unresolved problems. The original mass M, contracting to its critical radius, is a single body far away from important disturbing influences. The subsequent break-up of each of the masses M', M'' . . . is disturbed by the presence of the others nearby. We do not know what effect this has.

We could go on like this, but perhaps we have said enough. The hierarchical model obviously explains much, but also raises many problems. At best we are at the beginning of an understanding of the nature of quasars.

Many astrophysicists have contribued to the theoretical

TABLE III

	Location	*Source of Energy*	*Brief Description*	*Comment*	*Estimated* Probability of Correctness*
1	Distant	Gravitational	Large mass	Subject to instability	10%
2	Distant	Gravitational (plus nuclear)	Massive and dense cluster of stars		20%
3	Distant	Gravitational (plus nuclear)	Large mass, divided into hierarchy of condensations	Natural sequel to (1), quite similar to (2)	35%
4	Distant	Annihilation of protons and anti-protons	Large mass in a suitable region of Universe	May not produce radiation of suitable wavelength	15%
5	Local	Nuclear	Quasars are smaller objects, ejected by super-explosion 10^7 or 10^8 years ago	Difficult to understand super-explosion	15%
6	Local		Pairs of radio sources associated with peculiar galaxies	Proposed to explain coincidences in location. Perhaps (4) gives better explanation	5%

*We only assess the theories described here. No bets are laid on theories which have not been proposed yet.

study of quasars. We have been most strongly influenced by the work of Alfven, Axford, Burbidge, Chandrasekhar, Fowler, Gold, Hoyle, Iben, Terrell and Woltjer. We hope that we have shown why quasars have raised so much interest, and that our account has not been too biased.

Table III on page 111 lists some of the possible theories, with a few comments. In column 6 we give our estimate of their relative probability of being correct.